Logistics in the
Vietnam Wars
1945–1975

Logistics in the Vietnam Wars 1945–1975

N.S. Nash

Pen & Sword
MILITARY

First published in Great Britain in 2020 and republished in this format in 2022 by
PEN & SWORD MILITARY
an imprint of
Pen & Sword Books Ltd
Yorkshire – Philadelphia

ISBN 978-1-52679-814-5

Typeset by Concept, Huddersfield, HD4 5JL.
Printed and bound in the UK by CPI Group (UK) Ltd, Croydon, CR0 4YY.

Pen & Sword Books Limited incorporates the imprints of Atlas, Archaeology,
Aviation, Discovery, Family History, Fiction, History, Maritime, Military, Military
Classics, Politics, Select, Transport, True Crime, Air World, Frontline Publishing, Leo
Cooper, Remember When, Seaforth Publishing, The Praetorian Press, Wharncliffe
Local History, Wharncliffe Transport, Wharncliffe True Crime and White Owl.

For a complete list of Pen & Sword titles please contact

PEN & SWORD BOOKS LIMITED
47 Church Street, Barnsley, South Yorkshire, S70 2AS, England
E-mail: enquiries@pen-and-sword.co.uk
Website: www.pen-and-sword.co.uk

Or
PEN AND SWORD BOOKS
1950 Lawrence Rd, Havertown, PA 19083, USA
E-mail: Uspen-and-sword@casematepublishers.com
Website: www.penandswordbooks.com

Contents

Acknowledgements

I have been fortunate to have the support of Lieutenant Colonel W.W.T. Gowans and The Reverend Dr D. Coulter CB QHC who have each read my drafts and vastly improved them with their sage advice. At Pen & Sword my copy-editor was Pamela Covey; production manager Matt Jones oversaw the design of this book and has presented it with his usual skill.

I have acknowledged copyright of photos and maps wherever possible and where an attribution is not given, I will correct the deficiency in future editions if advised of the copyright-holder.

Preface

The three wars in Vietnam have produced a vast bibliography which has been picked over by skilled and erudite historians during the last fifty years. These scholars have been provided with a rich harvest of memoirs, political analysis and the accounts of individual battles, all of which fill groaning bookshelves. However, there is one aspect of the three wars in Vietnam over the thirty years (1945–1975), that has been taken for granted and that is the criticality of logistic support in all its myriad forms for each of the four nations concerned.

This book will, of necessity, comment on political issues because all soldiers, ultimately, report to a civilian politician. It will not dwell on battlefield tactics but will focus on the vast differences in the capability of the French, Americans, North and South Vietnamese and will examine the reasons why the sophisticated French and American armies were roundly defeated by a small, third-world country.

The measure of that success was summed up by a taxi driver in Ho Chi Minh City. He said to Christian Appy, 'Do you realize that we are the only nation to have defeated three of the five permanent members of the United Nations Security Council?' He was right, because France, the USA and China had all, in turn, been expelled from Vietnam.

This book seeks to single out the logistic factors that affected each army and to chronicle the measures taken to accommodate them. Where I have apparently strayed from my chosen path, it is to provide a backcloth against which the logistic systems functioned.

Glossary

AA	Anti-Aircraft
ARVN	Army of the Republic of (South) Vietnam
ATF	Australian Task Force
BPC	*Battalion de Parachutistes Coloniaux* (French)
CAT	Civil Air Transport
CEFEO	French Far East Expeditionary Corps
CIA	Central Intelligence Agency (USA)
CORDS	Civil Operations and Revolutionary Development Support
DBP	Dien Bien Phu
DIA	Defense Intelligence Agency (USA)
DMZ	De-Militarized Zone
DRV	Democratic Republic of (North) Vietnam
DZ	Drop Zone
FAF	French Air Force (*Armée de l'Air*)
FTNV	Commander, North Vietnam Ground Forces (French)
GNP	Gross National Product
GVN	Government of (South) Vietnam
HCMT	Ho Chi Minh Trail
ICP	Indochina Communist Party
JCS	Joint Chiefs of Staff (USA)
KIA	Killed In Action
KSCB	Khe Sanh Combat Base
LWL	Limited Warfare Laboratory
LZ	Landing Zone
MACV	Military Assistance Command, Vietnam
NVA	North Vietnamese Army
OCO	Office of Civil Operations (USA)
OSS	Office of Strategic Services (USA)
PACOM	Pacific Command
PAVN	Peoples' Army of (North) Vietnam
PROVN	Program for the Pacification and Long-Term Development of South Vietnam (USA)

RCP	*Regiment de Chasseurs Parachutistes* (French)
SAC	Strategic Air Command
S&D	Search and Destroy
SAM	Surface-to-Air Missile
TCK–TKN	*Tong Cong Kich – Tong Khoi Ngia* (General Offensive – General Uprising)
USMC	United States Marine Corps
VC	Vietnamese Communist (Viet Cong)

Chapter One

The Way It Is

'An adequate supply system and stocks of weapons and ammunition are the essential conditions for any army to be able to stand successfully the strains of battle. Before the fighting proper, the battle is fought and decided by the Quartermasters.'[1]

[Field Marshal Erwin Rommel]

Any soldier, of any rank, fighting in any theatre, at any time, if asked 'What would you really like?' would probably list 'a freshly-cooked meal and a dry pair of socks' high among his priorities.

The provision of that meal and those socks are the responsibility of his commander because keeping troops fed and clothed is a prime function of command, a matter wholeheartedly embraced by General Giap for one (see p. 36). It is incorrect to presume that 'operations' are in some way separate and divorced from 'logistics' because all operations are entirely dependent upon logistic support and the two are inextricably linked; it follows that logisticians are most emphatically combatants. Their role is usually unheroic and invariably unheralded.

This book will show that behind a successful general there is always an effective logistic and *transport* system. Logistics alone may not win a battle or a war, but they are a significant factor in victory or defeat, as they were in perhaps the greatest logistic exercise in war: the arrangements for D-Day and the battle for Normandy.

It is thought that the term 'logistics' dates from the nineteenth century and was coined by Baron de Jomini who adapted the French word *logistique* from *loger*, meaning to lodge. There is an alternative explanation and that is that the word stems from the Greek λογιστικός, meaning accountant or responsible for counting. In a military context logistics is the all-embracing word that covers every aspect of supply.[2]

The campaigns covered in this book were fought in the face of challenging geographic, topographic and climatic conditions. The fighting was hard, but surviving in the jungles of Indochina made that fighting even harder. The climate and topography were a constant and unremitting second adversary and, in combination, made re-supply all the more difficult.

Logistics are the poor relation in military historiography and those who publish military history recognize that logistics are not a high priority because it is 'muck and bullets that sells books'. It has ever been thus, and Kaushik Roy addressed this matter when he wrote that 'most military officers-turned-historians focus on strategy, tactics and the operational level of war ... The audience targeted by commercial publishers prefers campaign and battle studies that highlight the role of individuals and dramatise the exotic.'[3]

Similarly, Martin van Creveld remarked: 'Hundreds of books on strategy and tactics have been written for every one on logistics.'[4] This is illogical, as many if not most military campaigns are eventually decided by the superiority of one side over the other in supply terms. Examples of that are Napoleon in 1812 and Rommel at the Second Battle of El Alamein in 1942. In both cases, the defeated were at the end of vastly over-extended lines of communications and suffered the consequent supply difficulties. These are precisely the same circumstances that led to the loss of Kut in 1916.

Logistic support is mundane, routine and relatively unimportant, that is *until it fails*. Then, within forty-eight hours, it begets a crisis. Men (and horses) must be fed and watered, weapon systems must have ammunition, vehicles must have fuel and be maintained, the wounded must be cared for and the dead must be buried in marked graves. The list is endless and tedious. Roy is one of a small minority who have delved into the detail of logistics or 'supply', as it was called in 1914. He underscores the truism that 'without supplies neither a general nor a soldier is good for anything.'[5] This was a view expressed by Clearchus well over 2,000 years ago.

A perusal of a Waterstones bookshelf will offer a wide range of books on some aspect of military history. Some of the subjects have been done to death; for example, the Battle of the Somme, D-Day or the Battle of the Bulge. All have been extensively mined and reported on. They were centres of ghastly carnage. That carnage was the result of the combatants being furnished with the weapons and ammunition to kill the enemy in vast numbers; that is logistics in operation, although rarely highlighted.

Logisticians do not often attract public attention and when they do it is invariably because of a failure. Many years ago, the author was introduced to an elderly and long-retired American colonel. He was charming and, when asked about his service, he said that he was 'Patton's Petroleum Officer in the US 3rd Army in France, 1944.'

At the time, Patton's 3rd Army was rampaging down through Europe and was using about 350,000 gallons of petrol each day. To maintain the tanks the 'Red Ball Express' was set up to meet his demands and also those of the

US 1st Army. This was a non-stop convoy of trucks connecting supply depots in Normandy to the armies in the field; 6,000 trucks were employed. It was, by any yardstick, a major logistic exercise. As Patton advanced further, the demands placed on the 'Red Ball' grew faster than it was able to supply. Those 6,000 trucks were, themselves, consuming 300,000 gallons of fuel each day. On 28 August 1944, Patton's army was forced to slow its advance when its fuel allocation fell 100,000 gallons short. Even though gasoline was available in Normandy, the 'Red Ball' could not transport it in sufficient quantities to the 3rd Army's forward units. On 31 August, after the fuel supply dried up, Patton's spearhead came to a halt. I said sympathetically to the colonel: 'That must have been difficult?' He gave a wry smile and replied: 'You bet, he chewed on my ass!'

There were a number of knock-on effects resulting from Patton's immobility: the 3rd Army began to use its larger-calibre artillery weapons, causing an ammunition shortage. Ammunition stocks became a problem because all available trucks were transporting fuel. As the Lorraine campaign continued, shortages would also be felt in clothing, rations, tyres and antifreeze for the fast approaching winter months.[6]

This anecdote shows that in this instance Patton's generalship was flawed. He well knew of his dependence on fuel and must have realized that he would eventually outstrip his supply chain. 'Chewing on the colonel's ass' was unreasonable because the responsibility was Patton's and Patton's alone.

To reiterate, 'logistics are a function of command'. Wavell certainly thought so, remarking that 'logistics are the crux of generalship, superior even to tactical skill.'[7]

This book will consider the logistic issues in three wars. In these pages, the temptation to produce lists of stores, vehicles and aircraft supported by detailed annexures has been resisted. That is because to do otherwise would separate the logistic from the operational of which it is an integral part and would make for a very tedious book. This text examines logistic factors against their operational setting. Along the way it will show that the acquisition and stockpiling of supplies in their myriad forms is a valueless exercise unless there is, readily available, the means to distribute those supplies; in a nutshell, the transport capacity of a force must match its demand. Winston Churchill was a seasoned campaigner and, more than a century ago, he averred that 'victory is a bright-coloured flower. Transport is the stem without which it could never have blossomed.'[8]

This book will show that the great man was right on the mark and never more so than in Vietnam.

*   *   *

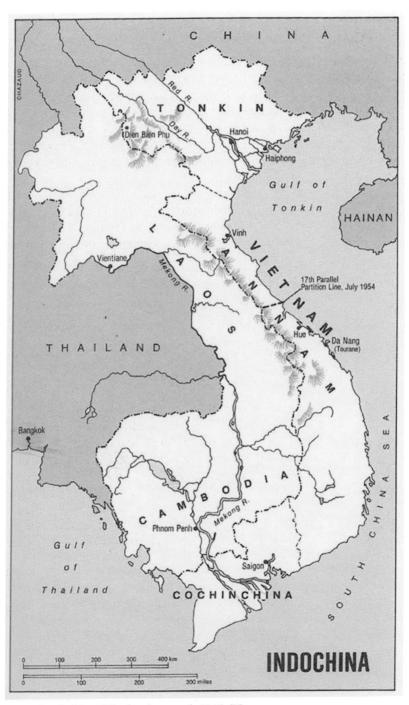

Map of Indochina. The battleground, 1945–75.

During the evening of 6 May 1954, in the north of Vietnam, French troops sheltered in their trenches as the Vietnamese artillery barrage thundered about them. Suffering an artillery barrage was then, and is now, one of the most frightening experiences known to man. When a shell hit a trench, the body parts of some defenders flew through the air. Other occupants of the unlucky trench were simply vaporized. Morale was low and the shelling drove it lower. The pungent smell of enemy dead outside the wire, decomposing in the hot humid climate, assailed the senses, as did the stomach-turning stench of latrines destroyed by the shelling.

The French troops, the majority of them colonial soldiers, only waited for the final assault on the 'impregnable fortress' of Dien Bien Phu (DBP) that they had defended since it was first besieged on 20 January. They knew that the enemy would come with grenades and bayonets; there would be no quarter. The men were exhausted, hungry and thirsty. There was no escape and many more were to die in the very near future. The French soldiers knew that there was no way out; 10,000 men had died or were 'missing' at Dien Bien Phu when the guns fell silent.[9]

By mid-May 1954, around the world, soldiers and historians were wondering how a sophisticated, modern Western army with massive American logistic support had been so comprehensively defeated by 'a bunch of little guys in black pyjamas', and who *was* this man Giap? It had been 'a war in which logistics decided the outcome.'[10] The USA had committed $3.5 billion to the fight – about 80 per cent of the total cost – but all for naught.

It is not the author's purpose to re-fight the battles of Vietnam; they are fully documented elsewhere, as the bibliography shows. Instead, the outline of key events will be sketched but with a focus upon the logistic operations of the four armies engaged in Vietnam between 1945 and 1975. It will examine their political aims, the effectiveness of their endeavours to meet those aims, and specifically the manner in which they prepared and supplied their forces. Finally, it will compare the results and the costs in matériel and human terms. It will, in passing, seek to put into an appropriate context the behaviour of all soldiers in Indochina.

Chapter Two

The Battleground

'The dominant feeling on the battlefield is loneliness.'[1]
[Lieutenant General Sir William Slim]

For hundreds, perhaps thousands of years, the combination of topography, climate and the dense forest made travel throughout Vietnam difficult for travellers and merchants alike. In 1945, some rivers could be navigated and the very limited and mediocre road/track system could be traversed with wheeled vehicles, albeit slowly.

Vietnam might well have been designed for revolutionary warfare but was absolutely unsuitable for conventional twentieth-century, Western-style, fast-moving, flexible military operations. Such operations depended upon the timely delivery of logistic support. The key word here is *delivery*. For that support to be effective, there had to be a defendable transport system in place.

For armies with a Western culture, Vietnam was a logistical nightmare. The difficulty of ground movement was exacerbated by the capacity of a guerrilla force to mount ambushes along rivers and roads.

It will be helpful to describe the territory over which, for thirty years, hundreds of thousands of people fought and died. The priority of the combatants was not ownership of this territory; it was but the setting for armed conflict.

In Vietnam, north of Hanoi and spanning the border with China, there is a range of hills and small mountains. The area is known as the Viet Bac and it provided safe haven for the Vietminh during the first war. The significance of Hanoi and its port of Haiphong is self-evident; they are both located on the delta formed by the Red and Day rivers. They access the sea in the Gulf of Tonkin by way of vast, centuries-old dykes built to channel the river water across the low ground. These dykes, despite their height and width, were thought by the USA to present Hanoi with a strategic weakness because, if breached, serious flooding would follow.[2] In fact, Hanoi has always been susceptible to flooding and today, heavy monsoon rain regularly inundates the city.

A spine of mountains runs for about 350 miles down the border with Laos and this high ground, covered with thick vegetation, provided cover from view for the Ho Chi Minh Trail (of which more later) which traversed the mountains. These mountains are not high, but they are steep. In some parts there are areas of karst; that is to say tall, limestone pinnacles that have abundant caves in their bases. Some of these caves are of sufficient size to provide the facilities for the storage of ammunition and weapons, others for workshops and hospitals. They were fully utilized by General Giap. (More of this in Chapter 7.)

The low-lying areas of the country, both north and south of the 16th parallel, were cultivated and the abundant rainfall was exploited in rice fields surrounded by dykes. Navigation across these areas was either by way of unpaved tracks surmounting those dykes or by wading through thigh-deep water. The Mekong delta is the dominating feature of South Vietnam. Located to the south-east of Saigon is the Ca Mau peninsula, the southern-most projection of Vietnam. It is flat, about 120 miles long and on average is only about 7ft above sea level. It had been formed by alluvial deposits from the Mekong River and was devoid of roads in 1945. Most of this area is mangrove swamp and all movement in the Ca Mau was dependent upon boats. Military operations in this area called for the development of appro-priate equipment and new tactics.

The topography, climate, vegetation and voracious insect life of Vietnam are the four immutable factors that affected all the combatants that contested control of this tropical wilderness. When they are combined with a dearth of roads, it will be understood why they impacted on key decisions as to when and where to fight and how to supply and support combat operations. Vietnam is about 850 miles long from north to south. It varies in width between 31 and 370 miles and has a land mass of 127,882 square miles. To put that into context, it is about the same size as Italy. China borders Vietnam to the north and it is bordered to the west by Laos and Cambodia. To the east is the South China Sea. The jungle was, allegedly, 'neutral', but the reality was that it strongly favoured guerrilla operations.[3]

The forest completely negated the possibility of the style of operations practised in Europe in the Second World War which was, in 1944, now run-ning to a close. The jungle was dangerous and unforgiving, particularly so to soldiers new to that environment. Secondary growth of vines, bamboo and assorted luxuriant shrubs impeded movement on foot and prevented all off-road mechanized movement. Visibility was limited to perhaps a few yards. Davidson correctly judged it to be 'good ambush country'.[4]

Another factor affecting operations in 1945 was that the country was virtu-ally unmapped, and any maps produced by the French colonialists were largely inaccurate. This deficiency in survey data had an adverse effect on military operations as artillery and air strikes, parachute insertions and route planning were all subject to guesswork. From 1956, the US armed forces filled the mapping gap with photographic aerial surveys and thereafter excellent tactical maps were available.

The climate varies depending on altitude: very cold in the mountains; humid and hot in the lowlands. The country is subject to monsoon between mid-May and mid-October. The south-west monsoon is particularly severe in the Mekong delta which, for practical purposes, is submerged. Elsewhere mechanized movement off-road is impossible and on roads always difficult as landslips and fallen trees often cut lines of communication. The south-west monsoon crosses Vietnam, then swings to the north and moves to the Red River delta and expires in mid-October. The north-east monsoon is a weaker version and begins in September and lasts until December. This particular weather phenomenon produces typical heavy rain but also light rain or drizzle. More importantly, it produces fog which the French called *crachin*. This fog has military significance as it limits air activity and precludes aerial re-supply and, although reduced visibility provided cover from view, nevertheless the Vietnamese curtailed operations during the monsoon. The continuous rain and deep mud affected morale and put a premium on endurance. The French, although they were equipped with wet-weather clothing, were still utterly miserable. Initially their opponents were not so equipped and the effect of monsoon upon them must have been akin to that of those soldiers of General Kōtoku Satō as they retreated from Kohima in the monsoon of 1944.

The climate of Vietnam had a debilitating effect on the health of all participants. Serious diseases including malaria, dengue fever, cholera, hepatitis, typhoid and tropical ulcers were all commonplace. Between 1950 and 1954 about a quarter of French troops were infected with schistosomiasis (also known as bilharzia, a waterborne disease), and leptospirosis or Weil's disease. The provision of medical care in this setting was a significant logistic burden. It was not until 1952 that the North Vietnamese Army (NVA) soldiers were issued with wet-weather clothing. One said 'We marvelled that mankind had produced a piece of paper that rain ran off.'[5]

The abject misery of living, let alone fighting, in this ghastly climate was described by an American officer as follows:

> And the rains came, did it rain! It rained several times a day and sometimes the winds that blew unimpeded across the plains drove the rain before them in horizontal sheets. The rain would fly right through any open doors or windows to soak everything within. We had to batten down every opening in the team house before each storm, an exercise that became tedious from constant repetition. Closing all ports kept out the wind and rain but kept in the stifling heat and fetid humidity …

Sometimes the need for a breath of air would overcome the desire to keep the rain out and we would open the bamboo thatch door a crack, accepting the spray that came in with the relieving breeze.

Sooner or later, everything was wet from the constant rain. Mattresses mildewed, matches disintegrated, cigarettes went limp, socks rotted, feet turned soft and pasty white from always being under water and jungle rot ate away at everything between our navels and our knees.

On combat operations we couldn't avoid getting soaked from either the rain, the sweat or a dunking. Damp, chafing clothing rubbed a man's neck, shoulders, groin, knees and waist. The raw patches of skin encouraged the multiple forms of fungus and general crud that were just waiting for a damp warm place to live. Since we could never get really dry or clean, our skin was constantly rotting off our bones . . . Small abrasions or scratches would turn into festering sores that refused to heal.[6]

A study of the chronology of Vietminh operations against the French between September 1952 and July 1954 shows that nineteen out of a total of twenty-six attacks were, quite reasonably, initiated by the Vietminh during the dry season. There is no doubt that the best campaigning weather is between early January and mid-May. On that basis it is no surprise that the North Vietnamese Army (NVA), later retitled 'The People's Army of Vietnam' (PAVN) and Vietcong (VC), mounted the Tet offensive in 1968, their Easter offensive in 1972 and their final offensive in 1975, all in that same time frame.

Vietnam has a lengthy coastline and in 1945 there were several efficient ports. In the north the principal port was Haiphong. In addition, it had Hon Gay and the port complex at Cam Pha. These were to be the ports through which the Russians would provide logistic support to the NVA in its war with the USA. Although Haiphong was the principal port, it also constituted a significant target. It was bombed and, in the early 1970s, the entrance was mined by the USA. In the south the ports of Saigon, Da Nang, Qui Nhon and Cam Ranh Bay were sufficient to feed logistic material into military operations.

The French, in less turbulent colonial times, had built a railway from Saigon to Hanoi. The railway had been neglected and its plethora of culverts, bridges and tunnels made it as vulnerable to attack as any of the main roads. The consequence was that it never played an important part in the logistic arrangements of any of the warring countries in the early years of conflict. However, the Chinese improved their rail network up to the Vietnamese border and by December 1950 a US intelligence assessment was 'It appears likely that if the Vietminh forces (aided by China) gain complete control of the Border Highlands they will be able to develop supply lines from bases in China to the northern edge of the Tonkin plain.'[7]

The technological advances of the twentieth century had revolutionized warfare. The invention of the tank and the aeroplane were not the least of these. The French harnessed aerial transport and built a plethora of basic landing strips all over their colony. Later, the Americans built on that infrastructure and introduced the helicopter. The advent of more sophisticated aircraft led inevitably to successful aerial re-supply, at least sometimes.

The first instance of aerial re-supply had been during the siege of Kut in Mesopotamia back in 1916 because, as they say, 'necessity is the mother of invention'. With Kut under siege, aerial re-supply was attempted for the first time and the potential of aircraft in the logistic chain was recognized. On 31 January 1916, newspapers, letters and small items were free-dropped. In the period from 15 to 29 April 1916, 30 Squadron RFC delivered 16,800lb of food to Kut – 22 per cent of the requirement – but the small squadron could not airlift the tonnage of food the 13,000 denizens of Kut required.[8] Molkentin summed up this first foray into aerial logistic supply by saying that

> aerial re-supply failed on two counts. First because the concept was not commensurate with the available technology and second because the available aeroplanes were unreliable and insufficient in number to deliver enough food to stave off starvation. However, history tells us that the obvious benefits of aerial re-supply were quickly realized and exploited during the war and further developed over the next three decades.[9]

That exploitation, to which Molkentin refers, was demonstrated by the Chindits in Burma (1943–1944) and later by the Americans in Vietnam (1964–1973). In Burma, for several months Chindit columns were wholly supplied from the air. However, only very few of their casualties could be evacuated; a significant weakness in the operations.

When two forces are in close contact, air supply is problematic. The accuracy of a parachute drop is subject to a number of factors. Timing of the release, wind conditions, weight of the burden and the condition of the drop zone (DZ) all affect the ability of the recipients to harvest the drop. There are many examples of the enemy benefiting from the inaccuracy of supply drops and the siege of Dien Bien Phu (see Chapter 7) in 1954 is one such.

Chapter Three

Why War?

'Guerrilla war is more intelligent than a bayonet charge.'[1]
[Colonel T.E. Lawrence]

In order to examine the three wars in Vietnam it is necessary to have a feel for the train of political events that led to armed conflict. With the benefit of 20/20 hindsight it is clear that the first two wars in Vietnam, from 1945 until 1973, achieved nothing and need not have been fought.

Had they been avoided, millions of lives would have been saved and a mountain of treasure could have been spent on something more productive than bombs and machine guns. However, the protracted wars were the product of the unrealistic, political, hubristic aspirations of first the French and then the Americans. Those aspirations were not tempered by an appreciation of the physical, social, cultural and psychological hurdles that lay ahead.

The world had undergone massive change between 1939 and 1945. The anti-colonial movement was unorganized but far-reaching. The British were facing independence movements across the globe; for example, in India, Malaya, Burma and Cyprus. Shrewdly and pragmatically, Britain withdrew from the Empire and, with the goodwill it generated, created the Commonwealth. The French did nothing of the sort.

The first flicker of self-determination for Vietnam was as far back as the uprisings against the French colonial government in 1885 and again in 1888. In 1911, one of the key players in Vietnamese independence, Vo Nguyen Giap, was born to an activist father in An Xa village, Quang Binh province, the 'waist' of the country and one of its most impoverished areas.

The country into which the boy was born had changed little in several hundred years and it had a simple rural economy. Educational standards were very low. 'Between 1883 when the French arrived and 1945 in the whole of Indochina (Vietnam, Laos and Cambodia) only 14,393 children gained the Diploma of Higher Primary Education.'[2] Young Giap was bright enough to gain a place, in 1924, at the Lycée National in Hue. The culture of the school was to provide a Western/Vietnamese education devoid of French overtones.[3]

Giap became politically active at the age of 14 and, by the time he had won a place at Hanoi University, his political views had crystallized. Only

408 lawyers graduated from that university in the twenty-five years between 1920 and 1945; Giap was one of the few and he graduated in 1937. Giap's political education was guided by Phan Boi Chau, a convinced revolutionary and committed communist.

In 1937 Giap joined the Indochinese Communist Party (ICP) and then quickly turned his erudition to good use. He wrote for several newspapers with a revolutionary bias, as did a P. Lin, later exposed as a pseudonym for Ho Chi Minh.

Ho Chi Minh was the leader of the independence movement and, until his death in 1969, a towering figure in Vietnamese politics. He was the mentor of Giap, whose political activities caused him to take his eye off the legal ball and he failed a key examination that would have allowed him to practise law. It was a setback, and so he was obliged to forsake the courtroom for the classroom and take a job teaching history at Thang Long Private School in Hanoi.

Giap's wife Quan Thai, who he had married in 1939, shared his communist fervour but was imprisoned by the French for her subversive activities in May 1941. She was tried and died in captivity. The circumstances of her death are unclear. Currey suggests that she was either beaten to death or she committed suicide.[4] Whatever the cause of her death, not unreasonably, it inflamed Giap's already well-developed nationalistic, anti-colonial, anti-French views and was the motivation for much of what was to follow.

Many years later, in 1982, General Raoul Salan, a former commander of French forces in Vietnam was interviewed by Will Brownell. He recorded Salan's confirmation that, despite his own personal antipathy towards Giap, 'a great crime had been done against him.' Quan Thai *had* been tortured. Salan added quickly, 'not by Frenchmen but by Vietnamese auxiliaries'.[5]

By any yardstick the conduct of the French in Indochina matched the excesses of the Germans in the Second World War. It was just not on the same industrial scale. It was noted by Brownell that

French police and Vietnamese jailers were willing to use any methods to persuade prisoners to talk, including the forced ingestion of water, electrical shocks, pulling fingernails and other brutal measures. With female captives they occasionally used a variety of electric shock methods that literally drove women mad. Jailers used eels – nasty, hard-biting creatures known for their strength and tenacity – and inserted them into the throat or vagina of women. Placed in these soft wet areas, the eels tried to swim and bite their way to freedom. The torturers watched as their victims were bitten and electrically shocked by the eels. Resistance was sometimes magnificent. One dying woman wanted to be sure that she did not speak and, allegedly, bit off her tongue and spat it at her interrogator.[6]

Vo Nguyen Giap and Ho Chi Minh (*aka* Nguyến Ái Quốc) in 1945.

It is little wonder that the French were hated by their colonial citizens and Giap worked to imbue this hatred in his soldiers. That hatred was a strong motivator and the reason that no quarter was given to the French in the many battles to follow.

In 1940 an aggressive Japan, already at war with China, had demanded that Japanese soldiers be allowed into Vietnam in order to police the Chinese border. The Japanese wanted to safeguard their supply of rubber. The French refused the Japanese demand but, after its catastrophic defeat by the Germans in June 1940, the French colonial government in Vietnam was dangerously weakened both morally and militarily. Notwithstanding diplomatic manoeuvring with the French and after winning significant concessions, the Japanese invaded Vietnam on 22 September 1940. The fighting was brief; nevertheless, 824 French troops were killed.

Japan took control of the country, but it suited its book to leave the French Colonial administration nominally in place. Vietnam, Laos and Cambodia formed French Indochina, a colonial possession since 1883. Initially Washington backed the French regime in Vietnam, hoping it would resist, although the authority of the French was significantly diminished. Nevertheless, the French worked at co-existence with the invader who was able to use Vietnam as a staging area and take advantage of its ports and airfields. It was from here that the subjugation of Thailand and Burma was later put into effect.[7]

After the invasion of Vietnam by the Japanese the US position changed and, by mid-1943, President Roosevelt was speaking frankly about the merits of Vietnamese independence.

In 1944, Washington recognized the need to involve itself in the situation in Indochina. Accordingly, the USA opened a military station at Kunming in southern China, while American advisers and Office of Strategic Services (OSS) agents supported both the Chinese Kuomintang and Vietnamese resistance groups. The Americans worked closely with Ho Chi Minh who was the political and public face of self-determination. He was something of an enigma.[8]

Ho had travelled widely and 'exuded an air of fragility, a sickly pallor. But this only emphasized the imperturbable dignity that enveloped him as though it was a garment. He conveyed a sense of inner strength and generosity of spirit.'[9] This judgement was made by one of his acolytes and cannot be taken at face value. It must be balanced by the realization that Ho was also utterly ruthless in pursuing his political aims. He caused the deaths of multitudes, many of whom were his own countrymen. Nevertheless, Ho was the undisputed leader of the resistance movement, the Vietminh, an abbreviation of *Viet Nam Doc Lap Dong Minh Hoi*, which translates as 'The League for the Independence of Vietnam'.

Japanese troops advance to Lang Son, Vietnam, 22 September 1940.
(*https://saigoneer.com/old-saigon*)

The Vietminh supplied the US military with information about Japanese troop numbers and movements. It was more of a working relationship and less of an alliance. However, it gave Ho Chi Minh hope that Washington might later support Vietnamese independence once the war had ended.[10]

Japanese military success against the French, British and Dutch had dramatically reduced the prestige of the colonial powers in the eyes of South-East Asians. The French nominally governed Indochina, but only with the acquiescence of the Japanese. The Vietminh, whose aim was self-government, was emboldened when by chance it found itself allied to the USA and Britain after the Pearl Harbor attack of 7 December 1941. The Vietminh received active support from the Chinese Nationalist forces under Chiang Kai-shek and used this support to fund their organization of communist cells in the north.[11] It was a complicated part of the world.

From October 1944 and the following year Vietnam suffered a famine. The cause was a combination of factors, the first being crop failures from 1943 to 1945, the second the neglect of the dykes around rice paddies.

A drought followed by catastrophic flooding that wiped out the remaining rice harvest was the final straw. The famine was exacerbated by ruinous logistic policies of the French and Japanese, both of whom used edible rice

Near Hanoi, 1945. Three orphans. (*Vo An Ninh*)

and maize as fuel in power stations. The loss of life is estimated to have been between 400,000 and 2 million. It was, however, a potent aid to recruitment for the Vietminh who encouraged the starving population to sack rice warehouses and to withhold their taxes. Approximately eighty-five warehouses were attacked. That did not materially alter the situation, but it did allow the expression of rising anti-colonial sentiment.

The Vietminh had a low profile at this time and, in July 1944, Vo Nguyen Giap sought to raise his profile by accelerating guerrilla activity. However, Giap had exceeded his brief and Ho countermanded Giap's initiative and questioned his political acumen. A little later, on 22 December 1944, Ho judged that the time was now right and he appointed Giap, despite his recent 'loss of face', as his military chief to command the 'Vietnam Propaganda and Liberation Front'. Initially titled the National Army of Vietnam (NVA), this was the forerunner of the People's Army of Vietnam (PAVN). It was a grand title, but it was only thirty-four strong, of whom three were women. Giap had no military training and, at this stage, was probably not even a competent private soldier.

Giap showed his recognition of the logistic imperative. He set up his own armoury. He saw the need to prepare for the conflict that lay ahead and to that end he 'moved blacksmiths into a deep valley behind a wall of several mountains. After months of dangerous experimentation, his men succeeded in producing their first land mine.'[12]

The mine is, of course, the favoured guerrilla weapon. It is inexpensive, easy to manufacture, does not require physical contact with the enemy, it is readily deployed, cost-effective and instils fear in the adversary. Where Giap went, generations of guerrillas since have followed, all over the globe.

In the mid-1940s Vietminh action against the French was sporadic and, in the order of things, not much more than a dangerous irritant. The French reacted with the utmost ferocity and their barbarous behaviour not only did them no credit, it was also ineffective and aided Vietminh recruitment. At about this time, Giap carried a hand grenade with him 'for protection' because he knew that if captured, he would not have a quick death. He wrote later that '(I) carried (it) constantly for its good effect on morale.'[13] He later discovered that the grenade was a dud.

As the Second World War ran to a close, the Allied powers, with the arrogance that flows from military power, decided how the planet should be governed. One of the items on the agenda at the Potsdam Conference in July 1945 was Indochina and its future government. It was agreed by the major powers that Vietnam should be divided at the 16th parallel and that Nationalist Chinese troops were to accept Japanese surrender in the north.

Hanoi, the bodies of three victims. (*Vo An Ninh*)

The USA, indisputably the most powerful military power in the world, was intractably opposed to 'colonialism' and worked assiduously to undermine those European states with colonies, not least the UK. It was reported in a State Department memo in 1945 that

> the President [Roosevelt] said he was concerned about the brown people in the East. He said that there are one billion brown people in many Eastern countries, they are ruled by a handful of whites and they resent it … He said that French Indochina should be taken from France and put under trusteeship.

The anti-colonial attitude of the USA was explored by Lawrence K. Freeman in his paper 'Roosevelt's "Grand Strategy" to Rid the World of British Colonialism: 1941–1945' and he quotes Roosevelt, speaking to his son Elliott, as saying at the Casablanca conference in January 1943 that

> I'm talking about another war. I'm talking about what will happen to our world if after *this* war we allow millions of people to slide back into the same semi-slavery! Don't think for a moment, Elliott, that Americans would be dying in the Pacific tonight if it hadn't been for the short-

sighted greed of the French and the British and the Dutch. Shall we allow them to do it all, all over again?

Roosevelt did not leave it there and, as an alleged friend and ally of the UK, he prophesied that 'we will have more trouble with Great Britain after the war than we are having with Germany'. To be quite clear, Germany was, at the time, an implacable enemy waging total war across Europe and engaged in the killing of American soldiers; lots of American soldiers. So much for the basis of the enduring myth of the 'special relationship'.

Pragmatically, in this case, the USA reluctantly supported French ambitions to return because the alternative was to accept the communist Democratic Republic of Vietnam (DRV) government.

In 1945 Indochina was a mess. On the face of it, seeking self-determination was not an unreasonable ambition for the Vietnamese. However, there were two significant obstacles. The first of these was French determination to hold on to its possession of Indochina and by force if need be. The second was the flavour of any possible Vietnamese government which was uncompromisingly communist. Those two issues, in combination, lit the blue touch paper for the first Vietnam War.

There were a number of players in Indochina. The French were seeking to suppress the Vietminh insurrection and to regain control of a country still occupied by Japan. The USA supported the French logistically, but also provided arms to the Vietminh on the basis that they would use them against the Japanese, although in practice the arms were used against the French. To describe the Indochina policy of the USA as 'fumbling and erratic' would be to understate the case.[14] Incoherent, ill-considered, inconsistent and irrational would also apply. This all suddenly changed on 15 August 1945 when Japan surrendered.

Major Archimedes Patti, US Army, landed with an OSS team at Gia Lam airport on 22 August 1945.[15] He was an OSS agent and immediately recognized that Ho Chi Minh was the leader of the *de facto* Vietminh government. The two men struck up a warm relationship as Ho played on Patti's 'considerable vanity like a lute'.[16] Patti described Ho Chi Minh as 'a gentle soul'. He added: 'Perhaps I was somewhat naïve ... but felt very strongly that the Vietnamese had a legitimate gripe or claim to really govern themselves. After all, what was it [the Second World War] all about?'[17]

Patti was the subject of a lengthy TV interview in 1981, having been particularly well-placed to view the events that shaped this part of South-East Asia. He opined that

We (the USA) had Ho Chi Minh, we had the Vietminh, we had the Indochina question in our hand, but for reasons which defy good logic we find today that we supported the French for a war which they themselves dubbed '*la sale guerre*', the dirty war, and we paid to the tune of 80 percent of the cost of that French war and then we picked up 100 percent of the American-Vietnam War.[18]

There was a power vacuum. The Japanese, until then effectively the masters of Vietnam, were stunned by the surrender of their home islands and their garrisons were disinclined to surrender. Ho Chi Minh promptly filled that power vacuum by persuading Emperor Bao Dai to abdicate and invite him to form a government in North Vietnam. That done, Ho led his acolytes into Hanoi and proclaimed independence for North Vietnam on 2 September 1945 in Ba Dinh Square, Hanoi.

Ho Chi Minh had declared independence from both the French and Japanese empires. He used a form of words from the American declaration of independence, guided by Patti. As the crowd cheered, US aeroplanes flew over Hanoi that day in what was, mistakenly, perceived to be a sign of tacit support for the new regime. The OSS people in Hanoi at this time seriously underestimated Ho Chi Minh. Major Patti was publicly supportive of the declaration and was photographed saluting the Vietnamese flag. It was into this chaotic, political mélange that the British came to play. The allies asked the UK for help and, in September 1945, 20,000 British and Indian troops under the command of Major General Douglas Gracey arrived in Saigon to take control of South Vietnam.[19]

The Japanese troops, although defeated, declined to lay down their arms. It would be true to say that Gracey had a problem and, compounding his problem, the Communist Party under Tran Van Giau became overtly aggressive. Public disorder reached such a degree that Gracey declared martial law. To make this effective, in a surreal move, he employed those same Japanese soldiers to help police the country. The communists were no match for Gracey's mixed force of battle-hardened soldiers and over those six months there were constant armed clashes. Gracey's orders were to take the surrender of the Japanese garrisons, evacuate Allied prisoners of war and to maintain law and order until such time as the French government in Paris could muster the will and the forces to assert control.

During the period November/April of 1945–46 British Indian troops were gradually replaced by French soldiers who took control in May 1946. This force was 46,513 strong and equipped and organized to fight a conventional battle along European lines. From here on, any fighting was between the French and the Vietminh.

Lieutenant Colonel A.B. Dewey, an officer of the OSS, arrived in Vietnam on 4 September 1945. Soon after, he complained to General Gracey about the

Lieutenant Colonel A.B. Dewey (1916–46), pictured as a captain.

conduct of the troops under his command. The general was offended by Dewey's tone and promptly declared him to be *persona non grata*.

On the day of his departure, the aircraft scheduled to fly Dewey out was late; he returned for lunch at the villa that the OSS had requisitioned in Saigon. Near the villa, he was shot in the head in an ambush by Vietminh troops who mistook him for a Frenchman.[20] Thus Dewey has the doubtful distinction of being the first American to be killed in Vietnam.

In these engagements with the communists, the British lost forty killed and Japanese and French contingents each about the same. The communists had suffered more than 2,500 dead. Latter-day historians such as Peter Macdonald have written that Gracey was the wrong man with the wrong attitude and that he exceeded his brief.[21] Stanley Karnow takes a similar view. There is no doubt that Gracey was unsympathetic to the communists and their political leadership. It is suggested that the imposition of martial law and support of the French return led to increased violence. This is unfair because Gracey was specifically charged with providing support to the French. In his magisterial book, Hastings comments that Gracey was 'merely a relatively junior soldier'.[22] Given the circumstances, martial law was the only available option. Gracey was certainly not subject to any criticism by HMG and he was later promoted and decorated.

Tran Van Giau saw the writing on the wall and took the residue of his irregular force north and combined it with the Vietminh.

Chapter Four

The 'Dirty War', 1946–1953

'Guerrilla war must have a friendly population, not
actively friendly, but sympathetic to the point of not
betraying rebel movements to the enemy. Rebellions can
be made with 2 per cent in a striking force and 98 per cent
passively sympathetic.'[1]

[Colonel T.E. Lawrence]

In 1946 the situation was confused. The French, now firmly back in government but incapable of mounting a major campaign, were being provided with
logistic support by the USA in their efforts to eradicate the Vietminh. The
'French' came in many forms: there were the French from Vichy, the French
from liberated France, the French from Giraud or North Africa, the French
colonials of Indochina and finally there were the French army personnel. It
was a thoroughly multi-race organization.

The political wing of the Vietminh was engaged in negotiations with the
French, while at the same time engaging in the killing of French soldiers.
It was not unlike the situation in Northern Ireland twenty-five years later,
when the leaders of the IRA orchestrated the killing but claimed to have only
a passive political role. No one believed Ho Chi Minh, just as no one believed
Martin McGuinness.

Ho Chi Minh directed Giap to represent the PAVN in welcoming General
Jacques Leclerc, the incoming French commander-in-chief.[2] Giap's hatred
of the French was such that initially he refused. Ho demonstrated his iron
will when he reiterated his command, but Giap did not carry off the event
well. When Giap greeted Leclerc at the airport he did shake his hand (the
general's) and pompously proclaimed 'the first resistance fighter of Vietnam
salutes the first resistance fighter of France.'[3]

In seeking to equate their military careers, Giap revealed an inflated ego
that would have an effect upon his performance when he served as vice chairman of the North Vietnamese delegation in its negotiations with the French.
Although he was viewed as a shrewd negotiator, Giap was also thought to be
unduly emotional.

Lieutenant General Jacques Leclerc.

The almost inevitable war finally came to Vietnam on 19 December 1946 when French and Vietminh forces clashed in Hanoi. The French attempted to seize a boat suspected of carrying contraband weapons. Both sides opened fire, the incident escalated and on 23 November a French cruiser, *Suffren*, opened fire on the Chinese and Vietnamese quarters of Haiphong. It was a very poor decision, both politically and militarily: many were needlessly killed for no purpose, but probably not the 6,000 claimed by Ho Chi Minh.

All revolutionary forces mass behind a charismatic leader and the Vietminh were following a pattern that includes Cromwell, Lenin, Gandhi, Castro, Kenyatta and Mugabe. The worth of these leaders as human beings was, and is, irrelevant; it is the persona and the promise that counts.

By December 1946 Ho Chi Minh drew saintly comparisons and many homes displayed his benign countenance. Nguyen Cao Ky said that 'The only name on my lips as well of those of nearly every one of my generation was Ho Chi Minh.'[4] However, the man was far from saintly; he was, in fact, utterly ruthless and disinterested in the human condition. He was prepared to spend as many human lives as it took to achieve his aims. He had sole ownership of the Vietnamese independence movement.

In 1946, France was about to fight another war, 8,000 miles from home. War is one of the more expensive activities known to man, and logistic matériel, its transport and protection account for much of that expense. It is germane to give a thought to the French economy at the time because, in 1945–46, France was recovering from a crushing defeat, enemy occupation and a loss of honour and dignity. From a population of 42 million, she had suffered 122,00 military dead and 335,000 wounded, 1.4 million had been made prisoners of war and 500,000 men, women and children died as a direct result of the war.[5]

Germany had held 2.5 million Frenchmen as forced labourers, that number made up of PoWs and civilians who were conscripted to this work force by the Vichy government of Marshal Pétain. By 1943 the French supplied 17 per cent of the German economy's labour. In 1945, the survivors trickled home to a country in crisis. Somewhere over 10,000 Frenchmen paid with their lives for perceived 'collaboration', although most of these killings were not as the result of any kind of legal process. France was divided, unhappy and the resurrection of the economy was of paramount importance. France was a broken state and, in addition, it was 'broke'.

The recovery was, in large measure, the result of the apparent altruism of the USA. France was still indebted to the USA for financial support in the Great War and repayment of these loans was suspended in 1931. It was on its financial knees in 1946 but, under a new agreement, the US waived the $2.8 billion debt and gave France a new loan of $650 million. The French agreed that, in order to resolve France's commitment to America – and to obtain further credit – France's markets would be open to American products, especially film productions. Film productions? Yes, apparently very important at the time.[6]

This does seem to be a very one-sided agreement. What was in it for the Americans? Only the most naïve believe that there is any friendship and charity in foreign relations. For example, the USA exacted, in full measure, from Britain the debt accrued during the Second World War; not that Britain sought charity.[7] It is suggested that, in 1946, the USA saw France as a useful proxy in its ongoing crusade against communism. That might not have been the rationale but, in reality, that is what happened. French historian Claude Fohlen was of the view that

> France received $7,000 million ($7 billion) which was used either to finance the imports needed to get the economy off the ground again … Without the Marshall Plan, however, the economic recovery would have been a much slower process – American aid restored equilibrium in the equipment industries which govern the recovery of consumption, and opened the way … to continuing further growth. *This growth was affected by a third factor … decolonization*[8] (or lack of it; author's italics).

Fohlen's remark about 'decolonization' hits the nail on the head. The cost of Empire was a factor in Britain's withdrawal from its colonies. However, the French, at vast expense, resisted to the bitter end in Indochina and Algeria. In Tunisia and Morocco, it delayed independence for as long as possible and only decolonized unwillingly.

General Leclerc, the first French general selected to preserve the French colonial system in Indochina, was a dry, humourless, bigoted man with a rigid outlook on life and was described by one of his aides as having 'one of the most brilliant minds of the twelfth century'. Allegedly, his appointment proved to be a serious mistake.[9] His first error was to underestimate his foe, which in doctrine, organization and training was quite different to anything previously experienced by Leclerc.

Leclerc's opposition may have appeared to be just a ragbag of part-time terrorists. The reality is that it was far from that. It was organized into three groupings and the first of these was the main force units composed of regular soldiers. It was these who took on the French and later the Americans in various guises: Vietminh, the North Vietnamese Army (NVA) or Vietcong. They were the cutting edge in large-unit fighting. Their organization and equipment evolved over time and with experience. Initially they were a single platoon but, in due course, were deployed as divisions. They were very high-quality, well-trained and totally committed soldiers. However, at this early stage the logistic support of the NVA was cursory.

A second-line female soldier.

The second category was the regional or local forces. These were semi-regular, second-line troops recruited from a given province or district, similar to the British Territorial Army of the 1960s. Some of these units were deployable anywhere, but others were only employed locally. They were self-supporting in terms of food and shelter.

The third category was 'guerrilla' and they were formed by individual villages. They fell into two sub-groups. The Dan Quan, which was composed of all ages and both sexes, was not intended to involve itself in direct operations but provided accommodation, medical and logistic assistance. Men aged between 18 and 45 were directed to the *Dan Quan Du Kich*. They were inadequately armed and they carried on their normal occupation during the day, during which they gathered intelligence. They were mustered for operations at night when they laid mines, prepared booby-traps and, when needed, acted as porters for main force units moving through their area.[10]

These soldiers, in whatever category they fitted, had one thing in common and that was a total, unrelenting commitment to their cause. Their opponents may have described them as 'fanatics' but Ho Chi Minh and Giap were masterly practioners of a 'hearts and minds' policy. Giap in particular was well aware of the dictum from T.E. Lawrence that appears at the head of this chapter because he was a disciple of Lawrence of Arabia.[11] Giap indoctrinated his subordinates unrelentingly and to very great effect. He developed in his troops a sacrificial courage seldom seen in that century (the twentieth), an accomplishment that was a major factor in Giap's success.

Ho Chi Minh and Giap had far and away beyond the 2 per cent active support of which Lawrence wrote. However, in 1946, Giap was not a general. He had led or instigated only very small and inconsequential actions. He was a student of guerrilla war but, as yet, not a capable practitioner.

The French army and its operations in South-East Asia did not enjoy support in metropolitan France. The French Far East Expeditionary Corps (CEFEO), as it was now titled, had to contend with public opinion that was, at best, tepid. This was because 'France had no vital interest in Indochina.'[12] The French were apathetic, and that attitude washed off on their armed force to a deleterious effect. There is a parallel: in the period from 1968 to 1972 the US armed forces fought the NVA/PAVN/VC while the American public were demonstrating in opposition to the war and spitting on soldiers returning home from operations. In neither case did attitudes 'at home' do much for the morale of soldiers fighting for their lives.

French forces were a composite of French, French Foreign Legion, Algerian, Moroccan, T'ai and Vietnamese.[13] The officers in the colonial units were French with a leavening of French senior non-commissioned officers in support. Of this force, a relatively high proportion were airborne troops and parachute insertions were commonplace. It was probably the last campaign in which multiple parachute landings were employed. The reason for parachute operations was that the French, who were otherwise road-based in a country with few roads, had no other option. The frequent dependence upon a sparse, inadequate and very vulnerable road system played into Giap's hands and contributed to his ultimate victory.

Parachutes and the aircraft to dispatch them were absolutely key to French operations. Their manufacture, provision and recovery from 1946 until 1954 were a logistic issue. Usually parachute insertions were on a battalion scale; that is to say, about 600 men in one wave of 26 to 30 aircraft. By 1953, the French had expanded their capacity for parachute operations sufficiently to be able to mount a three-battalion insertion. During the campaign the French conducted 150 parachute operations; it was the only means of reaching and supporting posts isolated in the rain forest. Charles R. Shrader remarks sagely (p. 33) that 'these airborne forces were "not well-suited for extended operations but were often misused for exactly that ... the siege of Dien Bien Phu being the most prominent example".' The parachute soldier, once duly 'inserted', could only be exfiltrated to secure French territory by marching through Vietminh-dominated jungle. The jump was mildly hazardous; the exfiltration process was often lethal.

The need for trained parachute soldiers led to an expansion of airborne forces from 'a few hundred in 1946 to 5,684 in 1950 and then the number almost doubled to 10,629 in 1951 as artillery, engineer, signal and medical units were added.'[14]

The requirement was a parachute for every man and for every 100kg (220lb) of equipment. In many cases the French dropped into 'hot' dropping zones (DZ) and, in those conditions, the airborne soldier's priority, on landing, was emphatically not retrieving and folding his parachute but, after every jump, about a third of the force was employed in recovering canopies.[15] By 1950 about 40 per cent of air-delivered tonnage was free-dropped and by so doing the capacity of the aircraft was increased by about 12 per cent.

The parachute was not a standard design or size and they had to be geared to the aircraft that were going to drop them. Most parachuting problems were overcome by the increasing experience of the practitioners. However, improving and expanding Vietminh air defence made it necessary for French aircraft to release their supply burden from higher altitudes and, for this to be effective, there was a need for an efficient delayed-opening device to ensure accuracy. The problem was never solved. The logistic units behind aerial re-supply were *Compagnie de Ravitaillement par Air* (CRA) and by 1954 the French had four such units. The 1,424 personnel were able to deliver a tonnage of 5,425 per month.[16]

Initially Leclerc had some success. His forces won several minor engagements with badly-organized groups of insurgents. Across the country small, well-protected stockades were built. These bristled with watchtowers, barbed wire, mines and hard defence works. These *miradors* were stand-alone, isolated and not mutually supporting. Their very existence generated an immediate supply problem unless they had an airstrip. The *miradors* were defended by small garrisons and minefields, but they were vulnerable to a determined assault. The Vietminh were not deterred by minefields; they were viewed as a source of supply as they lifted French mines in order to re-deploy them to their own advantage.

In late January 1947 the Vietnamese government of Ho Chi Minh and Giap's forces had withdrawn from Hanoi and established a base in the Viet Bac, that rugged hill country north of Hanoi and on the Chinese border. The area is subject to the south-west monsoon and between May and October receives about 60in of rain; this limited military operations in the jungle and there were no roads. Even a 'major' road such as Route 3 was only a single-lane track and movement along it was life-threatening. As a line of logistic supply, it was useless.

On 27 January 1947 the pattern for the 'Dirty War' was established when a large convoy of French vehicles carrying officials on an inspection tour was ambushed on Route 5 between Hanoi and Haiphong. Fourteen cars and vans were destroyed and many of the occupants were killed. The ambush was well-planned and very effective. It was evident that travel by road was hazardous and this one incident gave Giap the initiative and sowed doubt in the minds of his enemy. The brutality of the Vietminh, notwithstanding 'hearts and minds', was utterly ruthless.

As it was, villagers who survived a meeting with the Vietminh were at risk from their colonial masters and French atrocities easily matched those of the Vietminh. To look ahead, for example, in two bloody hours on 29 November 1948 at My Trach in Quang Binh Province, French troops murdered well over 300 civilians. Quite why they did this has never been explained. Of the dead, 157 were children. Many of the 170 women killed were first subjected to rape. Some 326 houses were destroyed. The scene of the massacre was a bridge close to the railway station. The incident is marked every year and there is a monument to the dead at the scene. It is a sad and enduring legacy of French rule.

Any dissension, any criticism or any failure by villagers to be supportive was met by the Vietminh with summary and immediate execution. Over the next twenty-eight years the Vietnamese slaughtered tens of thousands, perhaps hundreds of thousands of their own countrymen, all in the cause of 'freedom'. The French had been subject to Nazi barbarism for five years and so were

The people who suffered at the hands of their own countrymen and the French.

not strangers to cruelty. This writer – and others before him – is at a loss to understand why the Nazi experience had not impacted positively upon the French military. It may well be that the colonial troops, such as the Algerians and Moroccans, had not experienced life under the Nazis; however, they were led by French officers.

By the end of January 1947, the players in this military saga were in place. The French occupied the centres of population and controlled most of the low ground. The Vietminh had taken to the jungle and the high ground. It did not 'occupy' territory in the accepted sense but denied it to the French, other than in small cantonments. There was no discernible 'front line'. In a war of this sort, time was on the side of those fighting a guerrilla campaign. It was their aim to fight over a protracted period that would stress the French politically and economically. The guerrillas would avoid large-scale operations and would give force-building and training high priority. When in contact with the French they would only fight on their own terms. This would demonstrate the French inferiority in guerrilla warfare and would place psychological pressure on the French command chain. The French aim was, predictably, the opposite. They needed a military denouement and only a large set-piece battle would provide that. They were aware that, even with American logistic support, a long campaign would be expensive in both human and cash terms. The patience of Paris was finite. The Vietminh at this stage were simply not equipped for any large-scale, conventional operations. Dang Van Viet recalled years later that

> In 1947, defence in depth was made necessary by our poor equipment, as antiquated as it was deficient. A primer which did not ignite or hand grenade which did not explode were common occurrences in those early days of resistance against the French. None of us was deterred or appalled by such malfunctions because to own a firearm was already a matter of great pride for men like us newly freed from slavery. So, imagine how proud we were to sport a short-barrelled magazine rifle or a long Russian infantry rifle.[17]

The major stage for operations from January 1947 would be the Red River delta and in the country around Hanoi. It was a rich recruiting area for the Vietminh who drew on the population of about 6 million. A secure hold on Hanoi was the prize for both parties. Initially, the French were successful. They cleared Vietminh from the delta and took control of all the major centres of population. Importantly, they had possession of the major roads both in the north (Tonkin) and central Vietnam (Annam). Further south, their hold was rather more fragile.

The monsoon was due in May and it was critical that the French carry the battle to their enemy before the rain brought a halt to operations. Conditions were in the French favour. The enemy was on the back foot and Giap was not excelling. His experience was 'only about that of a major in a Western army'.[18] Despite the excellent reasons for cracking on, the French halted their operations. Ever since, historians have sought to establish why. It could be argued that there were still pockets of resistance in the lowlands and particularly in the cities. It could also be that the two months of the dry season remaining were insufficient to re-supply, reinforce and redeploy French forces to advantage. However, that is speculation and the consensus is that Leclerc dropped the ball, lost the initiative and by so doing gave Giap breathing space in which to recruit, train and indoctrinate his soldiers. It also gave him time to arrange the logistic support that was central to the plan.

It came as no surprise when Leclerc was replaced, on 18 July 1947, by Lieutenant General Jean Étienne Valluy.[19] He, like his predecessor, underestimated the foe and he would not be the last. Valluy did not perceive the Vietminh as a major problem and rather foolishly predicted that he 'could eliminate all organized resistance in three months'.[20]

About ten weeks later, on 7 October, after detailed planning and under pressure from Paris for 'results', Valluy initiated Operation LEA. Intelligence sources had identified Bac Kan, a nondescript little village astride Route 3,

Lieutenant General Jean Étienne Valluy.

as the Vietminh headquarters and the aim was to destroy that headquarters and the people in it. In addition, it was expected to eliminate Vietminh forces in the Viet Bac. Valluy had at least 15,000 troops at his disposal. It was an ambitious, all-arms operation that faced about 60,000 enemy in approximately 7,500 square miles of jungle sanctuary, which was a formidable task.

The operation was to comprise two pincers. The first, of three battalions of infantry, three regiments of artillery, three armoured regiments and one engineer regiment, was to advance by road from Lang Son to Bac Kan by way of Cao Bang and Nguyen Binh. The advance would be on the narrowest of fronts and as dictated by the 140 miles of unsecured road. The second pincer of three battalions of infantry and an artillery regiment would travel in French navy landing craft up the Clear River to Tuyen Quang. An airborne insertion of two battalions on Cho Don, Cho Moi and Bac Kan would initiate the action.

The airborne assault at Bac Kan surprised Ho Chi Minh and he only avoided capture by a hair's breadth by taking refuge in a camouflaged hole while paratroops beat the bushes nearby.[21] His office was discovered, along with current correspondence, and one could speculate on what impact Ho's death or capture might have had. It is suggested that the probability is that one of Ho's lieutenants would have stepped into his shoes; the battle for independence would still have continued unabated.

From the beginning, Operation LEA started to go awry. The Vietminh resisted the airborne soldiers and surrounded Bac Kan. The northern road-based pincer was easy meat for Giap's soldiers who, without difficulty, were able to stage a succession of successful ambushes. Each of these caused the loss of vehicles and men. The wounded had to be evacuated from whence they had come, and those vehicles were subject to further ambush. The sharp end of the pincer was on a ten-man frontage with a tank in support. There were logistic issues; every time resistance was encountered, time was lost. Along the route, bridges were destroyed and before the engineers could rig a replacement the infantry had to cross the river and secure the far bank. It was

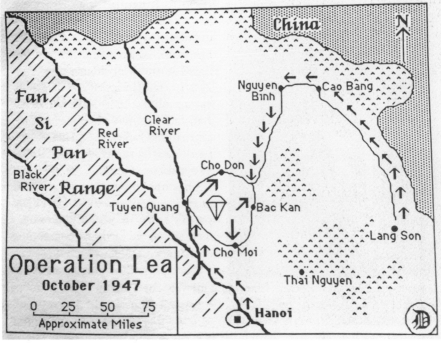

Operation LEA. (*Davidson*)

necessary for every convoy to carry large amounts of engineer stores for the repair or replacement of the route. A prodigious amount of ammunition was used in 'prophylactic fire' when the undergrowth ahead and to the sides of the road were sprayed to deter any enemy in hiding.

It was only on 13 October that Valluy was able to bring the Vietminh to what might be termed 'conventional' battle, and this was when the Vietminh 'dug in', figuratively, about 10 miles north of Bac Kan. It took three days' hard fighting for the pincer to break through to reach the embattled parachute battalions.

This element of Operation LEA is almost a case study in 'how not to fight a guerrilla force' and the riverine force did little better. Passage up the river was difficult as the craft negotiated sandbanks and other obstructions. The troops were off-loaded at Tuyen Quang and marched to join the fight, only to discover that the Vietminh had broken off contact. The two pincers closed together on 19 October, but with nothing in their grasp. There had been heavy casualties on both sides. The French lost about 6,000 dead and wounded and estimated the enemy casualties as 9,500.[22] This figure of 9,500 is probably an overly optimistic estimate. Years later, the Americans would

General Hoàng Văn Thái.

develop casualty estimation into almost an art form. Inflating enemy casualties is not in the accountant's best interest as it leads to a falsely-based sense of optimism.

The engagement around Bac Kan helped to enhance the reputation of Hoàng Văn Thái who acted as Giap's deputy and who, at the age of 30, had been the first chief of the Vietnamese General Staff of the embryonic North Vietnamese Army. Hoàng was an important player in the years that followed. The photograph was taken in 1986 just before his death at age 71.

The French troops had been in constant action for twelve days and their re-supply had been only by way of that 140-mile-long road. Aerial re-supply was not practical as the DZ was insecure. This operation provided Valluy with plenty of useful lessons. More significantly, it added to Giap's experience. 'He would never again leave a headquarters undefended against attack from the air.'[23] The battle polished his ability as a commander and his reputation.

Valluy licked his wounds. He returned to the fray on 20 November with Operation CEINTURE. This month-long operation was designed to clear out the Vietminh between Thai Nguyen and Tuyen Quang. The operation had limited success, but the French could not draw their opposition into a set-piece battle. In classic guerrilla style, the Vietminh simply broke off contact and melted away into the trees.

On 22 December 1947 Valluy withdrew his soldiers and recognized that, notwithstanding the ambitions of his political masters, this was going to be a long war and the elimination of the Vietminh 'was beyond the capability of the French'.

The French politicians continued their irresolute, incoherent and penny-pinching support of military operations while demanding 'decisive solutions'.[24] Valluy could not provide those decisive solutions, nor could he resolve the all-embracing transport issue. He added to the chain of fortified posts but, in order to reach and supply them, he was dependent upon control

A Vietminh soldier, little more than a boy, taken prisoner.

of *Route Coloniale* 4 (RC4). This road ran from Lang Son to Cao Bang. It was a two-lane highway that traversed very rugged country and ran through deep ravines and over innumerable bridges. The users of this road invited ambush and by the end of 1948 there had been thirty such actions. All of these were expensive in lives, vehicles and matériel. Valluy hoped, fervently, that eventually the Vietminh would come out to fight on his terms. There is little evidence that the French ever had an aspiration to own the jungle. The British in Malaya did. They pursued their enemy in his lair, and although the scale was different, it worked.

Valluy was not alone in having logistic problems. Giap had logistic issues too and he eschewed mechanization. He placed all of his logistic energy into people. Giap knew that one porter could carry 54lb of rice 15 miles in a day or 12 miles in a night. Horse carts could carry 473lb at 12.4 miles per day, and buffalo carts 770lb at 12 miles per day. Each soldier carried eight days' rations in a food tube. Then how many porters must begin working and *when* to sustain a 400-man combat unit in a ten-day assault on a target 130 miles away?[25] It may sound like a Staff College problem, but for Giap it was the real world. Phillip Davidson, a distinguished soldier, observed that

> Logistic support is the fuel which drives the military and an increase in (the size of Giap's) Main Force or any staff and command organization will not bring lasting results without a corresponding improvement in logistic capacity ... Giap had to convert the Vietminh from the 'cottage industry' type of support for guerrilla war to the more sophisticated logistic systems to support large, conventional forces. Of all the tasks facing Giap in 1948–50, this would be the most formidable; a Goliath of a problem facing a David of resources.[26]

Giap's logistic needs were dictated by the size of his forces and these had increased in size and capability. His main force had doubled from the 30,000 of June 1946 to 60,000 a year later. Commensurate increases were made to his regional and guerrilla formations. Where practical he moved his soldiers into the Viet Bac and, as a result, 'the French would have to come to him under conditions favourable to Giap.'[27] In the meantime there was a requirement to recruit porters. This was to be a massive work force and, as a rule of thumb, four porters per soldier was the scale. These porters, willing or not, had to be organized, provided with footwear, possibly clothed, some accommodated but all, when away from their village, had to be fed. The diet of soldiers and porters was unsophisticated, nevertheless the scale of the 'catering' (perhaps a misnomer!) operation was huge. The downside of employing so many porters was that, on a long journey, it was calculated that they consumed 90 per cent of the food they carried.[28]

The Vietminh were obliged to manufacture their own small arms and the production of mines, mentioned earlier, was expanded. In their jungle 'factories' and workplaces the Vietminh turned their hand to the manufacture of grenades, small arms, ammunition and some light machine guns. 'At Thai Nguyen the output was fifty rifles and ten pistols a day and three or four machine guns a month.'[29] Captured French ordnance was put to use, but the assembly and transport of the raw material for arms to manufacturing site was, in itself, a logistic burden. The victory of the communist Chinese over the nationalists in 1949 was of enormous benefit to Ho Chi Minh and he was the recipient of massive logistic support from that source thereafter. It was this logistic support and Giap's ability to transport the supplies that proved to be so critical to the campaign.

The French were blissfully unaware of the continuing development of a formidable adversary in the Viet Bac and their lack of offensive action would cost them dear ere long. Giap was emerging as a general. He learned from his mistakes and those of his enemy. Because he had not attended Sandhurst, West Point or St Cyr he had no pre-conceived 'school solutions' in his mind. Giap drew his own conclusions from the situations as he saw them and, having started to 'learn on the job', he had been more than the equal of General Valluy who was replaced in May 1948 by Lieutenant General Roger Blaizot.[30] The campaign season was over and, as Blaizot sat on his hands and waited for it to stop raining, Giap intensified the training and indoctrination of his troops.

The employment of hundreds and thousands of porters in support of Giap's soldiers, although acknowledged by Western historians, has not been the subject of the degree of detailed study it merits. There can be little doubt that these unsung multitudes, in their car-tyre sandals, were every bit as responsible for the defeat of both France and the USA as those who sported a rifle and bayonet.

At the close of 1947 the French contented themselves with responding to small-scale attacks that cost lives but allowed Giap free rein to go about his business in the Viet Bac. That business centred upon the 'Political Indoctrination and Education Programme'. Both Ho and Giap realized that they were unlikely ever to match the resources of a Western enemy and so they had to exploit what they had, and that was manpower. They

Lieutenant General Roger Blaizot.

had to beat their enemy on a man-to-man basis by ensuring that their soldiers were thoroughly proficient in the use of their firearms, politically aware of what they were fighting for and sufficiently indoctrinated in the cause that they would fight 'fanatically' and to the death.

The French colonial soldiers, although proficient enough in their skill at arms, had no political education and did not have the same sense of commitment as the Vietminh. Giap summed it all up when he wrote:

> Profound awareness of the aims of the Party, boundless loyalty to the army, the cause of the Nation and working class and a spirit of unreserved sacrifice are fundamental questions for the army ... Therefore the political work in its ranks is of the first importance. It is the soul of the army.[31]

Giap realized that he did not have to win large-scale battles to achieve his aim; he had only to cause French attrition and generate a defeatist attitude in France and that would be followed by a reduction in political support for the war. Time, most emphatically, was on his side. The political aim of uniting North and South Vietnam under a single communist regime, although distant, was entirely possible. That being the case, it was vital that the goodwill of the masses be claimed, fostered and fed. This could not be accomplished if his soldiers ill-treated civilians and Giap insisted that they treat civilians with dignity and concern 'in order to win their confidence and affection and achieve a perfect understanding between the people and the army.'[32]

This sort of philosophy should have been embraced by the French and the Americans but neither ever mastered or demonstrated an ability to win hearts and minds; their soldiers only served in Vietnam for a short tour while Giap's soldiers were there for life.[33]

In May 1949, the French government, blind to its own incompetence and indecision, did at least recognize the need for a reappraisal of their situation in Vietnam and decided to send the Army Chief of Staff, General Georges Revers, to conduct an investigation. Revers was a capable, quasi-political individual and he produced a first-rate forensic diagnosis of French problems in Indochina. His report was all-embracing and, inevitably, it ruffled feathers. Revers recommended that the chain of fortified posts that were strung out along the Chinese border be abandoned. He declared them to be 'a drain on French resources and could probably not withstand a serious attack.'[34] He suggested that the USA be asked for more logistic aid. He was of the view that the native Vietnamese army should be reinforced and that the population in the Tonkin delta be subject to a pacification programme; 'Hearts and Minds' if you like, but already far too late. However, the sting was in the tail: Revers recommended that diplomacy and immediate negotiations take priority over military operations. Revers could see that this was a war that could not be won and, tacitly, his report acknowledged that.

These recommendations made in 1949 were soundly based. With appropriate adjustments they would have been just as germane 'in 1952, 1964–65, 1967–68 and again in 1972'.[35] The French government took no action on the report and the document became wreathed in scandal and controversy.

Somehow, the report fell into the hands of the Vietminh and there was, and is, a strong body of opinion that it had been deliberately leaked. The leaking of the report reduced the options open to French government. To accept it at face value would throw into question all the glowing reports previously sent from the theatre, promising 'jam tomorrow'. Any number of reputations were at risk. Realistically, any negotiations could only end in the granting of independence and the immediate loss of national prestige, raw material and the markets that, it was hoped, would contribute to the French economy. Curiously, the forts along the Chinese border had a status beyond their military value. For example, the garrison at Cao Bang was the custodian of a military cemetery and the thought of leaving the graves to the Vietminh was anathema to senior French echelons. In summary, the Revers Report was mishandled for several incoherent reasons but, behind it all, was the need to maintain the perceived prestige of France. Revers was dismissed in December 1949, an entirely innocent casualty of a scandal not of his making.

The forts were a problem that would not go away. They were isolated, not mutually supporting and, as Revers commented, vulnerable to attack, difficult to re-supply and served no practical military purpose. Evacuating these outposts, which were of long standing, would not be easy. Enormous stocks of matériel would either have to be abandoned or transported out of the jungle. The evacuation would almost certainly be conducted under fire and the probable loss of life would be high. In 1949 the exercise would be very difficult but, if attempted in 1950, it was a disaster just waiting to happen. There had been a series of probing forays against these forts in April to June 1949. The French beat off these 'attacks' but Giap had no desire to take any of these positions. His forays had been to exercise his troops and test his systems. It was part of the master plan for Giap's major offensive planned for 1950.

Blaizot, who had achieved nothing during his tour, was replaced by Lieutenant General Marcel Carpentier.[36] Much was expected from Carpentier, who was described as being 'full of goodwill … deep-voiced, convincing promises'.[37] On his arrival in Saigon in late 1949 Carpentier found himself in a setting for which he had had no preparation. He needed a mentor to show him the ropes and to help him acclimatize. He selected Major General Marcel Alessandri, who was the same age but had served in Indochina several times before.

Lieutenant General Marcel Carpentier.

Alessandri had a blot on his record: he had been a soldier of Vichy and so he came with an unfair but slight taint of collaboration. Unfortunately, he was an unprepossessing character with a loud voice and strong opinions. He was not an attractive advertisement for *La Belle France*. Soon after Carpentier took command he met with Alessandri and to the amazement of the latter he was given carte blanche to conduct operations in Indochina. Incredibly, Carpentier had abrogated or abdicated his command and delegated it to Alessandri. This was almost without precedent.

Alessandri seized the opportunity and embarked, energetically, on a new strategy. In the Tonkin delta he cordoned off an area and then sought to destroy the Vietminh within his cordon. Then he moved his cordon and repeated the operation. Initially this process appeared to be successful and the maps showed an increasingly large area as being under French control. After the cordon operation, the area had first to be 'pacified' by local Vietnamese soldiers and then it had to be occupied by a garrison.[38] The majority of Vietminh assets in the delta were not main force, they were the *Dan Quan Du Kich* mentioned on page 26. These were farmers by day and guerrillas by night, and it was not their function to provoke confrontation with Alessandri's soldiers.

As the cordons grew in size, so too did the logistic requirement. Alessandri needed vast numbers of troops to secure the perimeter in addition to those now occupying earlier cordoned areas as garrison troops. There is no doubt that during this process many Vietminh sympathizers and communist officials were eradicated but crucially not all. As the French moved on, so the surviving communist cells regenerated, recruited and flourished, and those Vietminh who had been expelled by French action moved back.

Eventually Alessandri's strategy failed for two complementary reasons. These were first the lack of the required manpower and second the failure of the French to even start to win the 'hearts and minds' of their colonial subjects. This latter reason was the product of an inbuilt attitude towards the Vietnamese. They were viewed as second-class subjects and merely a source of labour and revenue. Because they were treated with contempt, many but

The product of a sweep: a very apprehensive captive.

not all Vietnamese returned the contempt in like manner. Giap prospered from the French attitude towards his people and, in 1970, he wrote:

> Our units operated in small packets with independent companies pene-
> trating deeply into the enemy-controlled zone to launch guerrilla warfare,
> establish bases and protect local people's power. It was an extremely hard
> war in all domains: military, economic and political. The enemy mopped
> up; we fought against mopping up. They organized supplementary local
> Vietnamese troops and installed puppet authorities; we firmly upheld
> local people's power, overthrew straw men, eliminated traitors and
> carried out active propaganda ... We gradually formed a network of
> guerrilla bases.[39]

Unknown to Carpentier, Alessandri's apparently failed strategy had, in fact, inflicted damage on the Vietminh and the damage was logistic. By his activities Alessandri had cut the supply of rice to the Vietminh by half. The effect was serious, and starvation was a real possibility. Giap had to consider major operations designed specifically to obtain food for his men. He realized that such operations would be difficult and might end in a catastrophic defeat.

He held his hand in 1949 and, in 1950, one of the most significant factors in the French war happened outside the borders of Vietnam when Mao Zedong won the Chinese civil war. By so doing, Mao assured the Vietminh of not only a safe haven but also a source of logistic support, especially rice and heavy weapons.

The French had been up against it, but now they were pitted against a proxy enemy in China. The chances of a decisive military victory to end the war had all but faded. Giap had no illusions and, writing of Mao's success, he said that 'This historic event altered events throughout the world and exerted a considerable influence on the war of liberation of the Vietnamese people.' The now hostile power on the northern border convinced Carpentier that he needed to retain and maintain the forts along that border, hopefully to

A Vietminh soldier unearthed somewhere in the delta. (*French Army*)

prevent the passage of matériel to the Vietminh. This was notwithstanding the Revers Report of the previous year. The border was about 300 miles long and to control cross-border traffic efficiently would call for a massive force that France could not provide. It was simply not practical. The forts, at best, provided bases for fighting patrols.

There were not many options open to Carpentier/Alessandri but, in practice, retaining the forts was not one of them because they made no military sense at all. They were isolated and easily bypassed by the porters making their way from China to the Viet Bac and, with the growing strength of the Vietminh, they were not secure. They were described accurately as 'tethered goats in tiger country'.[40] The initiative in this war was passing to the Vietminh.

Chapter Five

The Debacle of the Border Forts

'The art of defending fortified places consists in putting
off the moment of their reduction.'[1]

[Frederick the Great]

The French withdrawal from their positions on the Vietnam/China border
was a bloody affair marked by hubris, incompetence and great valour on the
French side and political savvy, sound planning and tenacity by the Vietminh
on the other. Transport was the key and the two sides embraced entirely
different methods to get their men and matériel in place. Churchill's dictum
(p. 3) was never more applicable than here.

The period between February and October 1950 during which the battle
was fought is, in many ways, a microcosm of the entire French campaign in
North Vietnam. This is because it illustrated the extreme contrast between
the flexibility of the jungle-based Vietminh and the hidebound road- and
vehicle-dependent French. It underscored the inadequacy of Western-style
operations against a guerrilla foe.

The one advantage of the CEFEO in the early days of the war was its
superiority in riverine assets, heavy weapons, artillery and aircraft in particular. This artillery was, however, tied to the roads, such as they were. It could
only engage a target that could be reached from the road and the Vietminh
had little difficulty in avoiding artillery strikes.

The Vietminh used small boats along the coast and on inland waterways,
especially in the two delta regions, and became adept at the laying of mines.
However, they could not match the French waterborne assets, many of which
were US-type landing craft but with the addition of armour and guns of up to
75mm. These craft when grouped were 'capable of transporting and landing a
battalion-sized force with its equipment, and of supporting the operations of
the force ashore while at the same time controlling the waterway.'[2]

The dependence upon roads, all vulnerable to sabotage, had the knock-on
effect of increasing the value of CEFEO engineers. A disproportionate
amount of infantry manpower was employed in protecting engineers engaged
in repairing the roads and bridges ahead of any convoy. French operations
had to be planned around the available roads and their condition. Each

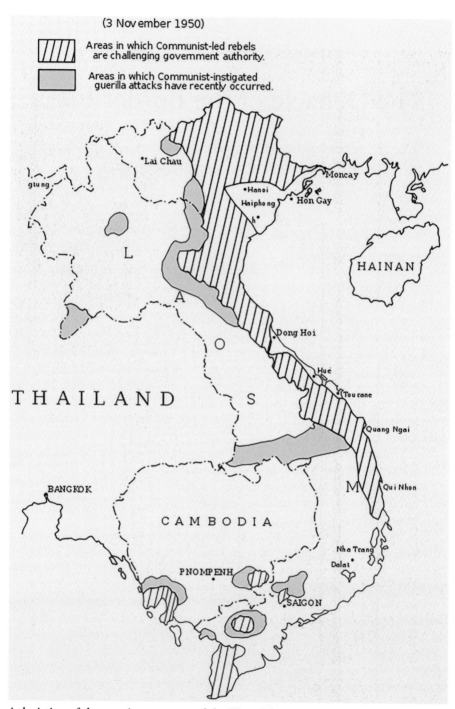

(3 November 1950)

Areas in which Communist-led rebels
are challenging government authority.

Areas in which Communist-instigated
guerilla attacks have recently occurred.

Lai Chau

gtu ng

Moncay

•Hanoi
Haiphong   •Hon Gay

h•

L

HAINAN

A

O

Dong Hoi

THAILAND   S

Hué

•Tou rane

Quang Ngai

BANGKOK

M   Qui Nhon

CAMBODIA

Nha Trang

Dalat•

PNOMPENH

SAIGON

A depiction of the growing presence of the Vietminh. (*Windrow*)

Building a punji trap. (*Peter Alan Hoyd*)

convoy carried with it the materials required to repair road surfaces and span rivers. On occasions parachute sappers were dropped ahead of convoys to take and repair bridges.[3]

Vietminh tactics against wheeled transport were unsophisticated but effective and so was its increasingly deadly use of mines and booby-traps. The mines were often French mines relocated or captured French ordnance. For the French soldier who stepped off a road there was the ever-present threat if not of mines then of the bamboo punji stakes which were placed, speculatively, where perhaps a soldier might pass or take cover. They were less expensive than a bullet but just as effective and they were difficult to detect

This photograph shows a field of punji spikes, sown in a depression that might be used as cover. They are as effective as barbed wire, but more dangerous. (*Peter Alan Hoyd*)

when camouflaged. The Vietminh perfected the punji pit with downward-facing spikes and here the victim would risk very serious injury as he tried to extricate himself. Those seeking to release the soldier by digging him out were then stationary for long enough to present an attractive target to a sniper.

To increase lethality the bamboo spikes were often smeared with animal venom or human faeces. A punji injury was intended to be disabling, but such measures could make them fatal.[4] In the Red River delta in the six months from September 1953 to February 1954, 75 per cent of all deaths and 56 per cent of wounds were caused by mines and booby-traps.[5]

Logistically, the mine and booby-trap could not be bettered because their components cost very little and were readily available. As a bonus they did not expose the 'sower' to danger and there were no countermeasures. Vigilance was the only defence and even the most vigilant and well-trained soldier was liable to fall victim.

Giap thought, optimistically, that he might win the war in 1950 or early 1951. He planned his offensive to start in February but, before that, he undertook a complete reorganization of his forces. He reformed his main force into divisions, each of about 12,000 men. These divisions were infantry-

The juxtaposition of the border posts, Giap's first target. Lao Cai is top left. (*Windrow*)

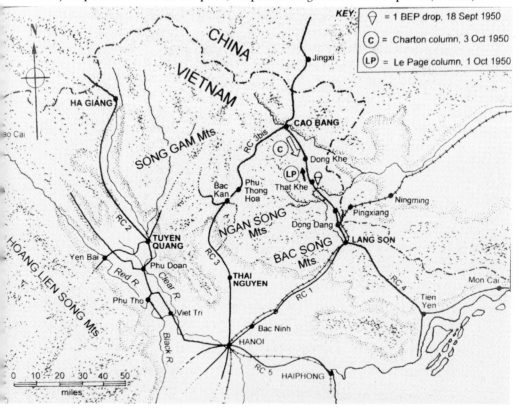

heavy and cannot be compared with a division in a Western army because they had only a company of 120mm mortars, no organic artillery and no mechanized transport. Gunners will always tell you that 'artillery is the queen of the battlefield', and they are irritatingly correct. However, as logistic matériel was about to start flowing in from China, this gunnery deficiency would soon be resolved. Until then, the dearth of heavy equipment made for a much more mobile force and, when supported by tens of thousands of porters, a Vietminh division was a flexible and versatile formation. Giap numbered his divisions the 304th, 308th, 312th, 316th and 320th. It follows that Giap had officers of the right quality to staff and command these divisions.

Carpentier had inherited a significant problem and that was the French dispositions along the northern border. These cantonments were numerous, but too small to be a viable military force. Due to their isolation in the rain forest, some could only be re-supplied by air. Others lined RC4. This road

> ran inland from the Gulf of Tonkin and closely parallel to the Chinese frontier, which it followed from Tien Yen north-west for 147 miles all the way to the major garrison of Cao Bang. The forward depot for all supplies and personnel, destined for the frontier forts, was Lang Son at the junction of RC4, RC1 and the Ky Cong River. From 10 miles north of Lang Son, at Dong Dang, the road was ideally suited to ambush. Here the road was only about 750 yards from the Chinese border, and it started to pass through gorges and tunnels to a perilous stretch on a mountain ledge overlooking the Ky Cong River for several miles before dropping down to the wet flats around That Khe.[6]

RC4 was not a smooth ribbon of tarmac with a helpful white line down the middle and parking places at convenient intervals. It was, in fact, little more than a narrow, pot-holed, unsurfaced jungle track. In many places there was insufficient room for two trucks to pass and the surface was such that speeds were very low indeed. The vehicles using this road were hard pressed and, lacking in maintenance, they broke down. A breakdown blocked the road and put the entire convoy at risk.

The forts were static assets and could not manoeuvre. Their maintenance and supply were costing lives, to no discernible purpose. Carpentier, abruptly, changed his mind and recognized his vulnerability. Accordingly, he planned to evacuate the forts as soon as possible. It follows that Giap, too, had a plan for the border forts. His intention was to pick them off one by one although they did not pose any threat to the Vietminh, but their eradication would allow unhindered movement in the rear base area of the Viet Bac and right up to the Chinese border. These posts had the added attraction as targets of being isolated; in some cases they were undermanned and, in every case, they were difficult to reinforce. They were easy pickings for Giap, but their losses would devastate the French. Giap held the initiative because he could select his targets and pick the time to attack, which put him in a very strong position. His strategy was solidly-based.

Once again Giap rehearsed his troops and he started, in February 1950, by mounting attacks on posts around Lao Cai in the far north-west. The object was not necessarily to take the post but to polish his command and control systems, train his troops and, by no means least, observe the French reaction. Pho Lu, a small mud and log fort on the Red River, was held by a company of about 100 or so soldiers (see Fig. 22). It was to be the scene of the first rehearsal and was assaulted by 10 Vietminh battalions, say 5,500 men. The French response was immediate. The insertion of a battalion of parachute troops was attempted. The conditions were poor, and the paras were dropped 20 miles from their intended dropping zone. This battalion then became a target as it cut its way through rain forest towards Pho Lu and it attracted the close attention of the Vietminh. The parachute soldiers were only saved from complete annihilation when six French fighter-bombers bombed and strafed the Vietminh to great effect. The paras were able to withdraw, but the defenders of the post were swept aside in an unstoppable human surge. The loss of Pho Lu was a minor episode, but it was symptomatic of what was to follow.

As the monsoon set in, it made for difficult flying conditions and gave Giap and his generals ample time to review the 'rehearsals'. Not much needed to be changed as the 'script' worked well. The only question was where to strike next.

There were any number of options open to Giap and few available to Carpentier. In the north and from east to west the most formidable defences were at Lang Son, Cao Bang and Lao Cai. These were manned by about 10,000 men in all. In the Lao Cai area, there were the satellite posts of Muong Khuong, Pa Kham and Nghia Do. All of these had company-sized detachments of around 100 men and mirrored the now destroyed Pho Lu on the Red River.

Cao Bang was a major installation with about 1,500 infantry and a further 300–400 logistic troops. It supported the satellite posts of Dong Khe and That Khe and each of these was home to a battalion of the French Foreign Legion. Lang Son was the headquarters of the northern perimeter of French posts and it held about 4,000 men.[7]

Carpentier had ample boots on the ground, but they were dispersed. His posts provided bases for patrol activity, but not for any form of serious

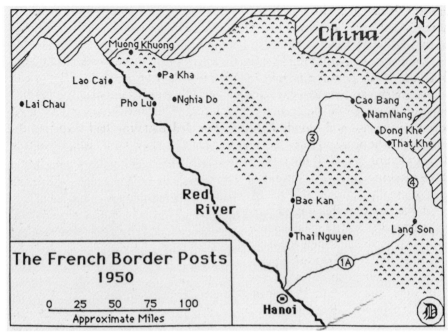

A less complicated sketch map. (*Davidson*)

offensive. Two posts, 20 miles apart in the rain forest, might just as well have been on opposite sides of the moon.

Nghia Do was selected by Giap as the next objective and, in March, it was assaulted by the 308th Vietminh Division. The attack was thwarted by the rapid insertion of a parachute battalion and the balance was changed. Giap withdrew, but achieved his aim when, a few days later, the French evacuated the post.

It is pertinent to consider these parachute insertions. Jumping into rain forest has all the attractions of jumping into water in the dark. It is hazardous and, after the jump, assembly on the DZ takes time. In an ideal world there are ten flat, dry, undefended football pitches grouped together that can be selected as a DZ. In North Vietnam, in 1950, those conditions did not exist and, more often than not, Carpentier's parachute battalions jumped into a 'hot' DZ. They were his elite force; a finite asset to be expended frugally.

In April Giap probed into Laos. His forces skirted French outposts on the Plain of Jars and reached Luan Prabang; the inhabitants all fled. He could easily have taken the empty town, but instead he withdrew. In 1990, when interviewed by Stanley Karnow, Giap explained that he 'never intended to remain in Laos. It was a feint, designed to distract the French and it worked.'[8]

He had demonstrated that he could march into Laos with impunity and by doing so, he fed the notion that Dien Bien Phu would act as bar to future Vietminh incursions.

Giap decided upon Dong Khe for his attention and selected five battalions from the 308th Division to take it. After two days of mortaring, the assault was successful and, on 28 May, Dong Khe fell but only temporarily because a counter-attack led by the French 3rd Colonial Parachute Battalion retook the fort after intense and bloody fighting. The 3rd Battalion had surprised the Vietminh who were so busy looting the post that they were taken unawares. The Vietminh lost '300 men, two howitzers (presumably Chinese in origin), three machine guns and countless small arms. The French lost the battalion that originally garrisoned Dong Khe less about 100 who escaped.'[9]

On the face of it this was a French victory. They held the ground, but what was that worth in the great scheme of things? Giap was bloodied, but much more experienced. When the dry weather came in September, he would be able to exploit it and made his plans accordingly. The French had no offensive plans and their posture was one of wary defence.

In June, the Korean War broke out between communist North Korea (DPRK) supported by China and the Soviet Union, and South Korea (ROK) supported by the United States and its allies in the UN. On the basis that China was supporting Ho Chi Minh and providing matériel support to the Vietminh, the government of the USA could well see that communist domination of the entire region was a possibility. The USA found itself engulfed in two wars against its proxy enemy China. Only the USA had the military capacity and wealth to fight this war against communism on two fronts.

In September 1950, the rain stopped and Giap briefed his generals. He had decided to surround Cao Bang and That Khe, both of which were located on RC4, the inadequate artery that served a number of posts along its ill-kempt length. Giap reasoned that such a move would present Carpentier with some unattractive logistic options. These options were (a) to reinforce the posts by road; (b) not reinforce them but re-supply from the air; or (c) evacuate both posts by road. The latter option would mean either (d) abandoning a mountain of war matériel that the Vietminh could then turn on the French; or (e) try to remove that matériel by road. To complicate Carpentier's situation but unknown to him, Giap proposed to take and hold Dong Khe and by so doing, cut RC4 between Cao Bang and That Khe (see Fig. 22). The stage was set for a military disaster with all the odds against Carpentier.

The single underperforming French military component during the war was, arguably, the Air Force. It was capable of providing aircraft for parachute insertions, but it was both under-equipped and under-trained to support ground operations. However, this is not to call into question the courage of the men who flew in this campaign. The French were dependent upon the USA for airframes and in part for aircrew. In July 1949 the 5th Fighter Wing equipped with Bell P-63 Kingcobras arrived from Tunisia and were stationed in Hanoi. More P-63s arrived in the theatre in November 1949.

In March 1950, General Hartmann, the commander of the French Air Force in Indochina, re-organized his force and advised the American Military Mission about his intentions to create a 'Battle Air Corp'. This would be composed of four jet fighter groups, two bomber groups and four transport groups. The transport capability was boosted with twenty Ju 52 Toucans. More P-63s arrived in the theatre in November 1949, pictured below.

In Hartmann's view jet aircraft were unsuitable for the Vietnam theatre and so he elected to employ the Grumman F6F Hellcat and F8F Bearcat. The twin-engine bomber Douglas B-26 (or A-26) Invader would also be used. Command arrangements were altered with the creation of three GATAC (Aerial Tactical Groups): North-Gatac in Hanoi, Centre-Gatac in Hue and South-Gatac in Saigon/Tan Son Nhut. It is presumed that Hartmann's conversation with the American Military Mission was in fact a request for the

Bell Kingcobra P-63s.

Kingcobras de la 5° Esc.de Chasse. TanSonNhut Juillet 1949

General Trình Minh Thế.

airframes specified. It was in 1950 that the French were first supplied with napalm, a frightful area weapon that was to be a constant in Vietnam for the next twenty-five years.

On 16 September 1950, Giap's offensive opened at Dong Khe. His force outnumbered the French by at least eight to one and it was led by Major General Trình Minh Thế.[10] The Chinese had provisioned the Vietminh with artillery and these weapons were dismantled into manageable pieces and carried upon the backs of porters to the selected area. Ammunition followed and was stockpiled. Dong Khe was garrisoned by about 300 French troops of the 2nd Battalion of the 3rd Regiment of the French Foreign Legion (3rd REI). The bombardment of the post was effective, and it destroyed French guns and fortifications and inflicted casualties on the defenders. It was a very one-sided fight; the French had no chance. On 18 September, the fort was finally overrun, after bitter fighting, by successive waves of infantry. Only twelve French soldiers escaped to reach That Khe. Learning from past mistakes, the Vietminh consolidated, took up defensive positions and prepared to resist an airborne counter-attack. It never came.

Dong Khe was lost and the Vietminh was ensconced astride the strategically vital RC4. This complicated Carpentier's plan which had been to evacuate the border posts, hopefully without a fight, but now that Giap had forestalled him it was clear that, from here, it was all about the movement of his troops, with or without wheeled transport. Despite the crisis staring him in the face, Carpentier still anticipated capturing Thai Nguyen by 1 October, a measure that would allow him to abandon Cao Bang. A force designated *Groupement Bayard* was formed at Lang Son commanded by Lieutenant Colonel Maurice Le Page. The force was composed of about 3,500 Moroccan colonial troops from I and II Tabors, supplemented by irregulars. This was a brigade-sized force and Le Page was relatively junior in rank for such a command. Carpentier's reasons for appointing him are unknown; it may be that he was the only man available.

On 16 September the bloody advance to join the 1st BEP (Foreign Parachute Battalion) at That Khe commenced. This was the prelude to the planned recapture of Dong Khe. The progress of Le Page was resisted and 'All along the track the Vietminh harassed the French troops by ambushes, mines, booby-traps and roadblocks. It became so difficult that Le Page had to send his artillery, trucks and heavy engineering equipment back to Lang Son.'[11]

Groupement Bayard was taking numerous casualties and the wounded, who had to be carried, posed another logistic test. It was not until 19 September that Le Page led his battered column into That Khe and met the 1st BEP who had parachuted in the previous day. They were to prove to be uncomfortable bedfellows. The Foreign Legion soldiers, many of them Germans, viewed the colonial soldiers with ill-concealed contempt. That was bad enough but, in addition, Le Page did not inspire confidence in the Legion's officers who noted his 'inexperience, indecisiveness and lack of confidence'.[12] The 1st BEP should have boosted Le Page's command, but the lack of trust in his capacity to command and low regard for his Moroccan troops led to a severe slump in morale. The prospects for future operations were not good, especially so as Le Page had no idea what Carpentier expected of him. Incredibly, the aim of the operation had not been promulgated.

On 30 September, Carpentier ordered *Groupement Bayard* to move north along RC4 and retake Dong Khe. At the same time he instructed Colonel Pierre Charton, the commander at Cao Bang, to destroy all his heavy equipment, abandon the fort and, at the head of his 1,500 legionnaires and Moroccans, meet Le Page at Dong Khe. Charton was burdened with about 500 civilian non-combatants and refugees.

Colonel Pierre Charton, commander of the Cao Bang garrison.

This was all military wishful thinking because Giap had massed ten battalions, say 6,000 men, around Dong Khe supported by an artillery regiment. He was well-prepared for Le Page and Charton. Le Page aspired to a double envelopment of Dong Khe, although he was not overly optimistic about success, saying to a fellow officer, 'We shall never come back.'[13] It is little wonder that he did not inspire his soldiers.

The 1st BEP attacked Dong Khe from the east and the three Moroccan battalions from the west. The thick jungle and broken ground made progress slow and, in the face of a well-entrenched and prepared enemy, both arms of the pincer were rebuffed. It was only on 2 October that Carpentier shared with Le Page his master plan and his original role in meeting the Cao Bang garrison, led by Charton, at Dong Khe. Le Page was now told that he should bypass Dong Khe and, by taking to the jungle, loop round and rendezvous with Charton at Nam Nang on 3 October.

This was much easier said than done. Davidson described the order as 'a death sentence for *Groupement Bayard*.'[14] Nevertheless, all vehicles were abandoned and Le Page thrust out into the unmapped jungle. All food, water, equipment, ammunition and the wounded had to be carried. Le Page was surrounded by overwhelming Vietminh forces who were at ease in the same jungle that was a new and frightening experience to many of *Groupement Bayard*.

The plan was that, at midnight on 2/3 October, the Cao Bang garrison would steal away onto RC4 without alerting the Vietminh. It was never going to work because the Vietminh realized that the fort would be evacuated at some point and by way of the road. The fort was under close observation. When Colonel Charton ordered the destruction of 150 tons of ammunition and other matériel, the major explosion signalled the garrison's imminent departure.

As it happens the garrison did not make a timely exit and was delayed until noon on 3 October, then it was led out of Cao Bang by the 3rd Battalion, Foreign Infantry Regiment (3 REI). In direct contravention of his orders, which were to destroy all heavy equipment and matériel of use to the enemy, Charton carried with him as much as he could cram onto his vehicles.

The predicable passage of Charton down RC4 was in the face of constant opposition. His large, unwieldy convoy could only move on a one-truck front and he suffered multiple casualties. The dead could be left but the wounded had to be carried. Air support for Charton was minimal. However, at Nam Nang (see p. 56) where Charton expected to meet Le Page, he found the village empty. Carpentier's headquarters responded to Charton's bemused enquiry by telling him that Le Page was in very serious difficulty; beset by a major Vietminh force, he faced total destruction. Charton was ordered to go, at once, to the aid of what remained of *Groupement Bayard*. This was a role reversal because the original plan had been for Le Page to aid Charton.

Charton was a shrewd, pragmatic soldier. He destroyed all his vehicles and their contents and decided that he might be able to reach Le Page down the little-used Quang Liet trail, if he could find it. Eventually Charton's native trackers found evidence of a trail that appeared to go in the right general

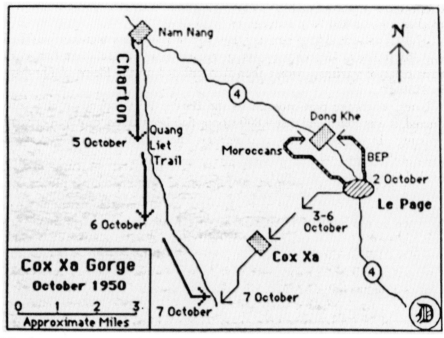

The destruction of *Groupement Bayard* and the Cao Bang garrison. (*Davidson*)

direction; the Cao Bang garrison and their refugees struck off in single file. Then the trail petered out and progress slowed as a passage had to be cut through the thick jungle. Two days later Charton was close to his beleaguered countrymen. In the meantime, the remnants of *Groupement Bayard*, still led by Le Page who was very ill, entered the Cox Xa gorge. This was a military death-trap to be avoided at all costs. As it was, the Vietminh occupied the rims of the gorge and, from there, poured fire down on the French column.

Le Page ordered the survivors of 1 BEP, only 130 in number, to break out and contact Charton and, with extraordinary courage and skill, they succeeded. The two groups joined up on 7 October. Short of water, food and ammunition, these two groups of French soldiers were logistically bankrupt and their destruction was only a matter of time. They were struggling to care for their wounded and this operation had, by now, taken on the characteristics of the British retreat from Kabul in 1842.[15] The Vietminh were as merciless as the Afghans had been. They were able to focus all their attention on the one position. The slaughter was all-consuming and unabated.

This was not the end of the French defeat and at That Khe further humiliation followed. A replacement company of 1 BEP (120 men) together with 268 men of 3 BCCP (*Bataillon Colonial de Commandos Parachutistes*) were dropped into the town on 8 October to assist survivors. A week later this body of elite soldiers had been reduced to thirty-seven.

The French could have retained their fort at Lang Son, 'but they panicked and abandoned it. Overall, this was the greatest single defeat in the history of their colonial warfare – worse than that suffered on the Plains of Abraham in 1759.'[16]

Later, when the post-mortem of the Border Forts operation was conducted, it was concluded that 4,800 troops had been killed, captured or were 'missing'. In military circles 'missing' is a euphemism for 'probably dead'. Some 2,000 wounded had survived. The loss of military hardware was significant: it amounted to 13 artillery pieces, 125 mortars, 450 trucks, 940 machine guns, 1,200 sub-machine guns and 8,000 rifles captured, destroyed or lost. Some of this matériel would be used against the French in the future. Giap summed up the Battle of Dong Khe by writing much later that 'the people's war had evolved from guerrilla war to conventional warfare. With the founding of the People's Republic of China our victory in the battle of the frontier zone put an end to the imperialist encirclement of the Vietnamese revolution. Our communication lines with the socialist countries were open.'

There is no doubt that Giap had control over the entire northern border region with secure lines of communication into China. This being the case, he set his engineers to work building roads from the Viet Bac to the Chinese border. Giap's premature belief was that he could now take on the French in conventional war is worthy of note, because it led him to make a series of very poor decisions that cost his cause dear.

Chapter Six

Escalation, 1951–1953

'War is an art, and as such is not susceptible of explanation or by fixed formula.'[1]

[General George Patton Jr.]

When 1951 dawned, no sane observer could envisage a scenario in which the French would defeat the Vietminh, seize Ho Chi Minh and Giap, and establish comprehensive control over the whole of Vietnam, all to the entire satisfaction of a quiescent population. It was simply not going to happen.

The debacle of the border forts had inflicted a deep psychological wound on the French. The success of a guerrilla force against a major European power had caused a rapid change in attitudes, not least in Washington where the communist invasion of South Korea had rung multiple warning bells. The anti-colonial attitude of the USA was swiftly revised and logistic support for the French was stepped up. This was to counter the Chinese logistic support, by now flowing across the border to the Vietminh, an organization growing in strength and capability and which now held the initiative in Vietnam.

Chinese support was not only logistic. Training was given at every level and the skill base of what had been a peasant army was raised across the board. Giap's men studied in Chinese schools, learning to be effective officers and non-commissioned officers to lead the 117 battalions Giap had at his disposal by 1951.[2] The title of this chapter is 'Escalation' and without detailing every battle it will show how a guerrilla campaign escalated into a full-on war and a disastrous confrontation.

From a distance of almost seventy years it is clear that the best the French could hope for was a negotiated withdrawal and cessation of the bloodletting. However, and despite the still tepid support for the war in France – all the more tepid after the border forts defeat – Carpentier was replaced by France's most favoured general. This was General Jean de Lattre de Tassigny who took command on 17 December 1950.[3] De Lattre was an accomplished leader and he took the CEFEO by the scruff of the neck and started work on re-building morale. He also introduced a logistic heavy new policy.

Despite the recent issue of the border forts, de Lattre determined to build a *ceinture* (belt) of new forts and blockhouses in order to defend the triangular

General Jean de Lattre de Tassigny.

wedge of the Hanoi-Haiphong delta. Logistically this was an expensive, labour-intensive exercise on a vast scale. De Lattre caused the building of 900 forts and 2,200 pillboxes, all supported by hardened bunkers. This was a new version of 'the Maginot line but by another name'.[4] Some 80,000 labourers were employed in the task and Macdonald speaks of the production of 15,000,000 tons of concrete for the project.[5]

The huge and vastly expensive *ceinture* project had just started when Giap started to believe his own publicity and, from January 1951, he led his army to a series of avoidable defeats. He was convinced that the need for guerrilla tactics had passed and he could now meet the French on equal terms. It was on that basis that he decided that he would start his *Tong Tan Cong* (TTC or General Counter-Offensive) by attacking Vinh Yen, a key road junction, about 25 miles north-west of Hanoi and which lay just inside de Lattre's projected *ceinture*. Giap's troops approached the town from the high ground and forested Viet Bac down the Tam Dau ridge. His multitude of porters struggled through the rain forest but, by 13 January, everything was in place.

Vinh Yen and the low hills in the vicinity were strongly garrisoned by about 6,000 men. Giap sent his two divisions – the 308th and 312th numbering around 20,000 – into the fray (see Fig. 28). As soon as the magnitude of the operation became clear, de Lattre flew in to take command. He experienced for the first time, as did many of his soldiers, the experience of the human wave assault. The French Air Force was a key player in this battle; it made extensive use of napalm to great effect. De Lattre called into the battle every available aircraft and deployed his reserve. The fighting was relentless, but de Lattre out-generalled his opponent whose attacks were uncoordinated and piecemeal in character. De Lattre kept his nerve and he took a very heavy toll on Giap's force.

A chastened Giap withdrew: he had suffered between 6,000 and 8,000 dead and an estimated 5,000 to 7,000 wounded in this, his first excursion into a battle of manoeuvre.[6] He had overreached himself and been defeated. Throughout the thirty years of war in Vietnam, casualty figures are usually no

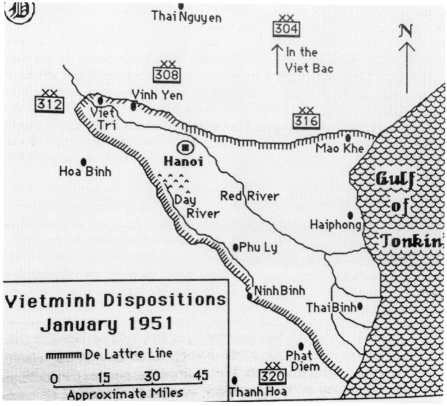

This map shows the French aspirations in January 1951: the defence of a very small part of North Vietnam by means of the de Lattre *ceinture* project. (*Davidson*)

more than an estimate and the 6,000 to 8,000 offered above is the range provided by several sources.

The Battle of Vinh Yen gave the CEFEO a welcome boost to morale and strengthened de Lattre's authority, which he exploited by accelerating work on the *ceinture*. The 'de Lattre line' now absorbed a great deal of manpower, for a strategy the validity of which had yet to be proved. The general removed as many soldiers as possible from security duties to man his line and to create a strong mobile reserve. He encouraged civilians to take responsibility for their own security, and he courted the USA in order to increase the American logistic commitment to the war. De Lattre was a human dynamo but, at this stage, a very sick man, although he might not have known it.

Giap licked his wounds and his damaged reputation, having shown himself to be a 'general of limited talents'.[7] His deficiencies at Vinh Yen were readily identified. He had committed his entire force and not left a mobile reserve to either reinforce success or cover failure. He had launched his attack without the assurance of well-schooled staff, capable of the manipulation of a corps-sized force. He had chosen to advance over open country in daylight and put his soldiers at risk from the French fire-power that had proved to be decisive.

However, Giap made further attempts to breach de Lattre's belt and force his way into the delta at Mao Khe on 29-30 March. This came to be known as the 'Battle of The Day River'. The 316th Division with elements of the 308th and 312th divisions engaged in fierce hand-to-hand fighting, but again sustained heavy losses with some 3,000 dead and wounded; more speculative figures. Naval gunfire support swung the balance in favour of the defenders and Giap withdrew.

In late May and early June Giap tried again; both attempts failed, and the Vietminh sustained heavy casualties for no gain. Giap was not prepared to change his tactics, despite the evidence that his ill-coordinated and piecemeal attacks were not working. He made a final push at Ninh Binh in the south-east of the delta. To do this it was necessary for Giap to move not only his soldiers but also his large logistic train some 150 miles overland without being detected by the waiting French. 'Supporting logistics efforts required the labour of 100,000 coolies each carrying his or her burden around de Lattre's half-completed *ceinture*.'[8] However, before he was ready, the monsoon broke. Thrusts at Phu Ly and Ninh Binh were countered by de Lattre who put together a composite force of eight motorized brigades with armour and artillery in close support. The battle swung both ways, but the weather and the ground conditions favoured the defenders and during the period 10–18 June Giap retreated in disarray. His losses were enormous: the 9,000 dead and 1,000 captured are an indication of his miscalculation. He had lost perhaps the equivalent of two divisions in the six months of his TTC and without any discernible benefit.[9] Despite his operational failure, Giap's logistic team had served him very well indeed, maintaining a corps-level force in the field for three months.

One casualty that had a strong impact on de Lattre was that of his son Bernard who died leading his men near Ninh Binh. De Lattre was predictably devastated.

Giap's poor performance did not pass unnoticed and he was called to explain himself to the Communist Party Central Committee. He went through the ritual process of self-criticism. His closest associates were removed from their posts on the basis of their incompetence. Giap had to accept the ascendancy of political commissars over the army chain of command and allow Chinese military advisors to be placed at all levels.

These measures did not satisfy all the members and one, Truong Chinh, demanded that he be sacked.[10] Truong Chinh (opposite) was an important member of the Communist Party and he ranked second only after Ho Chi Minh. His opposition to Giap was significant and could have been fatal. As it was, he now by far over-shadowed Giap.

The atmosphere was sufficiently volatile that even the revered Ho Chi Minh was criticized for supporting Giap. Giap's reverses had come as an unwelcome shock to the committee and called for a reality check. It was decided that the solution was not to sack Giap but to find another scape-goat. General Nguyen Binh was

Truong Chinh.

selected. He was accused of urging Giap's precipitate TTC and conveniently 'killed in a French ambush' while making his way north to face the committee.

De Lattre pursued the completion of his defensive belt around the Red River delta. The logistic requirements to build the multitude of separate blockhouses, all proof against 155mm artillery, was more than could be achieved with local resources. The general was obliged to obtain building material from across South-East Asia. Business was placed with a miscellany of civilian organizations of all sizes. A large labour force was recruited to build the defences that covered an arc of 235 miles. De Lattre was going first-class: his blockhouses were constructed in about 250 mutually-supporting groups, each of between three and six blockhouses. The smallest blockhouse accom-modated about ten men. Most had towers, and some had tank turrets installed. All had electricity provided by petrol-driven generators. The electricity was a boon for the men who had to garrison the *ceinture*. It powered the ventilation systems, but air-conditioning was not provided, although fans probably were.

The arc of 250 groups was aligned on the periphery. Some 600 blockhouses were complete by midsummer 1951 and the balance by the year's end. This policy of de Lattre does pose some questions. It took more than twenty bat-talions to man the belt. Davidson argued that the manpower bill was 'over two infantry divisions'. The *ceinture* was not impervious and Vietminh main force units had no difficulty in getting through it. That calls into question its validity as a defensive line. It was perceived that

> there was a need for a second inner belt to keep the enemy out of artillery range of the CEFEO's potential *final redoubt* – the harbour, base facilities

and airfields at Haiphong [author's italics]. This was an arc 31 miles long and 22 miles wide. All these defences had to be linked by a network of new roads allowing rapid reinforcement from the centre and capable of taking 30-ton tanks. At the same time, throughout Indochina, five airfields had to be built, enlarged or upgraded, complete with protected dispersal pens, workshops and living quarters.[11]

By any yardstick this was a grandiose scheme. Airfields and their ancillary facilities do not come cheap, but the USA was prepared to pay the bill.[12] The phrase 'final redoubt' smacks of defeatism. If the French had a need to plan for a final redoubt then, with that final redoubt, must have come evacuation plans. The fact that a denouement was anticipated around Haiphong indicated that the war was, at least morally, lost.

The efforts to put de Lattre's vision into place daunted many and, allegedly, when a staff officer expostulated 'But General, the cost ...', de Lattre replied succinctly, 'Fuck the cost.'[13] De Lattre was a very experienced and skilful general, but also a shrewd political operator. Leaving the building of his extraordinary defence works to subordinates to manage, he focused on logistic support and he was wildly successful.

In early 1951, the USA was furnishing de Lattre with 7,200 tons of assorted matériel per month. By September that year, that matériel had become a veritable flood. 'Within four months Washington shipped to Indochina 130,000 tons of equipment including 53,000,000 rounds of ammunition, 8,000 trucks and jeeps, 600 fighting vehicles, 200 aircraft, 14,000 automatic small arms and 3,500 radios.'[14] Eventually, and certainly by early 1954, the USA was funding 80 per cent of the costs of this war. That equated to $1 billion dollars per year; serious money from the US taxpayer.

From a distance the British government, with some expertise in withdrawal from Empire, observed affairs and was at a loss to understand the French position which, militarily, was increasingly untenable. The American posture drew from Selwyn Lloyd, the Foreign Secretary, the view that 'there is now in the United States an emotional feeling about communist China and to a lesser extent Russia which borders on hysteria.'[15] The role of the French as an American proxy was, by now, internationally recognized.

De Lattre hoped that, having concentrated his French forces in the delta and with an enhanced and larger Vietnamese army to man his *ceinture*, he would be well-equipped to launch a crushing offensive into the Viet Bac to destroy the Vietminh in its base. This was military pie in the sky. Neither de Lattre nor his successors were ever in a position to execute the master plan.

In October, a chastened Giap decided to assault Nghia Lo. This minor village was 95 miles west of Hanoi and 65 miles beyond the western limit of the de Lattre line (it is not shown on maps). It was the centre of the T'ai people who were active supporters of the French, providers of military man-power and it hosted a small French garrison that faced two regiments of the 312th Division. The initial assault was beaten off and the next day, 4 October, a parachute battalion was inserted to boost the defence, just in time. A further attack was repulsed at great cost to the attackers and two more parachute battalions were added to the garrison. Giap withdrew and had clearly learned from his earlier mistakes. Making frontal attacks on well-defended positions manned by experienced soldiers was folly. De Lattre had won again and the myth of Giap's invincibility had been further degraded.

De Lattre concluded that, hitherto, the French had merely been respond-ing to Vietminh initiatives and that he was going to have to be proactive in the future. He planned accordingly, but first he made an 'appreciation of the situation'. This is the time-honoured way that military men weigh up the factors before making a plan. It was at this important time that de Lattre was diagnosed with an advanced cancer that would kill him barely three months later. Devastating as the death sentence was, nevertheless de Lattre the good soldier 'continued the movement'.

In making an 'appreciation', it follows that the factors have to be assessed with ruthless accuracy if the eventual plan is to be valid. In this case de Lattre concluded that (a) airborne reinforcement and re-supply was a viable future policy; (b) the morale of his troops was high; (c) the morale of the Vietminh would be correspondingly low; (d) he had to demonstrate to the French government that CEFEO was in the ascendancy; and (e) the continued, active logistic support of the USA was imperative.

The net result of his appreciation was that de Lattre judged it was now necessary for the CEFEO to go onto the offensive. Some historians (includ-ing this one) believe that de Lattre knew full well that a military victory was highly improbable, but that a successful offensive would, at least, strengthen the hand of the French when a political settlement was negotiated.

The next issue was just where was de Lattre going to strike at his enemy? He was spoiled for choice because the Vietminh controlled the majority of the country. The objective had to be important to the Vietminh, and it had to be within only a few miles of the *ceinture* so that it could be readily re-supplied once taken. It had to be a place that the French could occupy long-term. The small town of Hoa Binh met all the criteria. It was to be at the centre of Operation LOTUS (see p. 66).

This operation is important because it once again emphasizes the com-pletely different approaches of the two adversaries. On the one hand was a Western army, the French, which would employ tanks, trucks, aircraft and armed river vessels. This combination would seize, by an airborne insertion, a town and airstrip. It would then seek to reinforce this airborne force with a 25-mile motorized thrust down a narrow dirt road in the face of very strong opposition. The lesson painfully learned in the battle of RC4 was to be disregarded. The aim was to take and retain the town in order to use it as a base for further aggressive operations.

The other side, the Vietminh, marshalled three infantry divisions of about 36,000 men through tropical forest and, in an operation that lasted for three months, it applied a vice-like grip on the lines of communication. It prevented the use of the airstrip and, by so doing, completely negated the French plans. With scant regard to personnel losses, the Vietminh overran a number of French positions and forced the withdrawal of the French army. The Vietminh employed a multitude of porters that provided the logistic support for the divisions and for themselves as well.

Operation LOTUS is, in miniature, characteristic of the French war in Indochina. It shows an absence of original thought and the capitulation of the jungle to the enemy. It was never envisaged that the Vietminh should be fought in the 'long grass', only from prepared defensive positions; a posture that ceded the initiative to the Vietminh and hastened eventual French defeat and humiliation.

Briefly, and in support of the observations above, it is necessary to provide a brief outline of the battle. Hoa Binh was a centre of Vietminh activity because it was a road (RC6) and river junction although the 'road' was, in effect, only an unsurfaced jungle track. The Black River that ran from French-controlled Trung Ha would, on the face of it, provide de Lattre with a second line of communication and re-supply. However, the forest covered both banks and provided cover for any Vietminh engaging the small river craft and *dinassauts* making the passage.[16] De Lattre's plan had a flavour of Operation MARKET GARDEN about it.[17] He was able to start the operation on 14 November when three parachute battalions jumped into Hoa Binh. They took the town without difficulty and awaited the arrival of a fifteen-battalion-strong mechanized force, with tanks, making its way along RC6. Meanwhile, a strong riverine convoy forced its way down the Black River and all three elements combined in the town on 16 November. Four days later de Lattre was evacuated to France where he died on 11 January 1952. Raoul Salan, de Lattre's deputy, assumed command on 20 December.[18]

Giap took his time in responding to the taking and fortifying of Hoa Binh but, when he did, he enjoyed success. He could see the glaringly obvious fact that the French lines of communication and supply were very vulnerable and so it was here that he focused his attention. On 12 January a Black River logistic convoy was unable to get through and was obliged to turn back in the face of very fierce opposition from both banks. Access to and from the town

General Raoul Salan.

by river was no longer viable; clear evidence of the impact of the three divisions of 35,000 troops supported by 150,000 porters that Giap had massed in the Hoa Binh area.

The town at this time was held by five French battalions, say, 3,000 men. RC6, their critical ground link with the *ceinture*, was secured along the 25-mile route by four thinly-spread battalions. These troops were grouped in small garrisons between Xuan Mai and Hoa Binh. Nevertheless, Giap interdicted RC6 and made passage along it hazardous in the extreme, if not impossible. The fighting along RC6 was as bloody as any in the war to date. Human wave attacks, although lacking in any sophistication or tactical polish, were very effective and they were employed along the length of RC6 and against places like Tu Vu on the Black River.

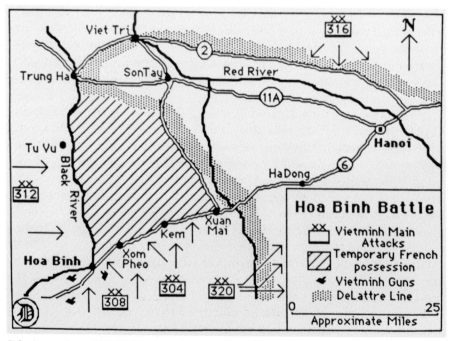

Salan's version of MARKET GARDEN. *(Davidson)*

The airstrip at Hoa Binh had been seen as a valuable asset by the French, but it soon became unusable after Giap's artillery cratered the runway with his artillery and any aircraft attempting to land was subject to direct fire. Supply and evacuation by air ceased.

In order to combat the vulnerability of his sole line of communication, Salan was obliged to launch another major operation to drive the Vietminh away from RC6. To this end he committed 'twelve battalions with air and artillery support; it took twelve full days to fight the 25 miles to Hoa Binh'.[19] The force reached the town on 29 January, at which point Salan decided to abandon Hoa Binh. His soldiers turned around and fought their way 25 miles back. It was a very long 25 miles and the French took grievous losses.

One can speculate that the soldiers might well have asked 'Was it all worth it?' The death toll was high on both sides, but estimates vary; the French lost about 890 killed and missing and 2,062 wounded; the Vietminh between 5,000 and 9,000 depending on the source consulted.[20] Despite the discrepancy in the butcher's bill, this was a victory for Giap. Operation LOTUS had failed in its objective and Hoa Binh returned to Vietminh control.

The engagement was significant for several reasons, not least of these being that once again it demonstrated Giap's capability to maintain and manoeuvre three divisions in the field and to feed, clothe and shelter them and provide for all their needs. He was able to bring to the battle 75mm guns and he effectively coordinated their fire with his infantry. For the first time heavy machine guns, probably Chinese or Russian, were deployed and they constrained the French Air Force and made low-level strafing attacks hazardous. This anti-aircraft capability was a growth area for the Vietminh from mid-1952.

All in all, it was a logistic tour de force by Giap. Although the size of the logistic train can only be estimated, Windrow suggests 150,000 porters were employed to support the three Vietminh divisions.[21] The coordination of such a body in a jungle, across broken ground, required exceptional skill. This stunning logistic capability made the Vietminh a formidable army and more than equal to their French opponents. This was an undertaking so vast that no one man could possibly control it and it can safely be presumed that Giap was, by now, served by a cadre of skilled logisticians. For example, the feeding of 150,000 porters in jungle conditions cannot be centralized; the food supply has to be obtained and distributed. Cooking might only have been rudimentary; nevertheless it was a logistic function that had to be managed at some relatively senior level.

De Lattre's aim of building an effective Vietnamese National Army was never realized by his successors, but his impact on this war was lasting and he remains the only general *not* to be defeated by Giap; however, that was only because he was not in command for the Hoa Binh operation that he had planned: Operation LOTUS.

*   *   *

The loss of life during this operation was enormous and the different value placed on human life by the two sides was demonstrated here. Giap was disinterested in casualties; he did not empathize with the wounded and expected the dead to be replaced. Macdonald commented after an interview with Giap, 'in future he would sacrifice units that were hopelessly trapped rather than be drawn into a meat-grinder situation ... if units already committed had to be sacrificed, so be it.'[22] Another biographer, Cecil Currey, titled his book *Victory at Any Cost*. That phrase amply sums up Giap's attitude, who said, in amplification: 'Every minute hundreds of thousands of people die all over the . world. The life or death of a hundred, a thousand or of tens of thousands of human beings, even if they are our own compatriots, represents very little.'[23]

Only Japanese and Russian commanders had that same mindset in the Second World War, which is anathema to a Western army. The Chinese adopted the same tactic during the Korean War. It would cost the USA many dead, years later, when it was thought, mistakenly, that in some way a high 'enemy body count' was the means to defeat the Vietnamese, to whom body count was of no importance whatsoever.

*   *   *

The monsoon brought operations to a halt in the spring of 1952. Giap turned to the training of his army. He had between 110,000 and 125,000 men in his main force now split into six divisions and a handful of independent infantry battalions. A seventh Heavy Division, the 351st, was also brought into being and this was composed of two artillery regiments, an engineer regiment and, significantly, some light anti-aircraft units. The artillery was equipped with 120mm mortars and 105mm howitzers, particularly suited to Vietminh needs.[24] The anti-aircraft weapons were 20mm and 40mm machine guns.

By mid-1952 Giap had under command 60,000 to 75,000 regional troops and in addition 120,000 to 200,000 militia and guerrillas, although many of those were of doubtful quality.[25] In addition to these armed individuals there were about 150,000 logistic porters in close support.

To counter this ever-expanding enemy force, the French, including Air Force and Navy, had about 90,000 servicemen. Of these, just over half were Frenchmen. The balance comprised Foreign Legionnaires, North Africans and French-led Indochinese. The Vietnamese National Army added 100,000 troops to the mix. Unfortunately, this latter group was of mixed ability, training and commitment. They were short of effective officers and subject to persistent desertions. When the campaigning season re-started in September 1952, Giap could put into the field 120,000 well-trained committed troops. The French could raise nothing like that and, with the burden of garrisoning the *ceinture*, they could at best raise 50,000 for offensive operations.[26]

The Vietminh held sway over great tracts of country, especially in the highlands, but that did not necessarily mean that the local population espoused Ho Chi Minh's philosophy or that they gave active support to Giap and his soldiers. Indeed, many were French supporters and France had a moral duty to defend these people, most of whom were either T'ai or Muongs. There were many isolated French cantonments carrying out that function. The decision facing Salan was would he support or evacuate these cantonments?

Giap's appreciation of enemy strength and aspirations was easy. He acknowledged the defensive capability of the de Lattre line and the capacity of the French to reinforce any operations close to that perimeter. He had to plan to counter the French aerial supremacy and its naval assets. On this basis he determined to exploit the French 'inability to sustain a large ground force any substantial distance from the de Lattre line'.[27] The French Air Force was obliged to operate from its facilities in the Tonkin delta and the further from these it was required to perform, the less effective it would be. The obvious solution was to fight the French as far away from its firm base as was possible.

During the summer of 1953, Giap enlarged his main force and his 351st (Heavy) Division was provided with additional artillery and mortars. Perhaps more importantly, anti-aircraft units were formed and equipped. The Chinese supplied machine guns, mortars and sub-machine guns. This latter short-range weapon was favoured by Vietminh infantry as the ideal assault firearm. To enhance the logistic line of supply, roads were either built or improved; all the better to accommodate the 600 Russian trucks and drivers.[28] It follows that hundreds of thousands of porters were mobilized as part of what was now a tough, well-equipped, experienced army.

Giap had had plenty of time to plan his next move; he selected as his targets the string of French posts between the Red and Black rivers and prime of these was Nghia Lo. This fell on 17 October 1953 with the loss of 700 French soldiers. It was only logistic difficulties that slowed Giap's advance. Nevertheless, he eventually reached the small garrison at Dien Bien Phu and its airstrip, which duly fell.

It lay in the future, but if Giap had been selecting a place to stage a final confrontation with the French, there is every probability that he would have selected Dien Bien Phu in which he now installed an infantry battalion, miles from the de Lattre line.

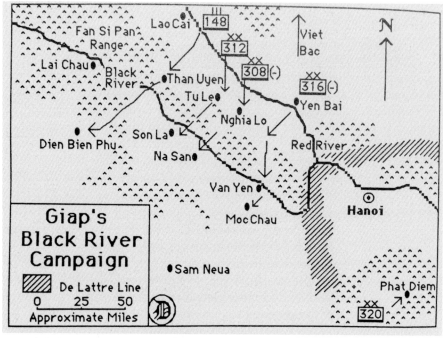

Giap's Black River campaign. (*Davidson*)

Salan launched Operation LORRAINE to counter Giap. This operation, which was initially a complicated, superbly-coordinated exercise in combined-arms operations, went very well indeed. Modest quantities of small arms were captured, along with 200 tons of ammunition. Interestingly, two Russian-built trucks were also taken; evidence that the Vietminh had, beside China, a second supporter.

Operation LORRAINE petered out thereafter and, when Salan withdrew his troops, it committed them to fighting a fierce, rearguard action over several days in mid-November 1952 before they regained the sanctuary of the de Lattre line. The butcher's bill was high. Some 1,200 French troops were lost, and the operation had only those small arms to show for it. French troops were painfully aware of the lack of support they had from their political masters and, when committed to jungle operations such as the withdrawal from LORRAINE, this became very apparent. For example, a French soldier recorded that

> we lived on rubbish – fish heads and rice. We were parachuted in some food once, and we could see that the tins were overpainted. A friend got a tin and made a hole in it with a bayonet. A sort of green mist flew out. He

scraped off a painted layer and (underneath) it said in French, 'For Arab Troops 1928'.[29]

A French fighting patrol, carrying everything, might possibly last a month in the jungle. Just like the Chindits of an earlier generation, they emerged with filthy, ulcerated skin. Their clothes were in tatters and their boots were rotted. Many were sick with either dysentery or malaria, or both. Others were extremely stressed. Living for a protracted period in very close proximity to 'poisonous snakes, scorpions, centipedes, spiders, stinging insects, blood-sucking leeches, soldier ants, burrowing ticks and microscopic parasites which could eat out a man's health for the rest of his life' were, in combination, sufficient to cause what is now called Post Traumatic Stress Disorder (PTSD).[30] Wounded men knew that, if they could not walk, their chances of survival were very low indeed. They could not be treated or evacuated and the best, perhaps the only option was an overdose of morphine and a painless death. It was in these same conditions that the Vietminh had to endure and Giap maintained a large and mobile army in the jungle for years. The fortitude and tenacity of the Vietminh invites admiration. The suffering of all soldiers was extreme.

Giap's plans were unaltered and Moc Chau was swiftly overrun, but Na San was most decidedly not. The defenders of Na San repelled massive assaults on 23 November, 30 November and 1/2 December 1952. By noon on 2 December 1,000 Vietminh dead littered the perimeter fence of the post. Giap suffered a total 4,000 casualties and he was nonplussed by his defeat. The likelihood was that, for once, his intelligence had failed him.[31] He thought he was facing about 2,000 men but, in fact, Na San held ten full-strength battalions with artillery and air support; say 6,000 men or more.

The garrison was maintained and re-supply by air was routine. A number of fighting patrols sought out the enemy, but they changed nothing of note, other than to demonstrate that a firm base *did* allow for forays of that sort. The French success at Na San was particularly significant because it had a disproportionate effect upon the thinking of the French high command. The concept of the fortified airhead or *herisson* (hedgehog) took root and it was the genesis of the Dien Bien Phu operation in late 1953. Na San was evacuated, successfully, in August 1953.

The reverse at Na San caused a reappraisal by Giap and that led directly to his first invasion of Laos, a French protectorate, which was almost un-opposed. He bypassed French border posts in mid-April 1953 à la George Patton and pressed on towards the capital of the local province Houaphanh, but then he outran his logistic tail (further shades of Patton, see p. 72) and was obliged to halt.

He was 'employing' but not paying thousands of lowland Vietnamese and T'ais. They were recalcitrant and, given half a chance, they dumped their load and melted into the jungle. This weakness in the vast logistic train brought the invasion of Laos to an abrupt end. Despite this rare breakdown in Giap's logistic arrangements,

> the rapidity of his … invasion of Laos is particularly noteworthy. His regiments averaged 10 air miles per day, which means that they walked and ran 20 miles daily on winding mountainous tracks. This is an extraordinary feat, particularly when one considers the primitive, cumbersome logistic system, a system based on the feet and backs of 200,000 coolies.[32]

Salan had countered the threat to Laos by creating two more fortified airheads at Lai Chau and Sam Neua in Laos. However, Sam Neua proved to be indefensible and when Salan ordered its denizens to evacuate and march south through the jungle, they were butchered and very few of the garrison survived.[33] This pattern was oft repeated. Whenever French troops attempted to advance or withdraw through the jungle, they were invariably slaughtered. However, successive French generals had not learned the lesson. The withdrawing garrisons would probably have been better advised to fight on; they had nothing to lose but their lives.

The Laotian capital of Luang Prabang was very vulnerable and Salan sent ten battalions to boost its defence. A further ten battalions were moved to a fortified airhead on the Plain of Jars. By late April 1953, the Vietminh's 308th and 316th divisions had surrounded that cantonment. At a stroke, the underequipped and undermanned French Air Transport Command came under severe strain as it sought to maintain the logistic flow at the extremity of its range. To the surprise of the participants, Giap did not attack either of the fortified airheads or Luang Prabang and, when the monsoon broke in May 1953, Giap withdrew.

Salan's tour came to an end in May 1953 and, before he departed, he prepared a memorandum for his successor. This document laid out, in stark unvarnished terms, a summary of the situation for Lieutenant General Henri Navarre. Navarre was left in no doubt about the capacity of his foe. Giap and his generals had made mistakes, but time was on their side. Almost unlimited manpower allowed them to apply pressure, at will, almost anywhere by dint of the unparalleled capacity of the Vietminh logistic system. In addition, Chinese support was all-embracing. Transport, ammunition, artillery, clothing, food and medical supplies were all provided in copious quantities.

Navarre had to understand that Vietminh soldiers did not do a 'tour' and then leave the theatre. They were committed for life, unless death claimed

Lieutenant General Henri Navarre.
(French Army)

them first. His army was not blessed with the same unqualified unity of purpose that was exhibited by Giap and his men. Navarre was aware that the French government had no strategic plan for Indochina. The government was at odds with the military establishment that it viewed as an expensive beast that was always asking for 'more'. Navarre was part of a system in which constant and routine posting of individuals from key military posts worked against a continuity of policy as 'each new broom swept clean' and created policy anew. He realized that the French people were disinterested and unsupportive of this war that was now his to fight.

The result of these factors was that Navarre was the latest commander-in-chief who had to fight a war with what could be provided, not with what he needed. It was only the ever-abundant American dollars and equipment that kept CEFEO afloat and in the field. The upside for Cs-in-C was that, at the end of their tours, they could leave Vietnam to take up a comfortable billet with NATO or the French Ministry of Defence, leaving their successors with the problem unresolved.

Navarre had under command, in late December 1953, 208,472 French troops (Army 187,494, Navy 9,975 and Air Force 11,003) and 294,562 personnel from 'Associated States' who were overwhelmingly soldiers. In total 503,034; manpower was not a problem if correctly deployed.[34]

Giap's army had many components. His regular army (*Chu Luc*) was distributed across Tonkin, Annam, Cochin-China, Cambodia and Laos and totalled 123,000. His regional force similarly deployed was 52,000 strong and his People's Armed Militia accounted for a further 115,000. His manpower base was 300,000 but of mixed quality.[35]

Navarre was but the latest commander-in-chief and his tenure would be the most problematic of them all. He was, arguably, not the ideal man for the job as he had spent part of his career as an intelligence staff officer and he had no experience of jungle operations. However, there is no doubt that he was intellectually gifted and his extensive experience of NATO 'fitted him to deal with political cant and evasion' and there was a lot of that around.[35] He was decisive and prepared to back his judgement over that of his subordinates.

One of these with whom he could find no accord was the commander of the Tonkin delta, Major General René Cogny. This officer was an extrovert given to self-advertisement, and he labelled himself 'Delta Man'. The soldiers called him 'Coco the siren' due to his predilection for being preceded by motorcycle outriders with blaring sirens. Navarre appointed him *Forces Terrestres du Nord Vietnam* (FTNV or North Vietnam Ground Forces).

A wise man once said 'One swallow does not make a summer'; however, the Na San battle and the successful evacuation of the garrison triggered in Navarre and Cogny a false sense of optimism, together with the percep-tion that summer had arrived.

Major General René Cogny, pictured as a lieutenant general later in his career. (Life Magazine)

Navarre considered his options. He had several and the first of these was to defend Laos by initiating mobile warfare in the rain forest and attack-ing his enemy where he could find them. The logistic burden of such a woolly, impractical idea was very evident, and so option number one was rapidly discarded.

His second option was to establish a linear line of defence to cover the Laotian border. This would call for the deployment of more troops than Navarre had available and the same logistic difficulties applied.

The third possibility was to protect the two Laotian capitals of Luang Prabang and Vientiane by placing a defensive circle around both locations. This idea foundered because both Laotian airfields were too far from the towns and the defensive circle would have to be far too large to be practical. In addition, the operation would be at the edge of the operating range of the FAF and consequently protracted re-supply was problematic.

A fourth possibility was for Navarre to mount a major attack into the Viet Bac to threaten the Vietminh government and the supply lines of Giap's main force. Valluy had tried something similar in 1947 but without success. In a reprise, in 1952 Salan's Operation LORRAINE had also failed in its aim and did not disrupt Giap's logistic arrangements.

Whatever choice Navarre made, it was going to be geared to his aerial superiority and his capacity to transport men and matériel. As a priority he was obliged to plan for the logistic support of his force. On this basis he was attracted to the idea of a fortified airhead, a *herisson*. He cheerfully accepted that it was '*une solution mediocre*', but it was the best of several bad choices.[37]

At this point Cogny advised that Dien Bien Phu should be re-taken and Navarre was in agreement because the 'fortified airhead' concept based upon the Na San model had worked before. On 2 November 1953, he proposed that Cogny retake DBP with six airborne battalions, the mission to be completed by 1 December. This would be an attractive target and, if Giap could be lured into battle there, he could then be destroyed.

Despite his earlier advice, quite illogically, Cogny resisted the order and went as far as putting together a strongly-worded refutation of the 'fortified airhead'. He preferred the use of DBP as a 'mooring point' from which 'light operations' could be mounted. The memorandum made several valid points. It observed that European tactics did not work in the jungle and blocking a road was no hindrance to this enemy. It concluded that a major base at DBP would suck in all available troops and, once there, they would be unavailable for redeployment on other operations. All available support air transport would be employed on this one operation. The memorandum, once prepared and polished, was not sent. Instead, on 6 November, Cogny sent Navarre an ambiguous letter which seemed to endorse the re-occupation of DBP (as he had suggested earlier), but did state his fears that he 'might not be able to hold the Delta'.[38] Cogny was covering his back against the possibility of failure. It was an unattractive device and readily discernible. Navarre was remarkably patient with the volatile Cogny, a man famously quick to take offence and nurse a grievance.

The objection to Navarre's plan was very much in character for Cogny, but after all, it was he who had first suggested to Navarre that DBP should be re-taken as it would be ideal as a base for light operations. The difference between the two men seems to have been a matter of scale and, either way, it promised to be a major logistic operation. Navarre wanted a secure, well-defended base with an airstrip. Quite how Cogny's 'mooring point' would function was never explained.

Laos was a current issue. It had been a French protectorate from 1893 until 1950 when it was nominally granted independence. However, the reality was that France continued to oversee the country through a puppet government. France saw Laos as a backwater and focused much more of its attention – such as that was – on Vietnam and Cambodia. In 1953, Navarre posed the question of the defence of Laos to the French government which vacillated over a decision until it was overtaken by events.

In November 1953 Navarre, not having been given any political direction, was unsure of his responsibility for the defence of Laos. This lack of policy was entirely typical of the ineffective and indecisive French government. Navarre believed that taking DBP would place French troops close to the Laotian border which, perhaps, they could then defend if ordered. Cogny's priority was the security of the Tonkin delta. His subsequent conduct caused Navarre to accuse him of releasing 'defeatist press releases' and ere long their relationship would completely break down.

It is worth giving some thought to what DBP had to offer and what implications its occupation would have. DBP was a cluster of hamlets with a total of 112 houses located about a third of the way down a large, flat 11-mile-long valley through which the Nam Yum River wended its way to the Mekong. The scattering of inhabitants, many of them opium farmers, numbered something around 1,000 souls. This opium had been a source of income to the French for years. In 1954 there was, in addition, a resident Vietminh battalion who would oppose any incursion.

Ground access to the valley was restricted to the *Route Provinciale* 41 (RP41) which came in from the north-east but was no more than a track and little more than a path where it exited, south of the valley. From Lai Chau there was another track that ran south to DBP, some 40 miles away. This very modest path was dignified with the name *Piste Pavie* after Auguste Pavie, an early French settler. Given that the valley was not accessible by road because there was no road, the overwhelming significance of the airstrip was evident. The downside of the airstrip was that it was 183 miles from the airfields around Hanoi. 'This distance placed it at a maximum operating range of the transports and fighters which would have to support it, permitting the fighters to spend only fifteen minutes over Dien Bien Phu and drastically limiting the carrying capacity of the ... (sixty-nine) transport aircraft available.'[39]

The airstrip would be the point of delivery of an anticipated 80 tons per day of logistic supplies and of the evacuation of casualties. As such, the security of the airstrip was obviously critical. However, it was vulnerable to shelling. Navarre was confident that the airhead could only be reached by artillery fire from the heights, about 13,000 yards away. He was assured several times by Lieutenant Colonel Charles Piroth, the designated artillery commander, that the enemy could not move artillery to the scene and, even in the unlikely event they did, his own counter-battery fire from his thirty medium guns would eradicate the threat.[40] Later, Bernard Fall refuted this, saying that, in fact, the airfield could be brought under direct fire from a hill line only 5,500 yards away.[41]

Navarre believed that DBP presented massive logistic problems for his adversary, far greater than those faced by himself. It was 190 miles from the

Lieutenant Colonel Charles Piroth. (*French Army*)

Chinese border over which Vietminh supplies flowed. The general assumed that the distance and lack of mechanical transport would inhibit the logistic capacity and thus the fighting strength of the Vietminh force.[42] This belief was fuelled by the intelligence staff who were advising Navarre. They had given insufficient credence to earlier, well-demonstrated enemy logistic ability and went as far as to assure the general that the operation carried *little or no risk* (author's italics). The French persisted in measuring Giap's logistic manoeuvrability by his lack of mechanical transport, an entirely irrelevant measurement. This blinkered and false attitude had existed even before Navarre took command because Salan had emphasized, in his study of May 1953, that truck shortage would prevent Giap from deploying heavy guns in any quantity. Both Salan and Navarre believed that Na San was the blueprint for continued success. They underestimated the Vietminh; a fatal mistake.

The reality was that the Vietminh had, by late 1953, American-built M2A1 105mm guns captured from the Chinese Nationalists and 37mm anti-aircraft (AA) guns. The field guns had a range of 12,000 yards and if they and their ammunition (each shell weighed 44lb) could be moved to the DBP area, they would present a serious threat to the airstrip and, by extension, to the entire French operation.

In September 1947 the logisticians of CEFEO numbered 13,271 and were 9.7 per cent of the force. By March 1953 their number had risen to 21,454 but they now represented only 5.4 per cent. This was not apparently a policy decision, but it is an interesting statistic in a 'Logistic War'.

The airhead at DBP – a vital element in this logistic war – was not a single, very large defended area, but was designed to be a series of fortified mutually-supporting hilltops around the airstrip (see Fig. 36). The valley covered an area of 75 square miles and so there was no possibility of building perimeter defences. That being the case, an enemy could infiltrate between fortified positions at will and attack them individually.

Navarre was aware that Cogny, who was in overall command of the proposed Operation CASTOR, and the senior air commanders were all opposed to the operation. Most of the objections were on logistic grounds, and none more compelling than those raised by Colonel Jean Nicot commanding the air transport force. He was adamant that he could *not provide a flow of supplies into Dien Bien Phu over an extended period, due to poor weather conditions and the probability of intense anti-aircraft fire*[43] (author's emphasis). Nicot put it all in writing; he, too, was covering his back.

Cogny's objections were supported by Brigadier General Gilles, the forces' airborne commander, and Dechaux, the senior airman in the theatre. The latter pointed out that the engine wear, fuel costs, crew fatigue and increased maintenance of his aircraft were all beyond his capacity. A reasonable man might think that this level of vociferous, professional opposition would cause Navarre to think again. He did not.

Chapter Seven

The Siege, 1953–1954

'Do not repeat the tactics which have gained you one victory, but let your methods be regulated by the infinite variety of circumstances.'[1]

[Sun Tzu]

French operations throughout the campaign were dependent upon their aerial superiority. Accordingly, parachute insertions were the routine method for the taking, reinforcing and re-supplying of isolated but tactically important locations. The flexibility and speed of deployment of French forces that was provided by the *Armée de l'Air* (French Air Force, FAF) was significant, though that was always inhibited by a shortage of aircraft. To counter the deficiency, reliance was placed on civil air transport (CAT). The civilian pilots, some American, were an asset but they were not 'under command' and flew only on a volunteer basis. By early 1954 these civilians were engaged in hazardous operational missions.

However, 'as late as November 1953 no effective procedures for the control of the available airlift had been put in place to regulate the flow of cargo or establish priorities.'[2] This did not auger well, particularly as

> The French expeditionary force in Vietnam was perhaps the first force to consciously employ pre-planned aerial re-supply as the *sole means of support for a fixed garrison* [author's emphasis] ... Conceptually the French had keyed into the potential impact of airlift but did not have an adequate air force, nor an understanding of the doctrinal nuances to ensure victory.[3]

In North Vietnam, air operations were heavily weather-dependent and a further ingredient in the mix was the lethargy and general lack of interest in improving the operational situation. French air operations were hindered by the parlous state of its equipment and the neglect of its ground facilities. The capability of the FAF was limited by inadequate maintenance, poor administrative systems, a dearth of qualified personnel and a general atmosphere of apathy.[4] It was on this ill-founded organization that Navarre rested his strategy and the lives of his men.

It was an appalling state of affairs; nevertheless, 'in the land of the blind the one-eyed man is king'. The Vietminh had not a single aircraft and, on that basis, total French aerial superiority should have been the winning factor in this campaign. The Vietminh, without an Air Force, pragmatically and prudently focused on equipping its formations with AA artillery. The Korean War had ended with an armistice in July 1953 and the Chinese were now able to turn their attention to fresh fields. They gave increased support to the Vietminh, including AA artillery.

Events would show that the battle and siege of DBP was to be the final clash between two vastly different politico/military systems. Each in turn had given rise to different military organizations with widely differing aims, priorities, intelligence arrangements, logistic support, personnel recruitment, education and training. It was the ultimate test of two competing logistic systems. They were as the pear is to the pineapple.

Navarre had the optimistic aim of dominating his enemy by establishing a *Base Aero-Terrestre* in the Vietminh's back yard. From there, it was his plan to strike outward from the base using armoured vehicles, of which he had only ten, and regardless of the unsuitability of the country.

Navarre was firm in his opinion that complete aerial superiority would allow unhindered re-supply to the base and its mixed nationality force. This was despite the clearly-expressed advice of Colonel Jean Nicot, his air commander. On the basis that aircraft would be Navarre's only logistic asset, why would an intellectually gifted, experienced general ignore the cold hard facts of logistic reality?

His rank and appointment gave Navarre the absolute authority to either take or leave the advice of his subordinates as he saw fit and all the players understood that. Nevertheless, logistic management is the responsibility of the commander and Navarre got the 'command' out of kilter with the 'logistic management'. Thus, based on a series of false premises and in a decision that might be termed aberrational, Navarre initiated the battle and siege of DBP. By so doing he played into the hands of his enemy.

The Vietminh responded by marshalling hundreds of thousands of deeply-committed Vietnamese in a logistic operation that exceeded in scale and aspiration anything ever achieved in human history before. The congregation of five divisions, supporting regiments of artillery and AA units, in combination, provided General Giap with overwhelming numerical superiority. He had met the French challenge head-on, and he had to hand all the tools he needed.

There was a downside. Giap did not have unlimited time because he headed a vast host that was living in the most arduous circumstances. The logistic support of his soldiers and porters was an ongoing problem, but the solution was almost at hand. Giap said that once DBP was invested in January, he 'was able to use our artillery fire to destroy the airstrips and our anti-aircraft guns to cope with the activities of enemy planes.'[5] As soon as Giap's artillery was in place the eventual capitulation of the base was assured; it was only a matter of time. The denial of the airstrip for re-supply flights led to the substitution of parachuted, aerial re-supply and the degradation of the logistic chain.

The sequence of events had all the characteristics of a slow-motion train crash. It could be argued that the problems stemmed from Navarre having had no political direction on the defence of Laos. Nevertheless, and in ignorance of his government's policy, he decided that he would proceed with Operation CASTOR. By doing so, he would keep his options open.

In his view, CASTOR had two functions. The first was to block Giap's supply route from China. This was absurd, because the lines of communication in a Vietnamese setting are not fixed along roads and the Vietminh could very easily evade any blocking movement in the jungle wilderness. Secondly, Navarre believed that his *Base Aero-Terrestre* would provide the launch-pad from which he could interdict Giap's installations. It was on that basis that he appointed Colonel Christian de Castries to command the post as soon as it had been secured. De Castries was a cavalryman and a protégé of Navarre. There was the expectation that armoured thrusts would be made from DBP and de Castries was suited to lead such actions. Apparently, it did not occur to Navarre that Giap could lay siege to DBP and so nullify all his aspirations.

On 20 November, the first sticks of airborne soldiers jumped into the 'hot' DZ of DBP. The airborne commander Brigadier General Gillies had been instructed by Cogny that he was 'to exclude any system designed to provide a belt of strongpoints for the airfield',[6] a curious instruction that belies common sense and military priorities.

In order to have an overview of the logistic battle it is necessary to sketch in the chronology of the period. The 6th *Battalion de Parachutistes Coloniaux* (6 BPC) dropped onto DZ Natasha and at the same time the 2nd Battalion, 1st *Regiment de Chasseurs Parachutistes* (11/1 RCP) dropped into DZ Simone. Both were engaged at once by the 148th Independent Infantry Regiment supplemented by a mortar company and an artillery battery of the 316th Division. The plan was for the 11/1 RCP to block any evasion by the Vietminh

Colonel (later Brigadier General) Christian de Castries. (*French Army*)

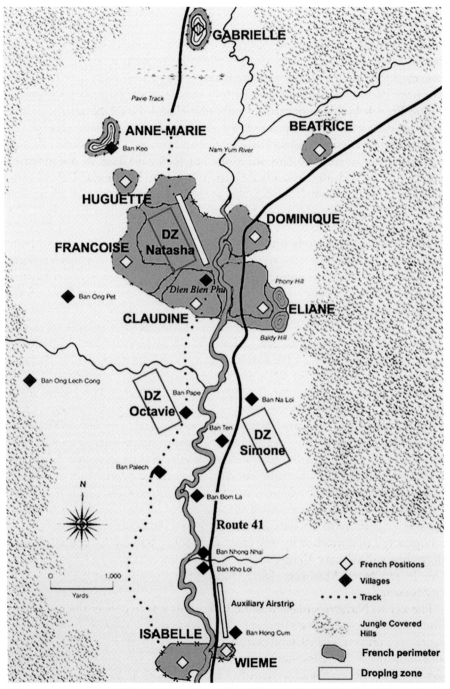

This map shows the widely-dispersed French positions in the DBP valley. The isolation of 'Isabelle' and 'Gabrielle' made their support difficult. (*Karta 3*)

to the south, but the airborne soldiers were so widely scattered after the drop that most of the enemy filtered out of the valley to the south. Nevertheless, they left ninety bodies as testament to the fierce, local action of that morning. French casualties were light, but eleven mothers lost a son.

The French build-up continued unhindered and, by 22 November, there were six battalions on the ground. Work started to repair the airstrip, dig latrines and weapon pits, clear fields of fire and produce range cards. Patrols pushed out to ascertain enemy locations but took casualties in the process.

Between 24 and 30 November Giap responded. He directed the 304th, 308th, 312th and 351st (Heavy) Divisions to leave the Viet Bac and move to DBP. The 148th Regiment and most of the 316th Division, already in the area, were to attack Lai Chau.

The die was cast, and the future of French Indochina hung in the balance. Navarre was optimistic and relished the chance to meet and defeat Giap. However, it was his miscalculation of the strength, flexibility and logistic capability of the Vietminh that, ultimately, led to humiliating defeat and the deaths of many brave men on both sides.

The battles of Vietnam have been fully chronicled by some outstanding historians whose work is referenced in the bibliography. The reader who wants chapter and verse on the battle of Dien Bien Phu is directed to Bernard Fall's masterly account, which is the definitive work on the subject.[7]

So far it had all gone very well. Cogny could recognize a good thing when he saw it and promptly embraced the operation, saying 'if the entrenched camp at Na San had been put on wheels, I would have moved it to Dien Bien Phu five months ago.' This was 'a striking about-face for the man who had been so vehemently against the operation only a few days before.'[8]

When the build-up was complete de Castries would have 10,814 soldiers under his command. That number would rise during the siege as further troops were added to the garrison. By the nature of the size and complexity this was a major general's command, not that of a colonel. On the subject of 'complexity', this was not by any means a Gallic garrison. Of those soldiers, more than a third were Vietnamese and in addition there were large numbers who hailed from Morocco, Syria, Chad, Guadeloupe, the Lebanon and Madagascar.[9]

The key to Navarre's plans was the FAF. This was to deliver the soldiers to DBP and to supply them throughout the operation. Available to Navarre were thirty-two fighters, forty-five fighter-bombers and about forty B-26 medium bombers, six C-119 transports and five Privateer anti-submarine bombers.[10] Also in the theatre there were forty-four helicopters, but these were not equipped for offensive action and were, in effect, airborne ambulances. It fell to Air Force Brigadier General Jean Dechaux, who commanded the 'Northern

Vietminh artillery being deployed. (*PAVN*)

Tactical Air Group' (GATAC Nord), to attack Vietminh supply routes and to strike in defence of the fortified areas of DBP. In practice, taking into account repair and maintenance and combat losses, Dechaux had a mixed bag of about seventy-five serviceable crewed aircraft at any one time. This was inadequate for the mission.

The six C-119s, the 'Flying Boxcars', were cargo aircraft but they were pressed into use in a bombing capacity and specifically for the delivery of napalm. Their payload of this frightful weapon was 6 tons and that represented a great deal of misery on the ground. It was and is an area weapon and so was most effective on Vietminh supply routes.

The French Air Force and French Navy co-operated in the air campaign. The Air Force fielded the B-26s, while the two fighter groups used Bearcat F8Fs. The Navy sent a carrier, *Arromanches*, and later that was replaced by the ex-American carrier *Belleau Wood*. *Arromanches* carried the 3rd and 11th Squadrons who flew SB2C Helldivers and F6F Hellcats. In addition, the French Navy had a few Privateer long-range bombers.

Giap took time to respond to CASTOR. He was unsure if the French planned to move out of DBP and, if so, where to: Laos? His first act was to move his headquarters 300 miles to a cave complex about 10 miles east of DBP. That simple statement does not begin to tell of the physical effort required. Those 300 miles were across jungle country, on foot, in a dangerous environment, in either hot and humid conditions or cold in the mountains. The climate was a danger to health. The physical strength and tenacity of the man and of all of those who accompanied him is noteworthy. Among Giap's

Napalm did not always hit the intended target. (*Horst Faas*)

entourage was General Wei Guoqing of the Chinese Advisory Mission. This general was a political commissar, and his presence was indicative of Chinese support throughout the campaign.

Giap's order to four divisions to congregate at DBP and join the 316th was a massive, unprecedented manoeuvre. Tens of thousands of soldiers and porters cut their way across country. Many must have died on the journey, either by accident, exhaustion, disease or of old wounds. Their numbers are not recorded and certainly not their names. They dragged with them their weapons, prime of which was their artillery. On the topic of the guns, a Vietminh officer Tran Do recorded that

> each night when freezing fog descended into the valleys groups of men mustered ... the track was so narrow (and) soon an ankle-deep bog, that the slightest deviation of the wheels would have caused a gun to plunge into a ravine. By sheer sweat and tears we hauled them into position, with men playing the part of trucks ... We existed on rice either almost raw or overcooked because the kitchens had to be smokeless by day and spark-less by night. On ascents, hundreds of men dragged the guns on long ropes, with a winch on the crest to prevent them from slipping. The descents were much tougher, the guns much heavier, the tracks twisting and turning. Gun crews steered and chocked their pieces, while infantry manned the ropes and winches. It became the work of a whole torch-lit night to move a gun five hundred or a thousand yards.[11]

It could reasonably be argued that the Vietminh logistic operation, prior to and during the battle and siege of DBP, was the single factor that led to the defeat of the French and the surrender of their colony. Giap has been described as a logistic genius and his vision certainly marks him out as exceptional. However, the logistic chain of command must have had thousands like Tran Do (see above) and included a large number of outstandingly talented individuals who made the system work on Giap's behalf. The general does not deserve all the plaudits, just a high proportion of them. It is interesting to note that, while Giap shared the hardship of his men, eating and sleeping alongside them, de Castries lived 'much higher on the hog'. He dined well with his officers and slept in a well-upholstered bed. He did not spend time in muddy trenches.

Giap gave his orders by radio and these transmissions were liable to be intercepted by French monitors. By this means Cogny learned that Giap had given orders for bridges and ferries over the Red River to be readied for the passage of 6,000 men every night and deduced that four divisions were heading for DBP to join the 316th. Navarre disagreed: he could not and would not accept that the Vietminh had the logistic capacity to support five divisions.

Instead, he speculated that the radio messages might just be a ruse.[12] This was a man who was losing touch with the world in which he lived.

On 29 November Navarre flew into the *Base Aero-Terrestre* where he was given further categoric assurances that he had nothing to fear from enemy artillery. Viewing the flat valley, Navarre could visualize his tank-infantry jabs against enemy positions in the foothills around the base. He pronounced himself to be content with the arrangements, decorated a handful of soldiers and, with Cogny, flew back to Hanoi, from where he was able to direct other ongoing operations much further south.

That same day Ho Chi Minh made public his willingness to negotiate an armistice with the French. This stunning revelation, at a stroke, increased the value of DBP to both sides. Its fate would be a significant factor in future negotiations. Both sides had to win the encounter. There could be no compromise here.

One of ten American M-24 Chaffee tanks which were air-lifted into DBP in pieces and then reassembled. They were a very useful asset. (*D. Starry***)**

In late November 1953 the only Vietminh formation in the area of DBP was the 316th Division and then only some of its elements. It engaged in low-level harassment of the French but focused on Lai Chau. A secondary role was to provide a cut-off should the French thrust towards northern Laos. Navarre nailed his colours to the mast on 3 December when he issued Personal and Secret Instruction No. 949 (IPS949). It said: 'I have decided to accept battle in the north-west to be centred on DBP which is to be held at all costs.'[13]

On 4 December the French government finally made a long-awaited decision on Laos and its defence. The government informed Navarre that he had no responsibility for that area. One wonders who did have the responsibility.

One of the reasons for CASTOR had been the probable need to defend Laos. This tardy decision-making by the politicians was typical of the inept leadership given to French generals throughout the war.

Bernard Fall took the view that the fate of DBP was sealed.[14] At this point Navarre still had open to him the option of withdrawing the garrisons of Lai Chau and DBP with his air fleet. On 8 December de Castries arrived and took command. The day before Cogny, aware that the 316th Division could easily overrun Lai Chau, ordered its evacuation.

Generals Henri Navarre, René Cogny and Colonel (later Brigadier) Christian de Castries in Laos, late 1953. (*Granger Collection*)

That post lay about 40 miles north of DBP, too far away to be in support and too small to challenge the Vietminh. The evacuation of the garrison was conducted superbly. Knowing that their radio transmissions could be intercepted, the French commander sent messages requesting significant reinforcements. When the Vietminh saw a fleet of aeroplanes arriving at Lai Chau it presumed, as was intended, that they were bringing in fresh troops. In fact, it was the first of 183 sorties of incoming empty aircraft that swiftly swooped up the garrison and bore it away. T'ai guerrilla units remained behind to destroy ammunition and other war stores.

This mission accomplished, 2,100 men and civilians set off for DBP along *Piste Pavie*. This was to be yet another re-telling of the story of the wholesale massacre of the French and their adherents trying to make their way through the jungle in the face of merciless opposition. On 11 December a three-battalion-strong force of the 2nd Battle Group was sent out from DBP to march north to meet the column. It not only failed to make contact with the column, but was badly mauled by the waiting Vietminh for its trouble. Of the 2,100 who left Lai Chau, only 185 eventually reached DBP. It had been yet another very painful debacle, despite the countless incidents of great fortitude along the way.

By 17 December, seven battalions of the 316th had assembled and the inexorable advance to DBP by the 304th, 308th, 351st and 312th Vietminh divisions continued. It took until 24 January 1954 for the entire Vietminh force to be assembled. They came bearing heavy guns and anti-aircraft guns. Giap had about 50,000 soldiers and they outnumbered the occupants of the *Base Aero-Terrestre* by about 5:1. In addition, Giap had a very large body of porters. Estimates of that latter group vary from 31,500 (Fall), 35,000 (Rocolle) and French intelligence 50,000–75,000.[15]

On 21 December the 2nd Battle Group made a foray to meet up with French Laotian forces moving north from Laos. They met at the Laotian village of Sop Nao after a slow and laborious trek through the very difficult country. Strategically this foray had only PR value: 'This demonstrated the bankruptcy of the concept that DBP could act as a base to harass Giap's supply lines or logistic installations; the enemy was too strong, the jungle too thick and the limestone cliffs too high.'[16]

On 29 December Navarre told Cogny to prepare an evacuation plan for DBP. Despite his obvious misgivings and although heavily committed at DBP, Navarre pressed ahead with his ambitious Operation ATLANTE. This operation was to be fought in three phases over a six-month period starting on 20 January. Fifty-three battalions of infantry and artillery were to make a seaborne assault on the low-lying and very wet country between Da Nang and Nha Trang in South Vietnam. The aim was twofold: first to defeat the

A few of the 185 T'ai soldiers who survived the withdrawal from Lai Chau. (*French Army*)

estimated 30,000 Vietminh in that area, and secondly to show positive support for the government of Bao Dai, the thirteenth and last emperor of the Nguyen dynasty; at this stage, in effect, South Vietnam.

Operation ATLANTE was under way before the ever-recalcitrant Cogny went through the motions of producing an evacuation plan. His slow and unenthusiastic response was probably because, by this time, the *Base Aero-Terrestre* was virtually surrounded and evacuation was not remotely possible. Events had overtaken Navarre.

ATLANTE was, at best, a qualified success. It failed to destroy the Vietminh in South Vietnam and, eventually, unacceptable French losses, in combination with an abject performance by the National Army of (South) Vietnam, forced Navarre to order a withdrawal. Of course, by mounting ATLANTE during the CASTOR operation it served to increase the burden on Navarre's air transport and reduce the logistic support available to DBP.

During 1953 the French had obtained eighteen Sikorsky H-19 helicopters and they represented a major upgrade in capability since they could carry six wounded and a medical attendant over more than 500 kilometres. At about the same time, the helicopters were transferred from the FAF (*Armée de l'Air*) to the army which formed the first all-helicopter unit in December 1953: the *Groupement des Formations d'Hélicoptères en Indochine* (GFHI: Indochina Helicopter Units Group), itself made up of the 1re and 2e *Compagnie d'Hélicoptères d'Evacuations Sanitaires* (CHES: Medical Evacuation Helicopter Company). In 1954 alone, helicopters evacuated 6,499 wounded from the various battlefields. Early in the siege, three H-19s were destroyed on the ground by artillery and one was shot down by AA fire. The Vietminh did not respect the red crosses painted clearly on their fuselage. This resulted in the suspension of helicopter flights to DBP in late March.

The fleet of forty-four helicopters (Hiller H-23, Sikorsky S-51 and H-19) played no part in combat, although eleven were lost to enemy action. Despite the technical limits of the early models, the value of these aircraft was quickly appreciated. The small number of helicopters evacuated 10,820 CEFEO casualties in 1951–1954 (roughly 1/7th of the total number of evacuations); the probability is that many of these men would have died had they not been airlifted out.

The French intention was to build helicopter assets during 1954, but that aspiration was overtaken by events. Nevertheless, the helicopters played an important role and by the end of July 1954 they had flown for 7,040 hours in 5,400 sorties. In addition, 'they rescued thirty-eight pilots and eighty escapees.'[17] The USA learned from French helicopter operations, and history shows that ten years later the first helicopter war was fought.

Sieges are invariably the result of logistic failure in some form. In this case the failure was the absence of a ground-based line of communication. In a siege situation the initiative always rests with the besieger and DBP was no exception. The least expensive and most certain weapon to capture a besieged position is starvation. Vicksburg (1863), Khartoum (1885) and Kut (1916) are examples. However, Tobruk (1941) was relieved, as was Chitral (1895), in

Vietminh AA guns. These played a critical role in disrupting and eventually destroying the aerial logistic lifeline to DBP.

both cases by relief columns that fought their way through enemy territory. Cogny realized that fighting the 180 miles into DBP and then 180 miles back out was simply not worth considering. He was entirely dependent on aerial re-supply, as had been Paulus and the remnant of his 6th Army at Stalingrad.

On the other hand, Giap did not have the time to starve out DBP because the supply and care of his own troops was an issue. Colonel Bui Tin observed that Giap was adamant that

> we took what precautions we could. General Giap issued special orders on hygiene ... Drinking water was to be boiled. The troops were to use clean socks after washing their feet in warm water and salt. They should have hot rice with adequate meat and vegetables at least once a day and sleep at least six hours every night ... Uniforms (were ordered to be) changed every two or three days.[18]

The logistic implications of Bui Tin's remarks are significant and open to question. For example, just how many pairs of clean socks, per day, were required? By what means was all that water warmed and in what did the soldiers bathe their feet? Probably a basin or large trough, but how many basins or troughs? A hot meal every day: who sourced the food, and who cooked it? The diet of the indigenous Vietnamese was limited, and the two staples were rice and dried fish. 'The Vietminh soldier's diet was of rice and salt supplemented by *nuoc mam* (a strongly-flavoured fish sauce rich in protein), fruits, vegetables, vegetable oils and salted fish. Sugar, tea, eggs, poultry and meat were all desired but very scarce.' The ration of dry rice is estimated to have been between 1.65lb and 1.76lb per day. With supplements, this produced about 4,110 calories per day.[19]

Those fresh uniforms raise a further question. Were the dirty ones laundered? If so where, how were they dried and redistributed? Clothing and equipment were degraded by the climate and although a French steel helmet might suffice for three years, a jungle hat, shirt and trousers lasted barely four months. French jungle boots succumbed to hard use and the climate after only three months. There was a need to entirely re-clothe CEFEO about three times per year. The Vietminh were subject to the very same circumstances and their clothing would also need constant replacement.

What degree of medical cover was there for the hundreds or thousands of Vietminh who would fall sick every day? The fact is that there was practically no medical support. Nevertheless, the sheer scale of the operation to provide basic needs to about 100,000 people living deep in a rain forest, bereft of any twentieth-century facilities or technology is way beyond the experience of any Western logistician. Events would show that, despite Giap's good intentions and Colonel Bui Tin's admiration, the Vietminh logistic system was far from perfect.

The subsistence of the CEFEO in Indochina was a considerable logistic task. The provision of fresh food in the tropics calls for cold storage and, as the war grew in scale, the French increasingly depended on the import of boneless frozen meat to meet the demand which in 1953 was for 22,700 tons. Of this, only about 60 per cent could be purchased in theatre. In addition, live sheep were required to feed Muslim soldiers. It follows that frozen meat generated a need for refrigerated trucks and long-term deep freeze facilities in ports and in major installations. In 1952 there was 92,660 cubic feet, most of which was in Saigon and Haiphong. Some 6,178 cubic feet were under construction and there were plans to double capacity in 1953 with an additional 102,370 cubic feet.[20]

The French calculated that the normal consumption of *Intendance* (food and clothing) was approximately 2.75kg per day (slightly over 6.6lb). In practice, and at Dien Bien Phu, the take-up was 3kg per European soldier, 2.5kg per African, 2kg per locally-enlisted soldier and 1.5kg per Vietminh prisoner.[21] The French did have the equivalent of the British Composite Ration ('compo') and the American K-Ration. They had a range of packed options, such as the *Ration Multiple F.O.M.*, somewhat similar to the American C-Ration, the *Ration Secours F.O.M. 101* for airborne troops and their *Ration Individuelle Guerre*. This equated to the British twenty-four-hour individual ration, the *Ration Conditionnée Spécialement Reservée*, for locally-enlisted troops.[22] These packaged, mostly tinned rations were supplemented by fresh vegetables whenever possible. Every British soldier who was fed on 'compo' for an extended period can affirm to its constipation-inducing qualities.

The transport of supplies by the Vietminh was not all on the backs of porters. Use was made of horses, mules, water buffaloes and elephants, some of which hauled sledges. Carts drawn by a water buffalo could move a load of 770lb about 7.5 miles in a twenty-four-hour period. A horse could move a lighter load: 474lb over 12.4 miles in the same time frame.[23] Bicycles carried up to 200lb of rice. Rivers were incorporated into the wider plan and rafts and sampans were employed where possible. Some 600 Russian 'Molotova' 2.5-ton trucks had been donated to the cause, but they had the same difficulties experienced by the French. Tracks had to be improved to accommodate them, especially RP41, the route into the DBP valley. Rice supplies from China were rafted down the Black River and unloaded at Lai Chau. From here, rice was portered down the *Piste Pavie* on those bicycles mentioned earlier.[24]

None of these activities were subject to effective interdiction by the FAF, although it employed American anti-personnel bombs that spread a shower of razor-sharp steel fragments.[25] To counter surveillance, the Vietminh tied the tops of trees together to form an all-embracing tunnel of vegetation. Where this was not possible, all movement was at night. By these means, they were able to stockpile artillery shells at DBP. Probably one shell was the load for one man. To measure the labour required to produce this stockpile alone is difficult and the arithmetic is mind-boggling.

Porters, male and female, with burdens carried on bicycles. (*PAVN*)

One of the first military principles taught to all young officers is that 'time spent on reconnaissance is never wasted.' Perhaps that was imparted to Giap in a Chinese military college; if not, then he knew it intuitively and applied the principle. He did not rush to attack the *Base Aero-Terrestre*. He bided his time and built an 18-mile circuit of concealed tracks around the perimeter of the valley.

This enabled him to observe the French positions and move his artillery and AA guns to the most advantageous place. He installed his artillery on the forward slopes of the surrounding hills where they had line of sight to their targets. This was a matter of necessity as his gunners did not have the skills to use indirect fire from reverse slopes. The guns were dug deeply into the hillsides and were completely concealed from view when not in action.

The tracks that had been cut around the *Base Aero-Terrestre* allowed swift re-supply of water, food and ammunition and also re-deployment of infantry when necessary. Vietminh re-supply was becoming more efficient and French intelligence calculated that a supply convoy from the Chinese border to DBP could journey along improved but unsurfaced tracks in about seven days.[26]

The strongpoints of DBP were allegedly named after eight former mistresses of de Castries; in which case he was a man with, if nothing else, a splendid libido. The strongpoints were divided: for example, 'Dominique' 1 to 5 and 'Elaine' 1 to 4, although, more realistically, they were simply named alphabetically, less 'F'. In all there were forty-nine defended sites[27] (see Fig. 38). The garrison of DBP occupied a very large footprint, spread out over several miles scattered around an airstrip. For example, 'Isabelle', which also had an airstrip, was about 6 miles from 'Gabrielle' and 'Beatrice' was about 2 miles from 'Elaine'. The wide dispersion of manpower was, initially, not an issue and the re-distribution of supplies effected by trucks worked efficiently. However, the separation of the defended localities made them individually vulnerable.

At first the re-supply system was satisfactory. Throughout North Vietnam 1,700 tons per month had been delivered to French garrisons in the period January to November 1953. Inevitably, this increased to 2,200 tons in December, 4,700 tons in March 1954 and again to 7,200 tons in April. In total 20,860 tons were delivered to DBP but, and it is a big 'but', only 6,584 tons were air-landed and the balance was either air-dropped or parachuted.[28] However, during the siege a high proportion of the parachute deliveries did not reach the French troops, and this was particularly galling because French ammunition fitted US-made Vietminh artillery. The logistic support of DBP was further limited by the availability of parachutes. Some 82,929 were required but after 14 March, none were recovered for future use. Of these, 2,390 malfunctioned.

The logistics of defence are formidable. Macdonald, one of Giap's many biographers, commenting on the defended sites, said that

The task of creating them was gigantic ... each battalion needed fifty-five dugouts and seventy-five machine-gun bunkers. Foxholes were not good enough; these positions had to withstand artillery fire. To construct them 2,550 tons of engineer stores and 500 tons of barbed wire would have to be flown in to entrench the garrison of ten battalions ... (this would require) 1,200 flights by C-47 from Hanoi and Haiphong with eighty of them available each day; it would take five months![29]

By the time that the *Base Aero-Terrestre* was surrounded, the French engineers were deficient in more than 30,000 tons of the appropriate defence stores. They had managed to build a hardened headquarters command post, a signals centre, the hospital and a water purification plant. Then, lacking the means to build more hardened positions, all the available trees were cut down, providing the Vietminh with line of sight across the valley. The preparation of defensive positions was not the first of de Castries' priorities and he was pressured by Navarre to push out on patrol. There were instances when half of the garrison was out on search-and-destroy missions. The result of those missions, up to 15 February 1954, was that 1,037 or 10 per cent of the garrison were casualties.[30]

When not patrolling, the garrison at DBP dug holes, very big holes. A ten-man bunker took a forty-strong platoon eight days to dig and prepare a fortification that was only vulnerable to a direct hit by an artillery strike. There was a need for every unit to dig for its life. There was insufficient barbed wire to complete the defences and this would prove to be a significant deficiency once the Vietminh had breached the perimeter.

The master plan for CASTOR was entirely dependent upon the logistic capability of the FAF which, it was anticipated, would fly in with supplies daily. This part of the plan had failed by mid-January 1954 when the airfield came under artillery fire. On the other hand, Giap, a master logistician, decided that the route to success was the elimination of the French logistic chain and, to do that, it meant that the FAF would have to be neutralized.

The Neutralization of the FAF resulted in forty-eight aircraft shot down, fourteen aircraft destroyed on landing and 167 damaged. The skill base to repair these damaged planes did not exist. The Vietminh launched Commando-style raids (à la David Stirling and the SAS) on an airfield at Cat Bi near Haiphong and this resulted in the destruction of eighteen transports; a further attack at Gia Lam was equally successful.[31] The impact on the FAF by Vietminh AA fire was to drive supply missions higher. The extra height increased aircraft survivability, but at the cost of less accurate logistic delivery.

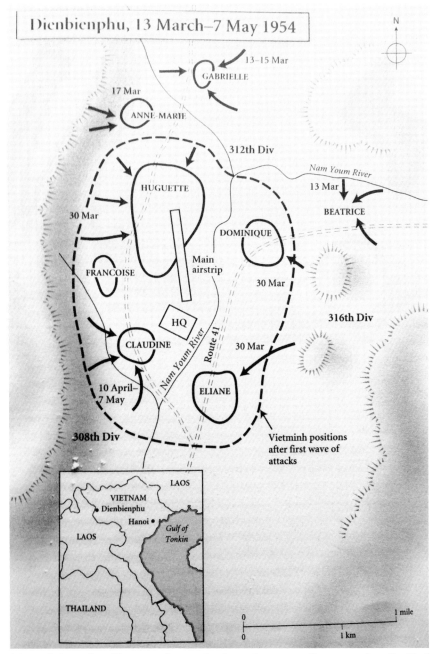

Dienbienphu, 13 March–7 May 1954

N

13–15 Mar
GABRIELLE

17 Mar
ANNE-MARIE

312th Div

Nam Youm River

13 Mar
BEATRICE

HUGUETTE

30 Mar

FRANCOISE

DOMINIQUE

Main airstrip

30 Mar

316th Div

HQ

CLAUDINE

Route 41

Nam Youm River

30 Mar

10 April–7 May

ELIANE

308th Div

Vietminh positions after first wave of attacks

LAOS

VIETNAM
● Dienbienphu
Hanoi ●

Gulf of Tonkin

LAOS

THAILAND

0   1 mile

0   1 km

Map of *Base Aero-Terrestre* shows the less than mutually-supporting fortified positions. These were spread out over a wide area protecting the airstrip, vital to the logistic operation. 'Beatrice', one of the most isolated of these positions, fell on 13 March 1954. (*weaponsandwarfare.com*)

By the end of January 'Giap had concentrated around DBP a force of five divisions including supporting artillery and anti-aircraft units. In addition, he had corps-level logistic support units.'[32] This assembly had required skilful staff work. Arrangements had to be put in place to select bivouac areas and water points. There was a need to provide food and shelter, not only for the 50,000 soldiers but also for the vast number of porters. Tracks had to be cut, existing tracks widened, and bridges had to be strengthened to accommodate the trucks now in the Vietminh inventory.

On 15 February, de Castries reported that the south-west of the garrison and strongpoint 'Claudine' was flooded. He warned that that situation would get worse if the rain continued. The large holes, dug with so much effort, started to fill with water. The bridge across the Nam Yum River was expected to be marooned in a large lake 300 yards wide. As the monsoon approached, the climate became as much of a threat as the Vietminh. The constant movement of 10,000 men, 118 vehicles and 10 tanks reduced the place to a quagmire. The burning of trees and shrubs made it impossible to camouflage weapon pits and gun positions. The *Base Aero-Terrestre* had much in common with the Somme in 1916.

On 6–7 March further raids on French airfields saw seventy-eight aircraft destroyed and most of them were transports. The saboteurs ignored other more available targets and clearly Giap was striking at the heart of the French logistic system. Then he started to crater the airstrip, in the process destroying aircraft on the ground. On 24 March a C-47 was shot down over the fortress and over the next few days a further four transport aircraft fell to the 37mm AA guns. These AA guns were well-placed to engage French supply flights that were obliged to make deliveries by parachute, at first from 2,500ft. On 27 March the CAT pilots withdrew their labour, complaining that the AA batteries were not being suppressed. Colonel Nicot wrote to General Lauzin, saying

> It is hardly necessary to insist on the necessity of stopping the carnage but the air crews, in addition to obvious physical fatigue, have suffered a psychological shock … it is necessary to immediately stop low-level parachute drops and I have given the order to do so as of tonight.[33]

Thereafter drops were made from 6,500ft and later from 8,500ft. The encirclement of the garrison had been completed in mid-January 1954. Nevertheless, throughout January and February the French sent out fighting patrols and paid for any short-term success in blood.

On 13 March 1954, eighty-five days since the initiation of Operation CASTOR, the Vietminh attacked. A key participant was General Văn Tiến Dũng. He had been by Giap's side from the earliest days and was

General Văn Tiến Dũng, a Vietminh commander at DBP. (*DRV*)

his chief of staff. Dũng was a very capable officer, closely involved in all aspects of the campaign and responsible for the coordination of the attack, not least of the artillery plan. Ringing the *Base Aero-Terrestre* were 144 field pieces, thirty 75mm pack howitzers, thirty-six other heavy guns of a mixed calibre and between twelve and sixteen Russian six-tube Katyushas. The 37mm AA guns were in addition.

On 14 March, the available tanks could not reach positions under attack because their manoeuvrability was hindered by the positioning of French defences.

'Gabrielle' and 'Beatrice' were the first targets. Vietminh artillery, so painfully dragged through miles of jungle, quickly neutralized many of the French guns. The observation posts (OPs) that provided French gunners with targets were all placed on high ground from where they could coordinate the work of six small spotter aircraft. Colonel Piroth, the artillery commander, had previously made his position clear and he told anyone who wanted to listen that 'Firstly, the Vietminh won't succeed in getting their artillery through to here. Secondly, if they do get here, we'll smash them. Thirdly, even if they manage to keep on shooting, they will be unable to supply their pieces with enough ammunition to do us any real harm.'[34]

Piroth did not know about the Vietminh's stockpile of an estimated 125,000 shells. He had no idea what he was up against. Within two days all his OPs and spotter aircraft were destroyed. He was now fighting blind. He apologized to his comrades for his failure and then placed a grenade on his chest and pulled out the pin.

'Beatrice' was taken on 13 March and two days later so was 'Gabrielle'. The Vietminh lost heavily, but that was not an issue for Giap or for those who embraced his philosophy. They were prepared to pay any price for DBP:

Two events during the course of the battle stand out as pivotal. First, the failure of the French to hold or re-take 'Gabrielle' on 14 March which exposed their northern border and provided the first crack in the dyke of aerial re-supply. Second, the loss of 'Huguette' 6 on 16 April which proved to be even more costly, as it shrank the drop zone to the point where re-supply was actually counterproductive; from this point forward CAT, FAF and the commercial airlines supplied the Vietminh with nearly the same effectiveness as they did their own forces.[35]

As the perimeter shrank, so did the DZ for any form of parachute activity. Nevertheless, on 14 March, two more battalions of troops were dropped on the diminishing perimeter. Supply drops that went astray were serious, especially those of 105mm US-made ammunition that was later fired into French positions. The redistribution of supplies became much more difficult as the ground transport was eliminated by artillery strikes. Those of the original forty-nine defended positions that survived existed on whatever it was able to scavenge from a re-supply parachute that fell close by. The priorities were water, ammunition and food, but not all were readily available.

On 20 March, the French Chief of Staff, General Paul Ely, met his American counterpart, Admiral Arthur Radford, President Eisenhower and Secretary of State, John Foster Dulles. Ely warned that the anticipated loss of DBP would have serious knock-on effects in South-East Asia. Radford promptly proposed Operation VULTURE: the employment of sixty B-29 bombers from the Philippines escorted by 170 fighters from two aircraft carriers in the China Sea. This force would eliminate Vietminh artillery and if that was not successful then the *use of three atomic weapons* (author's italics) 'properly employed'.[36]

This extreme militarily and politically disastrous measure had surprising and worrying traction. It was discussed as a viable option if European allies would support the move. Radford was unable to specify just where these atomic bombs were to be dropped and a siege situation is probably the worst scenario for such action; the besieged would be as much at risk as the besiegers.

Predictably, Churchill would have nothing to do with this preposterous operation and, in late April, the idea withered and died. Meanwhile, the Vietminh saps drew even closer.

Between 17 and 30 March there was a lull in the ground fighting, although during this period Giap was not idle. He prepared for the upcoming assaults on 'Elaine', 'Dominique' and 'Huguette' 7 and 6 and to this end 'the Vietminh dug 100 kilometres of trenches during these twelve days.'[37] The demise of 'Beatrice' and 'Gabrielle' had created a command crisis for the French as de Castries, now promoted to brigadier, had withdrawn to his bunker and abrogated his command responsibility. It was evident on 24 March that he was not competent and Cogny, who was of a mind to take his place,

Lieutenant Colonel Pierre Langlais, commander of 2 GAP.

was dissuaded by his staff. Lieutenant Colonel Pierre Langlais, the very capable and resourceful commander of the 2nd *Groupements Aéroportés Parachutistes* (2 GAP) was accepted as the de facto commander.

After the lull, Giap renewed his efforts and, at great cost, took 'Dominique' and parts of 'Elaine' and 'Huguette'. 'Isabelle', about 2 miles south of 'Elaine', and its 1,700 men was isolated. A bizarre arranged meeting between Navarre and Cogny on 31 March was delayed when Cogny failed to appear. Later both generals were seen to be yelling at each other and Cogny even threatened his superior with violence! This extraordinary event baffles historians, especially those with a military background. Navarre should have sacked Cogny on the spot, but he did not.

On 2/3 April reinforcements were parachuted into DBP. There was no formal DZ and the men of the 2nd Bn/1st *Regiment de Chasseurs Parachutistes* (11/1RCP) were just dumped over the fortress area; much to the surprise of all concerned there were very few casualties. This insertion of reinforcements continued right up to the very end of the siege; on 4 May 383 men jumped into a hopeless situation. Of these, 155 were ethnic Vietnamese and they could expect no quarter from the Vietminh who regarded them as traitors.

On 4/5 April 'Huguette' 6 was held and French artillery and fighter-bombers wreaked havoc among the attackers, who left 800 dead. The French suffered 200 dead, but this imbalance in casualties was irrelevant. Giap would spend as many lives as it took. The French resisted strongly and effectively, and Vietminh dead littered the slopes and wire around all the French positions. The execution had been massive and, for example, an assault on 'Elaine' 1 on 10 April failed; 400 fresh corpses were the result.

It is not surprising, given the numbers killed, that Vietminh morale started to crack. By 13 April, Vietminh losses at DBP had reached 16,000–19,000 of whom at least 6,000 had been killed and many of the 8,000–10,000 seriously wounded would succumb later in the jungle. Notwithstanding Giap's logistic brilliance, he was unable to counter the dire living conditions, the mud and the persistent rain, all compounded by irregular food. However, the greatest blow to Vietminh morale was the minimal medical support available. A wounded Vietminh soldier would almost certainly not receive professional medical aid. This was a legacy of French rule, which restricted the education of its subjects, not least in medical training. The consequence was that Giap could only muster 'one surgeon and six assistant doctors to care for his 50,000 soldiers' and tens of thousands of porters. In effect, there was no medical aid available and uncounted thousands died of medical neglect.[38]

Within the French perimeter, defenders listened to Vietminh radio broadcasts from lower-level commanders informing their superiors that some units were refusing to obey orders any longer. Prisoners taken by the French told how, during an advance, they were at risk of being shot by their own officers if they faltered.[39]

Giap's response to this slump in morale and martial ardour was to launch a campaign of ideological education. In Giap's view, 'the (educational) campaign was a great success and one of *the greatest achievements ever* [Giap's italics] secured in the history of struggle of our army.'[40] It can be assumed that this would not have been much comfort to a wet, hungry and badly-wounded soldier, dying of gangrene.

On 14 April, Giap had to fill the gaps in his ranks and so he ordered three battalions to move from Laos to DBP. For the French the movement of water and ammunition to 'Huguette' 6 was the priority, but the delivery of even 25 gallons of water cost more lives. It was evident that, with Vietminh saps ever closer, 'Huguette' 6 was no longer tenable and it was decided that the small band of survivors should break out. This was duly attempted, but only a handful of men made it to transient safety.

The French medical team was sorely pressed. Dr Grauwin, the senior doctor, performed near miracles, at least on the men who could be brought to him. They had two main medical underground facilities, albeit bunkers. There were also the eighteen battalion medical officers, each at their unit aid posts. They tried to treat the less seriously wounded on the spot. They were functioning in muddy trenches, knee-deep in blood-stained bandages, vomit and faeces. They were supported by men with only a cursory knowledge of first aid. Nevertheless, the result was that the survival rate for French troops was significantly better than that of their adversaries. The generators kept the most critical equipment running and the refrigerators, X-ray machines and lighting in the operating theatres continued to function. The provision of stored blood was vital, and a blood bank was established. Blood was parachuted in, packed in dry ice, but it had a shelf life of only three days and so its recovery after a supply drop had to be effected very quickly. Up until the first week of May it was only blood and plasma shortages that caused serious concern.[41]

'Huguette' 1 was surrounded by the 308th Division and the soldiers of that division dug their saps ever closer to Captain Chevalier and his men of 11/1 RCP. The position was overrun on 22 April and, as a result, the drop zone shrank even more. A counter-attack to retake the hill of 'Huguette' 1 was an expensive failure. The whole of the airfield was now dominated by Vietminh artillery in all its forms and shellfire knocked out the last three of the original seventy-three trucks. Only a handful of jeeps were left to move the wounded and supplies.

It is estimated that throughout the siege 75 per cent of French casualties were caused by artillery, with a commensurate impact on plant, buildings and aircraft. The distribution of food was becoming a hit-or-miss affair and was dependent upon the vagaries of geography and the proximity to and contents of the last palette to land nearby.

By 24 April the perimeter enclosed an area of only 520 acres, about a third of the original fortress, and Giap was planning his final offensive. By 26 April his logistic arrangements were in place. It was, by chance, the opening day of the Geneva Conference where Ho Chi Minh and the French would start to negotiate, if not 'peace', at least a cease-fire.

Newspaper *Le Monde*, which should have known better, published an article on 24 April revealing plans for Operation CONDOR. This was to be an advance of 3,000 men from Laos to relieve DBP. It was clearly futile, unworkable nonsense. It did not happen.[42] It was on the same day that the civilian pilots once again expressed their reluctance to continue flying re-supply missions given the weight and effectiveness of the AA fire. They had to this point, in April alone, flown about 428 sorties and delivered around 2,500 tons. Colonel Nicot had a problem, but as an airman himself, he was also sympathetic. The monsoon now arrived in full fury, driving rain and low cloud producing conditions that limited re-supply for three days to a modest 60 tons per day.

Reinforcements were still dribbling in and, on 26/27 April, thirty-six men arrived by parachute, a further indication of how the *Base Aero-Terrestre* concept was totally dependent on aerial re-supply, reinforcement and casualty evacuation, although the latter had fallen by the wayside some weeks before. Many neutral observers had thought that the *Base Aero-Terrestre* was military madness, and by now the participants were not overly enthused either. Responsibility for the lives of the men at DBP lay with the FAF and its civilian attachments. The airmen could not and would not simply opt out. They stuck to their task, even as the situation below them went from bad to worse.

It was late in the day but, on 27 April, 300 body armour vests were dropped and priority for the issue was the gunners. These vests were American-made and had only been requested on 14 April. The US Army delivered them within five days, but it took the French a further eight days to drop them. Had the vests been requested three months earlier, one wonders how many lives might have been saved.[43] At this point and 'after nearly sixty days the French garrison, representing only 4 per cent of the total CEFEO and South Vietnamese forces, were still holding out and tying down 60 per cent of the People's Army regular force [PAVN].'[44] That is an interesting statistic but notwithstanding, one by one the Vietminh rolled over the defended positions. This was despite the utmost courage of the defenders. Lives were given selflessly, and none could gainsay the stoicism of the majority of defenders.

That was as maybe, but now the death throes of the garrison of DBP were as painful as they were inevitable. Late on 6 May, a mine filled with 3,000lb of TNT was detonated under 'Elaine' 2. The logistic effort to stockpile the TNT and then to move it, under fire, to the mine entrance is notable. The position was vaporized, as were most of the defenders. The few survivors fought on for five hours before they were put to the bayonet and 'Elaine' 2 fell at 0530 on 7 May.

Victorious Vietminh troops on de Castries' bunker. (*PAVN*)

That day Vietminh soldiers stormed de Castries' bunker and flew their flag triumphantly overhead. That same day, and a world away, the Geneva Conference toiled to determine the future of Indochina in general and Vietnam in particular. Simplistically, the French had no cards to play and the aces appeared to be held by Ho Chi Minh. However, there were other more powerful players at the table. One of these was the United States, represented by the arrogant and bigoted John Foster F. Dulles. The American view of the world in 1954 was to have long-term consequences.

In North Vietnam the killing continued as the Vietminh continued to apply effective pressure on the dying embers of French colonialism. At about the same time, a Privateer four-engine bomber of the French Navy was shot down while bombing Vietminh communication lines along RC41. The crew of nine were possibly the last Frenchmen to die.[45]

Chapter Eight

The Reckoning

'Calm yourself, young man. One may be beaten by
my army without dishonour.'[1]

[Napoleon Bonaparte]

On 7 May 1954 the French lost not only the battle of DBP but also its colonial future in South-East Asia. The United States, the proxy participant in the war, also suffered a humiliating defeat and apparently learned little from the experience.

The French had been thoroughly beaten, but the individual soldiers had no cause to be ashamed. They had fought with astonishing courage but against a better-organized, numerically-stronger, better-led, better-supplied, extremely committed enemy. On their own ground the Vietminh would have beaten anyone and, a decade on, they were to do it all again. The quotation above applies here.

Why did the French lose the war in Indochina? It is a simple question that begets a rather more complicated answer. There were a number of factors. The most fundamental of these was the lack of political will to negotiate a peaceful withdrawal from the colony in 1946. Similarly, and perversely, a lack of political will to defend that same colony thereafter. Although French losses were heavy, they only amounted to 6 per cent of the CEFEO, despite having occupied 50 per cent or more of Giap's forces.

A succession of French generals failed to understand the determination, tenacity and political philosophy of their Vietnamese opponents who they consistently underestimated. The Vietminh would, quite literally, pay any price to expel first the French (and later the Americans). Ho Chi Minh said 'You can kill ten of my men for every one I kill of yours. But, even at these odds, you will lose, and I will win.'[2] This complete disregard for human life is what separated the Vietminh and later the Vietcong from their opponents. The culture of Western democracies, when compared with those of the Vietminh, was as the apple is to the coconut.

The initiative was gifted to the Vietminh early in the campaign by a road-bound French army and they, the Vietminh, never relinquished that initiative, coping easily with sporadic, disastrous, French forays into the jungle. The final and crucial factor was the overwhelming superiority of the Vietminh logistic system that overcame all the physical, environmental and psychological problems that stem from a protracted period of living in a hostile environment. This was the 'Logistic War' and the Vietminh won it, hands down.

The logistic superiority of the Vietminh is demonstrated in the artillery statistics. To feed Giap's 144 field guns, thirty recoilless cannon, thirty-six heavy AA guns and twelve to sixteen Russian Katyushas, Jean Farran calculated that 350,000 rounds were stockpiled.[3] This number strains credibility and Fall, quoting French artillery observations, suggests that the Vietminh fired 103,000 shells of 75mm or larger into DBP, of which 12,000 were misplaced parachute deliveries.

This artillery capacity of the Vietminh took Navarre, Cogny, de Castries and Piroth entirely by surprise and, when it disabled the airfield, the balance of the conflict was irrevocably changed. Nevertheless, the French artillery did fire 93,000 shells, but their counter-battery fire was generally less effective than the fire of their opponents.[4] This imbalance in effectiveness is important, but it was not the single, battle-winning difference.

The battle-winning factor was, without question, transport capability (author's emphasis). The reader will recall Churchill's pronouncement (on p. 3) of the criticality of transport in all its forms. The role of the multitude of porters who either carried their burdens or who wheeled load-bearing bicycles long distances through the jungle has been briefly discussed in earlier chapters, but it is germane to observe that 8,286 tons of assorted stores were moved several hundred miles from China to DBP. This included 4,629 tons of petrol products, 1,360 tons of ammunition, 1,700 tons of rice (of which 400 tons were consumed on the trail) and 46 tons of weapons. As the war progressed, Giap was able to make more and better use of his 600 Molotova 2.5-ton trucks over the vastly improved roads and tracks that now accommodated this fleet.[5] The movement of Vietminh artillery was part of that logistic burden. Giap acknowledged the part played by those porters when he wrote:

> The supply of food and munitions was a factor as important as the problem of tactics: logistics constantly posed problems as urgent as posed by the armed struggle.... Our people never made so great a contribution as in the winter 1953–spring 1954 campaign in supplying the army ... On the main DBP front our people had to ensure the supply to a big army, operating 500–700 kilometres from the rear and in very difficult conditions. The roads were bad, the means of transport insufficient and the supply lines relentlessly attacked by the enemy. There was, in addi-

General Vo Nguyen Giap, logistic genius, the victor of Dien Bien Phu, architect of the Ho Chi Minh Trail and implacable foe of the USA. (*PAVN*)

tion, the menace of heavy rains that could create more obstacles than bombing.[6]

The extract above does not tell the reader anything he/she does not already know. The significance is that Giap, the victor, was not, in British terms, 'a nice chap'. He was a vain, egotistical, selfish, totally ruthless and unpopular individual. Giap was loath to share his glory with subordinates and it is difficult to ascertain who, precisely, was the Vietminh's quartermaster general (in British nomenclature). In the quote above he shared at least some of his glory.

Stanley Karnow wrote:

He commanded the communist forces that defeated both France and the United States and his brilliance as a logistician, organizer and strategist ranks him with Wellington, Grant, Lee, Rommel and MacArthur in the pantheon of great military leaders. Unlike them, however, he owed his achievements to innate genius rather than to formal training.[7]

Bernard Fall remarked that 'The little history professor with his largely self-taught military science had totally outguessed the French generals … with their general-staff school diplomas.'[8] Philip Davidson who fought against Giap opined that

> as a military strategist and tactician he started as an amateur and finished as a professional. He earned even higher marks as a logistician; his ability to supply his forces around DBP was an achievement of the first rank. It was in the field of organization, administration and motivation that he excelled. In this area he was a genius.[9]

Giap may be the world's only self-taught, four-star general. He died aged 103 in 2013, undefeated.

The logistics of defeat usually put the onus on the victor, who is honour-bound to sustain his prisoners. However, the Vietminh did not subscribe to that philosophy and, to be fair, they too were hungry, wet, cold and tired. Since 21 November 1953, the garrison had had, at a conservative estimate, 9,000 casualties. Some 885 were handed over to the French after the battlefield truce on 8 May. That left about 7,000, many seriously wounded, who were now prisoners of war. These 7,000 were now sent off on a 500-mile trek to prison camps north of the Red River or south to Thanh Hoa province. The one situation that cannot be ignored is that of the internal desertions, formally recorded as numbering 1,161 (but probably nearer to 3,000) who had left their posts but who would join their erstwhile comrades as prisoners. Had these deserters stayed at their posts, one can speculate at the effect. Remaining at DBP were the estimated 2,000 French and 8,000 Vietminh dead. They were buried where they fell.

The prisoners were undernourished, intensely fatigued, and in some cases psychologically damaged. They were required to walk to their death on a diet of 14oz of rice per day and ten peanuts every tenth day. Un-boiled water and sometimes weak tea were the only beverages. Dysentery was rife, immobile men had to be carried and that hastened the demise of the men carrying the litter.

The neglect of PoWs by the Vietminh matched that of the Japanese and Russians in the Second World War. Of the total of 36,979 French troops captured by the Vietminh during the campaign (1946–54), only 10,754 or 28.5 per cent were repatriated in July 1954 and of these, 6,132 needed immediate hospitalization; 61 died within three months.

The killing continued after May 1954 and until the last French soldiers left on 28 April 1956, leaving a swathe of spiteful destruction behind them. Neither the Democratic Republic of Vietnam (DRV) nor its successor since 1976, the Socialist Republic of Vietnam, have ever revealed publicly the total

The meaning of defeat. French prisoners march into captivity, 8 May 1954. They presented an immediate feeding problem for their captors. (*Stringer AFP*)

casualties suffered by their armed forces between 1945 and 1954, but estimates of those killed range from 175,000 to 300,000. The French have suggested the rough figure of 500,000 Vietnamese killed during their campaign, apparently including civilians.[10] More methodically-sound estimations put the number at 300,000.[11]

Casualty figures were first published in the French Fourth Republic's *Journal Officiel* of 12 January 1955 and have been revised by specialists since then. In all the forces of the French Union, the number killed has been calculated as 92,800. Wounded were calculated as 76,400. In all, the Indochina War took some 400,000 lives.

The Vietminh, having defeated the French, believed that they had an entitlement to the whole of Vietnam. This was wishful thinking because, at the Geneva Conference in 1954, a wide group of interested parties, among them communist China and Russia, compelled them to accept partition of the country at the 17th parallel reunification until reunification elections were held in 1956.

Despite Chinese and Russian ambivalence, both communist regimes did support, at least in principle, Vietminh ambitions for a single Vietnamese state. Mao Zedong well understood the desire for reunification, but he believed the prospect was as remote as his own dream of capturing Taiwan.

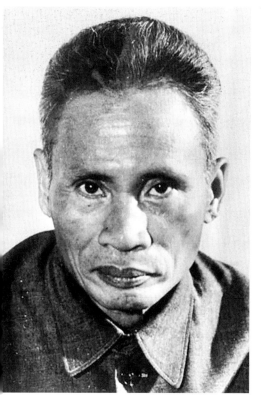

Pham Van Dong in 1972: deputy prime minister of the DRV 1947–55; prime minister 1955–76; a significant player during the first two wars in Vietnam. (*DRV*)

He cautioned Pham Van Dong, saying 'I don't have a broom long enough to reach Taiwan and you don't have a broom long enough to reach Saigon.'[12]

The participants at the Geneva Conference were the Vietminh (in effect the Democratic Republic of Vietnam), France, South Vietnam, China, Russia, Cambodia and Laos. The conference was chaired by Anthony Eden of Britain. The conference lasted for seventy-four difficult, acrimonious days filled with distrust and tension.[13] Dulles was frustrated by the UK's decision not to support the USA's position on Indochina and left Geneva in a huff on 3 May. He was replaced by Walter Bedell Smith, a much more reasonable and pleasant individual, but a man who had been given very specific 'riding instructions' by Eisenhower and Dulles.

The Americans hoped for and planned a unilateral, military alternative by a US-led Western coalition in South-East Asia. However, they failed to win the support needed and so armed intervention was rejected, for the moment. Nevertheless, the Central Intelligence Agency (CIA) was already active in both north and south.

Pham Van Dong, the Vietminh representative, was in no mood for compromise and he demanded a political settlement first under which the French would leave Vietnam and allow the Vietnamese (north and south) to settle their own affairs. This suggestion was anathema to Bao Dai because it would hasten the end of his country's sovereignty and his personal rule as emperor. Pham Van Dong made a case for the recognition of the communist movements in Laos, the Pathet Lao and the Free Khmer in Cambodia. The French rejected these demands outright.

Zhou Enlai, representing China, exercised his considerable intellectual, diplomatic and negotiating skills as he sought to arrive at an agreement that would obviate any pretext that the USA might exploit in justifying military intervention in Vietnam and, by association, threatening China. On this basis he supported the French. This was at a time when China was continuing to pour military aid into North Vietnam, still nominally a French colony; a bizarre political machination. Zhou believed that a divided Vietnam suited China's book because for 2,000 years Vietnam and China had had unfriendly relations. Although, briefly, they were both currently against the French, a unified Vietnam presented a future threat to China. He supported the partition of Vietnam. Zhou also had bigger fish to fry: he wanted to court other large, non-aligned states in Asia such as India, Pakistan and Indonesia and, by demonstrating his moderate and conciliatory approach, hoped to win hearts and minds.

Chapter Nine

Interlude

'Peace is an armistice in a war that is continuously going on.'[1]

[Thucydides]

On the departure of the French in April 1956, the USA assumed the role of world policeman. The USA perceived it to be its duty to combat communism worldwide. The domino theory 'had great resonance with American political culture in the 1950s and early 1960s and there was widespread public support for intervention in Vietnam that lasted through the years of escalation.'[2] The US government had a fear of the 'domino effect' in which communism would spread throughout Asia and that, one by one, countries would fall into the maws of people like Ho Chi Minh and Mao Zedong.

The Geneva accord was not accepted by the United States and, accordingly, they did not feel any moral obligation to abide by its recommendations. These had called for the cessation of all hostilities in Vietnam, Cambodia and Laos and the temporary separation of north and south at the 17th parallel at the Ben Hai River. This latter measure was a face-saving measure for the French to stave off total defeat by the Vietminh and was temporary, pending re-unification elections in the south to be held in 1956. The 17th parallel later became the centre of the Demilitarized Zone (DMZ), an area 5 kilometres on either side of the demarcation line, out of bounds to the military of both sides.

Just after the Geneva Conference, in 1954, North Vietnam and South Vietnam established themselves as separate entities on either side of the 17th parallel. Ho Chi Minh was the well-established leader in the North and Emperor Bao Dai led the South. This generated a move of populations and although about 1 million North Vietnamese crossed to the south, only a tenth of that number moved the other way.

The USA grudgingly accepted the reality that the northern half of Vietnam had now embraced communism. Nevertheless, it immediately authorized the CIA to open clandestine operations against the DRV. The prime mover in these operations was Colonel Edward Lansdale.[3] One of his subordinates was Major Lucien Conein; both officers meddled in Vietnamese politics and were responsible for acts of sabotage in the north.

In violation of the Geneva accord, Conein and his team formed secret squads of anti-communist activists that were intended to harass the Vietminh. They were trained at Clark Air Field in the Philippines and infiltrated back into Vietnam aboard US Navy vessels:

> The Conein team were well supported logistically and hid their arms and ammunition along the banks of the Red River as well as in Hanoi cemeteries by organizing phony funerals ... The undercover squads were not expected to stage major uprisings, but merely to ferment unrest that could be exploited for psychological purposes.[4]

Colonel Edward Lansdale, USAF and CIA.

It was the aim of the USA to maintain a non-communist southern state, ruled by the playboy emperor. He was personally ineffective and selected Ngo Dinh Diem to be his prime minister; the latter took post on 7 July 1954. It was a poor decision because Diem was totally dishonest.[5]

He turned South Vietnam into a despotic dictatorship with members of his family in key positions. His brother was head of the political police, which herded suspected opponents into prison camps. The favour the regime showed to Roman Catholics and its hostility to Buddhism helped to power rising discontent, while the Communist Vietcong movement formed in the south and the Americans, who had poured millions of dollars into South Vietnam to keep communism at bay, had growing doubts. An American official in South Vietnam memorably described Ngo as 'a puppet who pulled his own strings'.[6]

At the time, in South Vietnam life was reasonably well-ordered. The Mekong delta was 'the most productive rice-growing area in South-East Asia, the countryside was unscarred ... there was much less enthusiasm for communism.'[7] However, in October 1955, Prime Minister Diem forced a confrontation with his sovereign, Bao Dai, and held a referendum in his self-interest. Diem won with an unlikely 92.2 per cent of the vote, and he promptly declared himself to be president. From that day in October 1955 until his assassination in November 1963, Diem was a key player in the politics of

South-East Asia. Initially, he was thought to be merely an American puppet, but Diem had his own ruthless agenda and the Americans were not always successful in constraining him. Eventually, Washington lost patience with Diem and connived in his murder.

The referendum result in 1955 was clearly fraudulent and indicative of the debased state of public affairs that would haunt the Americans in the years ahead. Lansdale was the confidante and advisor of Diem and the conduit of American foreign policy as it applied in Vietnam. He had a high level of influence, out of kilter with his relatively junior rank and had had a part to play, prior to the referendum, suggesting to Diem that a vote in his favour of more than perhaps 90 per cent would be excessive.

Working towards its political goal, the USA supported Diem when he refused to hold the planned elections in the south. It appeared to be possible that, in a re-unification election held across the whole of Vietnam, the communist Ho Chi Minh might well win. That could not be risked, and so democracy, a fragile flower in this part of the world, took a back seat. The result was that the partition at the 17th parallel became permanent until 1975. Diem's rule of South Vietnam was marked by continuing conflict between different political factions and the government.

Ngo Dinh Diem.

General Nguyen Chi Thanh. (*Malcolm Browne*)

In 1956, and after the aborted election, it was the stated aim of the DRV to unite the whole of Vietnam and by force if necessary, but not yet. In the meantime, Hanoi directed 10,000 Vietminh to remain under cover in South Vietnam and to engage South Vietnamese forces when ordered. The remainder trekked north to an uncertain future. Ho Chi Minh bided his time because he had urgent domestic issues to address first.

Giap, although the victor, found that peace brought problems of a different hue. His army was put to work 'rebuilding roads, repairing dykes, restoring villages and harvesting crops'. The troops dealt with flood relief. All very necessary, but it went further and, in 1958, some main force units were required to operate collective farms.[8] Giap found this employment of his army demeaning and he fell into conflict with Ho Chi Minh and his old adversary Truong Chinh, who had initiated the policy.

The argument went against Giap and to underscore that, his previous subordinate and rival Nguyen Chi Thanh, a protégé of Le Duan, was promoted to full general (four stars).[9] Although his influence was diminished, Giap focused on the military education of his officers and senior NCOs. To this end he established a range of schools and he depended upon Chinese officers to provide the instruction. Giap took an all-encompassing approach, and his experience of air power in the recent war was such that he sent men to China to be trained as pilots. He also built a maritime facility that would concentrate on coastal defence in small craft. The construction of small arms and artillery ranges gave a clear indication that, like all good generals, Giap was preparing for the next war.

In 1956 342 US military advisers were dispatched to aid the South Vietnamese government against residual communist insurgents, not least those 10,000 mentioned above (known as the Vietcong or VC or 'Cong'). This modest gesture by the USA, although it was not realized at the time, in effect heralded the start of the second war. These military advisors, often young, junior officers, were in most cases embedded in Vietnamese communities with small teams. They were given wide-ranging political and military responsibilities, some beyond their experience. They were usually isolated and always vulnerable. They confronted the VC with mixed results, but their contribution to South Vietnam made with unheralded, day-to-day courage was notable.

Giap's post-war army was equipped with a mixed bag of French, Chinese, Japanese and American arms and equipment. There was a clear need to re-equip and standardize at the same time. This was a logistic and financial test that could not be resolved overnight, and the decision was taken to equip the NVA with largely Chinese weaponry. The logistic support of an army extends into the national infrastructure and so roads and railways were built, and the

Le Duan, the prime mover for insurrection in South Vietnam. *(DRV)*

ports of Haiphong, Hon Gay and Ben Thuy were modernized. Radio and telegraph systems were installed. Giap had wide horizons and he recognized the criticality of transport as part of his reforms. He enlarged his holding of trucks and trained men and women to drive and maintain them.[10]

Truong Chinh initiated the North Vietnamese Land Reform Programme. This brutal administrative measure was ruthlessly applied and resulted in wholesale imprisonment, violence and the execution of thousands of 'rich peasants', a contradiction in terms if ever there was one. On 2 November 1956, the Vietnamese peasantry rebelled, to the shock and bewilderment of Ho Chi Minh and his acolytes. Local police and militia forces could not control the situation and as the insurrection spread, Giap was ordered to employ the army. The 325th Division was closest, but it was recruited from the rebelling area and its loyalty could not be guaranteed. Nevertheless, it went into action and expunged the insurrection. The death toll has never been established. O'Neill suggests that 1,000 peasants were killed and 6,000 deported.[11] That is over and above those killed as part of the programme.

In political circles the government of DRV was split. There were those, such as Truong Chinh, Giap and Pham Van Dong, who favoured a concentration on domestic issues, a development of the economy and the building of 'socialism'. They were the 'North Vietnam first group'.

The opposing view was that of the 'South Vietnam first group'. For them, the highest priority was the need for a 'national democratic people's revolution' in South Vietnam and the re-unification of both Vietnams. This was the position of Le Duan, Nguyen Chi Thanh and Le Duc Tho.

Until 1959, the North Vietnam group had the ascendancy and, in some measure, because Ho Chi Minh anticipated the collapse of Diem's chaotic government, police force and army, all of which were riddled with corruption. A bloodless (well, relatively) takeover by the Communist Party would be the result. The reality, however, was that despite Diem's incompetence and corruption in most things, he had excelled in taking on and defeating the Communist Party in South Vietnam.

The balance changed and, in January 1959, the Fifteenth Plenum of the Central Committee took the decision to instigate an armed insurrection in South Vietnam. The casting of that die caused the lives of millions to be irrevocably altered, a multitude to be killed and, across the world, sociological change would result. Yet ultimately, and despite the cost, Vietnam would be re-unified.

Chapter Ten

The Second War: Early Days

'There is only one thing worse than fighting with allies,
and that is fighting without them.'[1]

[Winston Churchill]

The second Vietnamese war was as unnecessary as the first. North and South Vietnam were both relatively stable (by the standards of the time) independent states and there would have been no pressing issues between them had the promised elections been held in 1956. The refusal by Diem and the USA to hold those elections fuelled anger in the North.

The war that resulted was completely ideological in origin and an expression of the political philosophy and ambitions of a group of North Vietnamese government officials. The people of North Vietnam were not asked if they wanted another sixteen years of bloodshed and the people of South Vietnam were not consulted either.

North Vietnam meant business. Its first priority was to rapidly form the 559th Transportation Group, well understanding the criticality of transport in the campaign that it could see ahead. Ho Chi Minh placed responsibility for operations in South Vietnam in the hands of Le Duan and Le Duc Tho. The military commander was to be Giap's younger but very effective rival, Nguyen Chi Thanh. This was a blow to Giap, and more was to follow as he was demoted in the hierarchy from fourth to sixth. Giap withdrew to nurse his wounds. He was down but not out, and he recalled:

> My army had gained a lot of experience from the battle of Dien Bien Phu. It was also from this battle that I knew … our logistics were a key factor amongst many. At the beginning we thought that the Americans with their strategy of flexible response would escalate the war and that the American soldiers would come here. We therefore had to look long-term.
>
> I knew that if we were to win in the south of Vietnam where there was already a guerrilla war, we would have to expand our front line and fight larger battles. Therefore, in May 1959, I directed the opening of the Ho Chi Minh Trail.

At first the trail was only passable on foot. Later, roads were opened. To camouflage the trails, we planted climbing plants. We erected fences on either side of the tracks so that the vegetation could climb, forming planted domes. I learnt this from Dien Bien Phu.[2]

After Giap had issued his orders for the construction of the Ho Chi Minh Trail (HCMT), Colonel (later General) Vo Bam was selected as the first commander of the 559th Transportation Group.

The proposed north-to-south line of the trail traversed some of the most difficult terrain in South-East Asia. The mountains that ranged in height up to 8,000ft were covered in thick rain forest that was largely unpopulated. There were existing but little-used paths in the region and these were utilized in the greater plan. Initially, only foot traffic could use the trail and so bicycles were the favoured means by which supplies were transported.

The HCMT was quickly established, but often the road 'East *Truong Son*' was impassable. Giap ordered the building of a parallel road, 'West *Truong Son*', to be built. This would be on Laotian territory but, in this part of the world, national boundaries were little more than lines on a map. The second road was to traverse very difficult mountainous country of hard limestone, and the message sent back to Giap was that it was all 'too difficult'. Giap was not the sort of man who took 'too difficult' as an answer. Despite the extraordinary physical hurdles, at the third attempt the *Ta Le* or Route 20 was completed. The labour had been arduous, lengthy and pressurized. The casualties were buried, but unnamed and uncounted. The logistic flow into South Vietnam was enhanced.

The labour had come from the PAVN and the role of the 559th was to provide the means of moving logistic matériel from north to south in support of the Vietnamese Communist Party (Viet Cong or VC) which was now setting up training organizations to prepare for increased armed conflict. Of those Vietminh who had emigrated north in 1956, about 4,500 returned to form the nucleus of VC units.

By now North Vietnam was starting to receive increasing amounts of military aid from its Communist allies, China and the Soviet Union, with some support from Eastern European nations. It was not only small arms, but mortars, artillery and tanks. In addition to war matériel, China and the Soviet Union provided personnel ranging from labourers who helped to build and maintain the HCMT to soldiers who helped man and maintain AA sites. About 300,000 Chinese and several thousand Russians served in Vietnam.[3]

On the other side, the United States persuaded and, in cases, paid for a handful of nations to enter the war, ostensibly on behalf of the South Vietnamese government but in effect as participants in an American-led crusade.

Thailand, Australia, New Zealand, South Korea and the Philippines supplied more than 300,000 troops who fought in Vietnam.[4] So perhaps it was 'even Stephens', in manpower at least. A notable absentee from the war was the UK. It consistently declined to fight in a conflict in which it had no discernible stake. UK/USA relations were adversely affected as a result.

The VC, with a logistic line established, enjoyed early success, 'especially in the Mekong delta, the Central Highlands and on the coastal plain'.[5] They controlled not only vast areas of territory but the lives of the people who lived there. This was despite the active opposition of the American military 'advisors'. As the situation worsened, an attempted military coup by a Lieutenant Colonel Vuong Van Dong at the head of three battalions of ARVN paratroopers in November 1960 came close to success. Some 400 people were killed in the ensuing battle, in which the rebels were defeated. Diem survived and soldiered on, diverting American dollars to his personal use.

The American political aim, to deter communism, had to be executed with the military support of South Vietnam but without provoking two of the largest and best-armed communist regimes in the world. Domestic politics also came into play, as did national prestige. It was a complicated mix, made more so by the aggressive Nikita Khrushchev. The debacle at the Bay of Pigs in April 1961 damaged the military credibility and resolve of the USA. Thus, in 1961, it fell to President J.F. Kennedy to steer his ship of state through this political shoal water. Notwithstanding his rousing rhetoric, he had to determine a strategy for his armed forces to apply. Kennedy and his successors were bound by contradictory principles which were: (a) do not lose Vietnam to Communism; (b) do not get involved in a major ground/air war in Asia; and (c) do not use any military strategies that might invite Chinese and Russian retaliation. Kennedy had as his right-hand man Robert McNamara as Secretary of State for Defense.[6] McNamara had previously been the CEO of the Ford Motor Company. He held his appointment in Defense for seven years, during which he sought to apply business methodology to warfare, with a marked lack of success.

The armed forces of the United States in 1961 were, by some considerable degree, the most powerful on earth. However, they were to be shackled by detailed political intervention in military operations over the next dozen years and were never able to exploit their strength to the full. In August 1961, responding to the continued success of the VC, Kennedy approved, *in principle*, the deployment of 200,000 men in support of the Army of the Republic of Vietnam (ARVN). At this stage the role of those 200,000 men was not specified, but they were not expected to fight! 'The plan was that they would train ARVN soldiers and perhaps relieve ARVN from routine static defence duties.'[7]

Meanwhile, military technology was advancing quickly and across a wide range. The United States was leading in the embrace of new technology and it had recognized the potential benefits of helicopters in future wars. It was giving thought to how they might best be used and was preparing organizational change to accommodate the new flexibility that helicopters provided. Rotary-wing aircraft, just like fixed-wing, incurred a high initial cost and an ongoing maintenance commitment. They did, however, go a long way towards solving the transport problem presented by Vietnam's jungles and flooded paddy fields. Elsewhere, military researchers were not idle. The Chinese were perfecting surface-to-air missiles (SAMs) and were providing them to North Vietnam as well as MiG fighter aircraft. Logistic support had moved on a long way from the bags of rice in 1954.

The guerrillas did not have electronic aids and most of their weapons had been captured, but they excelled in the ancient art of camouflage. This capacity to hide was 'low-tech' but a battle-winning skill.

Diem's government, such as it was, limped from crisis to crisis and Washington despaired at his deficiencies, although there did not appear to be a viable alternative. The security situation in South Vietnam deteriorated and, whereas in 1959 239 government officials were assassinated, in 1961 there were more than 1,400 similar political murders.[8] The VC grew bigger and bolder, and in a single year its strength grew from 5,500 to 25,000. It was confident enough to mount a major assault on and take Phuoc Binh, a provincial capital about 40 miles north of Saigon.[9] This was a game-changer and Kennedy realized that he could not sit on his hands any longer. Vice President Lyndon B. Johnson visited South Vietnam in May in 1961 and, on this visit, he promised American support for the government and went as far as describing Diem as 'the Winston Churchill of Asia'.[10] Ludicrous and wildly over the top as it was, nevertheless, Johnson's unequivocal language locked the US government into a military alliance with Diem and his government. Lansdale worked assiduously behind the scenes to further the case for the injection of American combat troops into the theatre. Just after the Johnson visit, 400 Special Forces soldiers (Green Berets) landed in Saigon and they were followed by forty US Army helicopters together with pilots and maintenance staff. The American logistic account was open.

Kennedy was now obliged to take positive action and his first initiative was to appoint a vastly experienced individual to manage American affairs in South Vietnam. He selected General Maxwell Taylor who had, previously, filled all of the most prestigious appointments in the US Army. The task set him was to advise on Diem's situation and manage it to best American advantage.

Taylor was politically aware and, although his report of 24 October 1961 was robust, he realized that any recommendations had to be palatable to the voters at home. He outlined the parlous state of ARVN intelligence systems, assessed the military situation as 'critical' and he recommended the injection of American combat troops, ostensibly in the guise of logistic troops, brought in to assist with 'flood relief'.

The 'flood relief' plan was quietly dropped, and Taylor wrote again. He was a wise man and he told his president that American troops should be deployed to the Western Highlands and the coastal plain (neither of which had been subject to flooding). He said that the US strategic reserve would, of necessity, be reduced for an imprecise period, the prestige of the USA was already tied to Vietnam and it would be more so with the addition of extra troops. He also predicted, presciently, that if the first contingent was insufficient it would be difficult to resist further reinforcement. He raised the spectre of a major war in Asia.

The optimism of the USA in these early years was perhaps the product of the national propensity to swear allegiance to the flag at regular intervals, to proclaim American superiority in all fields and a reluctance to accept that the USA was not the fount of all wisdom. It could be argued that the education of young Americans was not so dissimilar to that of young North Vietnamese. It was of course softer, more persuasive, more attractive and more sympathetic, but the end result was that generations of Americans, convinced then (and still so convinced) of their superiority, did not come to terms with the commitment and martial qualities of their adversaries. This was exemplified, in July 1962, at a conference in Honolulu. General Paul Harkins advised that victory would be achieved 'by the end of 1963'. The Defense Secretary, McNamara, was less optimistic and planned for the defeat of the VC by the end of 1965. Both men were seriously deluded. In later chapters the disillusionment of the American public and of some American soldiers will be addressed.

Despite the downside, clearly explained by Taylor, by mid-1962 there were 8,000 'advisors' embedded in ARVN and the 'Military Assistance Command, Vietnam' (MACV) had been established. In Hanoi there was no doubting the significance of the MACV: it was clearly a device to allow for the management of further troop reinforcements. 'By November 1963 there were 16,000 Americans on the ground: soldiers, sailors and airmen; technicians and pilots; electronic eavesdroppers and agriculturalists; academic social analysts and flamboyant Special Forces cowboys; spooks and geeks of every hue.'[11]

These 16,000 people were accommodated, fed, watered and given all the creature comforts that an affluent nation can provide. The logistic accountants were busy and US aid to South Vietnam was rising steadily and had reached a rate of $400 million per year. To put this into context, the USA military budget in 1963 was $368 billion. The support of South Vietnam was fractionally more than 1 per cent of the pot; financial peanuts and, to mix metaphors, the end of a financial wedge.[12]

The British Army avers that 'any bloody fool can be uncomfortable'. During its long history it established well-served cantonments around the world where it thought its presence was permanent, such as in India, Malaya (that was), Egypt, Burma (that was) and many others. It is in the nature of armies to build settlements; everyone does it. The Romans did it in Britain (43–410AD). Now in 1961 the Americans were, quite reasonably, importing a little of their homeland into South-East Asia.

The cantonment, when and wherever it is, brings with it a new raft of issues. It invariably employs local people to provide the domestic services needed. These people are potentially a security risk. The cantonment has to be fenced and defended and thus part of the deployed army is employed in either static defence or the management of locally-enlisted soldiers to do the same. The US armed forces expected a very high level of domestic service when not physically engaged in operations. This served to build a gap between the soldiers engaged in the jungle to those in the logistic tail, described as 'rear-echelon mother-fuckers' (REMF). In contrast, the PAVN and VC lived spartan lives, they did not have any luxuries, and neither did the internal divisions that followed in their wake.

The affluence of the American visitors jarred with the largely rural South Vietnamese. The Americans were very generous and wholly well-meaning, but their medical support, inoculation programs, food, farm equipment and all manner of vehicles freely and willingly given were not accepted with reciprocal gratitude. There was a major culture gap that was never satisfactorily filled.

The conflicts in Vietnam, from 1945, were all marked by complete insensitivity to the indigenous people who suffered great privation at the hands of successive armies: Japanese, British, French, Vietminh/PAVN, American, VC and ARVN. There was much glib talk over a period of thirty years of 'pacification' and 'hearts and minds'. The 'Land Reform Program' had caused unrest and rebellion in the North. It showed that the Vietnamese people were the constant victims, often at the hands of their own countrymen. In the South, an example is the 'strategic hamlets' programme initiated by Diem in April 1962. The aim was to distance the peasant population from the VC behind punji stakes and barbed wire. It was a laudable aim, but its execution was clumsy and took no note of the strong ties felt by those peasants to their home village and the family cemeteries close by. When questioned about the impact the forced relocation of thousands of people would have, Major General Victor Krulak, a US Marine officer, responded by saying that 'it was necessary to force the peasants to make the programme succeed.' The absence of compassion is marked and the alienation of those peasants was inevitable.

Roger Donlan, who won the first Medal of Honor in July 1964, commented in an interview with Christian Appy that the object was

> to give people a sense of belonging to a program that came from central government. Our job was to make sure these people could defend these outposts of freedom scattered throughout the whole country. We trained a Vietnamese strike force of about 300 men – A Civilian Irregular Defense Group.
>
> Some of them were coastal folk. Their families had been fishermen for centuries, and they were relocated as part of the strategic hamlet program and told to make their new homes there in the mountains ... of the 300 members of our Strike Force it turned out that about 100 sympathized with the enemy.
>
> We never had a sense of the magnitude of the problem ... we were babes in arms in every way. We were working with and against cultures that were 2,000 years old. They could manipulate us.[13]

In February 1962 there was a second attempt to unseat Diem when two disaffected officers, members of the South Vietnam Air Force, bombed the presidential palace. Diem was unhurt, but three palace staff were killed. Diem blamed the Americans and said that the American media was hostile. He introduced restrictions on press freedom and political association. The relationship between Diem and the USA was hastening to a conclusion.

The military advisors' tour was for one year and the regular turnover of personnel negated any chance of continuity. Relationships between young American advisors and their usually much older Vietnamese counterparts had limited chance of success, although both parties tried to make the best of the situation. The military advisors worked with the ARVN which they found to be of mixed quality. The ARVN never enjoyed the wholehearted respect of its allied soldiers. The commander of a Special Forces team in the winter of 1962 commented that 'it could be hard to get them out on an operation ... sometimes we had to bribe them with extra food or clothing.' Regular and professional American soldiers were frustrated by 'accidental' discharges that served to warn the VC and avoided contact or the wilful display of smoke from cooking fires. That same commander reflected that 'It takes a while to learn that the American way isn't always the right way...in Vietnam, the poor bastards had been at war for fifteen years. And we come along full of piss and vinegar, wanting to win in six months.'[14]

The year 1962 saw the start of 'airmobility' and a solution to the transport problem in a jungle setting. The forty helicopter aircraft sent in May 1961 had given the ARVN vastly increased mobility and with these aircraft they could now land troops at will. However, the old H-21s were not ideally suited to their new role. In addition, they were not supported by 'gunships' or by heavy-lift helicopters to consolidate any landings. The tactics of the helicopter war had still to be devised, as had the drills for helicopter-borne troops. It was an inauspicious start but, initially, the VC were stunned by the innovation when they were attacked in their bases and killed in large numbers.

Briefly, the ARVN had the initiative but it was just as at the Battle of Cambrai in 1917 when tanks were first introduced to the battlefield piecemeal. There, after great success on the first day, mechanical unreliability, German artillery and infantry defences discovered the frailties of this new weapon. In Vietnam there were insufficient purpose-designed helicopters, and while the numerical and design issues were addressed, the VC responded to the threat of helicopters and worked out counter-tactics.

The year 1963 was a significant one in the second Vietnamese War. The Buddhist population of South Vietnam rebelled against the Catholics, their number swollen by VC agitators. Diem was a Catholic and did not handle the delicate situation well. He lost much of his residual public support. In September/October the Americans finally gave up on Diem and 'acquiesced'

A Buddhist priest, Thich Quang Duc, immolates himself in protest over the government of Ngo Dinh Diem on 11 June 1963. The event triggered the Buddhist uprising that contributed to the overthrow of Diem. (*Malcolm Browne*)

in his assassination on 2 November.[15] The Strategic Hamlet policy was not working, and many were overrun by an increasingly bold VC.

On 22 November President J.F. Kennedy was also assassinated and Lyndon B. Johnson was the unwilling recipient of the political and military mess in South-East Asia. The Americans had observed at close quarters the shambles that the French had made in Vietnam and they had learned of the criticality of transport in a jungle setting. However, American generals had not recognized the quality of their adversary and were convinced that they could overwhelm their enemy by the power of their arms and the depth of their logistic base.

On 24 November, Johnson met with his ambassador, Cabot Lodge, who briefed him on the current situation. Lodge said: 'If Vietnam is to be saved, you, Mr President, will have to do it.' President Johnson had no doubts and replied: 'I am not going to lose Vietnam. I'm not going to be the president who saw South-East Asia go the way China went.'[16]

The future conduct of the war in Vietnam flowed from that conversation.

Chapter Eleven

Managing a War

'Given the same amount of intelligence, timidity will do a
thousand times more damage than audacity.'[1]
[Major General Carl von Clausewitz]

President Johnson recognized the need to take assertive action and in January
1964 he appointed Lieutenant General William Westmoreland to be the
Deputy Commander of Military Assistance Command, Vietnam (MACV).
The commander in post was General Harkins and his tenure was to expire
in June. Westmoreland would then move into the top job. Westmoreland
had filled many of those appointments previously held by General Maxwell
Taylor, the ambassador to South Vietnam, and his journey to the top of the
army seemed to be almost pre-ordained. Along the way, he won adherents.
'The most gracious and gentlemanly officer with whom I served,' said one.[2]
However, another who was less enthused remarked that he was 'awed by his
own magnificence'.[3]

Westmoreland was perceived by many, but by no means all, to be the best
man available. Brigadier General Amos Jordan appealed to Cyrus Vance, an
old friend and Secretary of the Army, saying 'it would be a grave mistake to
appoint him. He is spit and polish, two up and one back. This is a counter-
insurgency war, and he would have no idea how to deal with it.'[4] Jordan was
to be proved right.

Westmoreland would have to work hand-in-glove with Robert McNamara,
the Secretary of State for Defense, but they had similar mindsets and together
they embarked on policies that have since been debated endlessly. To execute
their policies, they had to hand an overwhelming military capability that
stemmed from vast national wealth. The logistic depth of the USA exceeded
that of North Vietnam by multiples of ten.

Post-war, the Americans were brutally honest in their appraisal of the Vietnam War and of the people who 'managed' it. McNamara drew heavy fire and
Jeffrey Record pulled no punches when he observed that

no American official more epitomized the managerial approach to war
than Robert McNamara, the insufferably arrogant auto-executive upon

General William Westmoreland: COMUSMACV, 1964–68. (*US Army*)

whom it apparently never dawned – until it was too late – that managing a large bureaucracy, be it Ford or the Pentagon, had little to do with forging success in a shooting war. Maximizing productivity at Ford taught nothing about defeating an Asian revolution. The most disastrous American public servant of the twentieth century, he combined a know-it-all assertiveness with a capacity for monumental misjudgment and a dearth of moral courage worthy of Albert Speer. McNamara transformed the office of Secretary of State for Defense into a temple of quantitative analysis. Infatuation with the countable was established as the foundation of not only force structure and weapons choices.[5]

Unfortunately, McNamara's bureaucratic characteristics were also to be seen in Westmoreland, 'who saw the war as essentially an exercise in management'.[6] The two men, in combination, made for a toxic top leadership team.

They were not short of advice. The 'Advanced Research Projects Agency' and the RAND Corporation were just two of the many organizations that dispensed plans for counter-insurgency and technology and grew fat on the spending of public money. Given McNamara's numerical bent, they provided him with quantifiable advice. Three features of McNamara's reign were his hubris, intellectual snobbery and ill-concealed contempt for the military who were obliged to dance to his tune.

Westmoreland explained that his strategy was not to *defeat* (author's italics) the North Vietnamese Army. It was to put pressure on the enemy which would transmit a message to the leadership in Hanoi that they could not win, and it would be to their advantage to either accept a divided Vietnam or negotiate.[7] Fighting a war with no intention of defeating the enemy was nothing if not different.

In order to achieve his aim, Westmoreland would wage a war of attrition using 'Search and Destroy' (S&D) tactics, the measure of which would be the enemy body count. This policy would be pursued until the 'crossover point' was reached. The crossover point was the day that communist losses could no longer be replaced and thereafter its strength could be rapidly degraded.

However, on 16 March 1964, McNamara commented, rather gloomily, on Giap's re-equipping of the NVA which was proving to be successful. He made mention of 75mm recoilless rifles, Chinese heavy machine guns, US .50 calibre heavy machine guns on Chinese mountings and 90mm rocket-launchers. More importantly, he noted the readily-available Chinese version of the excellent 7.62mm AK-47 assault rifle.[8]

In Hanoi a decision to open the trail to trucks was the source of furious debate, but Giap ruled that the army must make best use of its assets. That decision had serious implications and Giap said, 'I then ordered a comrade to be made the commander in charge of transporting petrol along the trail. It was a horrific project.'[9] General Dong Si Nguyen, the longest-serving commander of the HCMT, was responsible for that pipeline and he said

General Dong Si Nguyen. (*DRV*)

the Americans were well aware of this petrol supply line. It ran from the Chinese border to a point just outside Saigon. They set out to bomb it out of existence and were successful. Within a month of the pipeline's construction, in about June 1966, they had destroyed 80 per cent of the surface storage capacity for petrol, oil and lubricants. However, as an insurance the VC had constructed under-ground storage and the movement of trucks went on unhindered.

Despite Giap, his re-arming and his building of the HCMT, on the face of it, and given the political will, the engagement of the USA in Vietnam with its vast strength could only have one outcome. At this early stage Westmoreland did not lack for advice and Major General William Yarborough who was commanding the Special Warfare Centre at Fort Bragg wrote to Westmore-land on 26 February 1964, saying

> I cannot emphasize too greatly that the entire conflict in South-East Asia is 80 percent in the realm of ideas and only 20 percent in the field of physical conflict ... Under no circumstances that I can foresee should US strategy ever be twisted into a 'requirement' for placing US combat divisions into the Vietnamese conflict as long as it retains its present format. I can almost guarantee that a US division ... could find no targets of a size which would warrant a division-sized attack ... Nothing is more futile than a large-scale military sweep through Vietcong country, since always there must be left behind a tangible symbol of governmental power and authority.[10]

Notwithstanding, this expert advice on 'the large-scale military sweep through Vietcong country' was firmly eschewed by Yarborough. Westmore-land ignored the advice and strongly favoured and embraced it. His policy that he put into effect was termed 'Search and Destroy'. It was based upon the rapid growth of helicopter assets and the flexible, far-reaching range of opera-tion provided by these aircraft. 'Search and Destroy' was inextricably linked to the 'body count' process.

Until 1964, the country had been subject to continuous guerrilla war and its defence by the USA had been restrained. There had been American fatalities; initially only a few, but the trend was clear. Between 1956 and 1960, nine Americans had been killed. In 1961 the toll was sixteen and in 1962 it was fifty-two. Then 1963 saw the doubling of casualties when 118 American servicemen died.[11] From June 1964 with the advent of 'Search and Destroy' there was a commensurate very significant increase in fatalities.

During 1964, the USA demonstrated either laudable and statesman-like restraint or callow timidity, depending on the reader's point of view. There was ample and frequent provocation. Over the period 3–6 February, the VC mounted a major operation against the ARVN in Tay Ninh province and in the Mekong delta. They attacked the American advisory compound in

This captured communist photo shows a VC fighting patrol in the Mekong delta in 1966. The photograph is clearly posed. (*George Esper*)

Kontum City. On 7 February the VC set off a bomb in the Capital Kinh Do theatre and killed three Americans. The US did not retaliate to any of these attacks. The military's desire to take the battle to the enemy was thwarted by the politicians in Washington and this timid political attitude was to be a feature of the war to come.

Westmoreland had had an early introduction to the politics of his host nation when General Duong Van Minh, who had led the coup that murdered Diem in November 1963, was himself overthrown three months later by General Nguyen Khanh in January 1964. Khanh held power only until February 1965 when he, in turn, was ousted. Westmoreland, and those who served under him, toiled manfully for years to build a military structure in South Vietnam, but they were building on political sand because South Vietnam was in a state of almost permanent chaos, the product of wholesale corruption at every level. It was calculated that about 10 per cent of all matériel sent to South Vietnam by the USA was stolen on arrival. Retail outlets throughout the country were stocked with goods normally only available in a US Post Exchange (PX).

Giap and his acolytes dispatched about 7,000 North Vietnamese soldiers down the HCMT to the south. The Vietnamese were not homogenous, and

Sunlight filters through the canopy on the HCMT onto NVA soldiers. (*Le Minh Truong*)

A Vietnamese Marine and a Vietcong prisoner carry the heads of three Vietcong away from an engagement 20 miles south-east of Saigon. The severed heads are suspended from a pole with vine strung through their ears. Heads were collected by both sides. (The New Face of War, *M.W. Browne, 1965*)

these northern soldiers had different dialects, culture and customs. They were not readily assimilated by southern VC; the historic, long-standing animosity between north and south was a factor. In the north, because of wartime food shortages, people had to mix cassava into their rice.[12] General Vu Hiep observed that

in the Central Highlands there was so little rice we used to say that our cassava carried rice on its back. Whenever possible we caught fish and

Uniformed members of the NVA descending a pinnacle on the HCMT in the Karst country. (*Nguyen Trong Thanh*)

killed animals including tigers, monkeys and bears, but every soldier had to care for 500 cassava plants so we could continue fighting even when we could not kill enough game or didn't get rice from the North. From commanders down to ordinary soldiers, we all grew cassava. Every year we grew it closer to our objective.[13]

The VC, now supplemented by the NVA, reorganized and formed the 9th Viet Cong Division. VC battalions were augmented into brigade-sized 'regiments' (US equivalent). Giap started another of his training programmes and General Taylor, the US ambassador, recorded that 'in terms of equipment and training the Viet Cong are better armed and led today than ever in the past.'[14]

The USA was at a decision point.

Chapter Twelve

Search and Destroy

'Principles of strategy never transcend common sense.'[1]

[Leon Trotsky]

All armies are subject to political control, and politicians, the world over, work assiduously to direct, define and limit their forces. The US was no exception. In 1964, the role of US forces in South-East Asia was picked over, refined and defined in NSAM 288.[2] 'Although American rhetoric grew hotter, American actions remained lukewarm.'[3] The helicopter-carrying USS *Card* was attacked and sunk by a VC underwater demolition team in Saigon harbour on 2 May, but the USA did not retaliate, nor did it retaliate when a VC regiment overran a Special Forces' camp at Nam Dong, killing fifty South Vietnamese and two Americans.

The 23,300 US troops in Vietnam in August 1964 were rapidly reinforced after the 'Gulf of Tonkin Incident' (see Table 1 overleaf). The Tonkin affair was little more than a minor skirmish between North Vietnamese torpedo boats and the USS *Maddox*. One torpedo boat was sunk. A few days later a second destroyer, the USS *Turner Joy*, joined the *Maddox* on patrol and the two ships might or might not have been the subject of a further attack. The fact that no evidence of an attack could be produced speaks volumes.

Nevertheless, the 'incident' gave rise to 'The Tonkin Gulf Resolution' in which the US House of Representatives voted 416-0 and Congress 88-2 'to give the President authority to use whatever force was necessary to assist South Vietnam and other allies of the USA in South-East Asia.'[4] The troop build-up, shown above, was an immediate consequence.

Australian involvement in Vietnam had started in 1962 with the deployment of thirty military advisors, not reflected in the table above. Within seven years the Australian force level had risen to 7,670. Approximately 60,000 Australians served in the war; 521 were killed and more than 3,000 were wounded.[5] When the Australians entered the Vietnam War, it was with their own 'well considered … concept of war', and this was not necessarily in harmony with US concepts.

The Australian infantry had experience of jungle warfare gained in the campaign in Malaya against the Communist insurrection and, in this area of

Table 1. US and Allies' Manpower Assets, 1959–1973.

Year	American	SVN	Australia	Korea	New Zealand	Philip	Thai
1959	760	243,000	–	–	–	–	–
1960	900	243,000	–	–	–	–	–
1961	3,205	243,000	–	–	–	–	–
1962	11,300	243,000	–	–	–	–	–
1963	16,300	243,000	–	–	–	–	–
1964	23,300	514,000	198	200	30	20	–
1965	184,300	642,500	1,560	20,620	120	70	20
1966	385,300	735,900	4,530	25,570	160	2,060	240
1967	485,600	798,700	6,820	47,830	530	2,020	2,200
1968	536,100	820,000	7,660	50,000	520	1,580	6,000
1969	475,200	897,000	7,670	48,870	550	190	11,570
1970	334,600	968,000	6,800	48,450	440	70	11,570
1971	156,800	1,046,250	2,000	45,700	100	50	6,000
1972	24,200	1,048,000	130	36,790	50	50	40
1973	50	1,110,000	–	–	–	–	–

Source: US Army Department of Defense Manpower Data Centre.

operations, it was more skilled than its US allies. Australian tactics for patrolling, searching villages (without destroying them), ambush and counter-ambush were criticized by US commanders. For example, General Westmoreland is reported to have complained to Major General Tim Vincent, the commander of the 1st Australian Task Force (1ATF), that the Task Force was 'not being aggressive enough'.[6]

It was normal practice for US forces to flush out the enemy and employ, decisively, 'massive firepower'. Australians cheerfully acknowledged they had much to learn from the US forces about heliborne assault and joint armour and infantry assaults. However, the US measure of success – the body count – was apparently held in contempt by many of the battalion commanders in the 1st ATF.[7] In 1966, journalist Gerald Stone described tactics then being used by Australian soldiers newly-arrived in Vietnam:

> The Australian battalion has been described...as the safest combat force in Vietnam … It is widely felt that the Australians have shown themselves able to give chase to the guerrillas without exposing themselves to the lethal ambushes that have claimed so many American dead …
>
> Australian patrols shun jungle tracks and clearings … Picking their way carefully and quietly through bamboo thickets and tangled foliage … It is a frustrating experience to trek through the jungle with Australians. Patrols have taken as much as nine hours to sweep a mile of terrain. They may move forward a few steps at a time, stop, listen, then proceed again.[8]

The Vietcong accorded the Australians considerable respect and they conceded that the Australian approach to jungle warfare was effective. One former Vietcong leader is quoted as saying:

> . . . worse than the Americans were the Australians. The Americans' style was to hit us, then call for planes and artillery. Our response was to break contact and disappear if we could . . . The Australians were more patient than the Americans, better guerrilla fighters, better at ambushes. They liked to stay with us instead of calling in the planes. We were more afraid of their style.[9]

Albert Palazzo commented that 'as a junior partner, the Australians had little opportunity to influence US strategy in the war, the American concept (of how the war should be fought) remained unchallenged and it prevailed almost by default.'[10] It is worth noting that although the Australian and New Zealand contingents were dependent upon US logistic support, nevertheless their governments footed their share of the bill. The remainder of the non-US forces were funded by the USA.[11]

The VC accelerated its attacks and, on 1 November (just before the US presidential election), they mortared the US airbase at Bien Hoa, outside Saigon. Four Americans were killed, five B-57 bombers were destroyed and eight other aircraft were badly damaged. The USA took no action. It took no action after an attack on US officers' billets in which two were killed and thirty-eight wounded. The VC and NVA were, predictably, buoyed by the somnambulant posture of the USA, whose only response to date had been to raise the size of its in-country force.

The logistic effort of moving 150,000 US troops across the world is huge. On arrival they had to be comfortably accommodated in secure barracks or tented camps, they had to be fed, clothed, armed, acclimatized and briefed. While this force build-up was progressing, in December 1964, an NVA main force regiment moved down the HCMT to the Central Highlands. Two other regiments were close behind and by the end of the year, the 325th Division of the NVA was settled in the north-west of South Vietnam but living rather less comfortably than the Americans. This deployment of the 325th from North Vietnam changed the nature of the war in the south from an insurrection to an invasion. The USA had now got a dangerous tiger firmly by the tail.

By the middle of 1964 the USA had established, in South Vietnam, an awesome base. It had injected vast sums of money with a singular lack of appreciation for the culture of its host. Americans experts were to be found in every field. The US government posted in doctors, school teachers, accountants – lots of accountants – mechanics and even the disc jockeys to run an American radio station. The impact on the South Vietnamese who came into contact with this largesse and alien culture was life-changing and corrupting.

American military technicians were introducing and testing new weapon systems. The CIA was building on its spy network. All these activities were funded by the US taxpayer which also paid for medicine, milk, petrol, oil and lubricants (POL), fertilizer and other products, sold locally to generate cash to pay the Government of South Vietnam (GVN) and its armed forces, now 642,000 strong. The US logistic aid to South Vietnam, over and above the support of its armed forces, was vast. The war, although still only in its early stage, had become the principal pillar of the South Vietnamese economy.[12]

The background to the American troops build-up merits further attention, as does Westmoreland's employment of this awesome force. The enormous demand for manpower by the MACV from 1965 had, by 1968, created a crisis. In July 1965 President Johnson had, in an unprecedented move, decided that he would not call up his very significant reserves of over 600,000 trained and experienced men. He determined that, instead, he would rely on conscripts and he would initiate the draft. This was 'a system that was grossly inequitable and permitted many of the brightest and best young men to escape service in Vietnam. It contributed substantially to a dangerous depletion in the US strategic reserve as well as a marked decline in the quality of US military manpower.'[13] This was epitomized by the commissioning of people of the calibre of William Calley, the mass murderer of My Lai infamy. It is interesting statistically that of the almost 16 million eligible men, 57 per cent were exempted.[14]

The president's decision triggered a series of significant consequences and not the least of these were social but others were logistic in nature. The draftees had to be identified, selected, screened and assembled at training camps across the USA. The appeals process had to be staffed and administered across the country. The training organization had to be expanded to cope with the influx of recruits. This was an expensive measure, even for a very rich country.

Some, when selected, sought to avoid conscription and as many as 100,000 draft-eligible men fled the country.[15] Others were deferred on educational or medical grounds. Some young men enlisted in the reserves, well knowing that they would not be deployed. Among those who avoided the draft were three future presidents and a vice president of the USA.[16]

Some 80 per cent of the men conscripted were from working-class backgrounds and many of them had not completed high school (secondary school in UK terms). The percentage of black soldiers enlisted was 14.1 per cent compared with a national black population of 11 per cent. The black casualty rate was running at 20 per cent in 1965–66 and after protests from community leaders President Johnson ordered that black participation in frontline units should be reduced and, by 1969, the casualty rate had been cut to 11.5 per cent.[17]

The manpower resources of the United States were overwhelmingly greater than that of North Vietnam and, between 1964 and 1975, 8,744,000 served in the armed forces and, of these, 3,403,000 in South-East Asia.[18] Notwithstanding the magnitude of these numbers, Westmoreland reduced any numerical advantage it gave him by 'instituting a personnel policy about as detrimental (to the war effort) as if it had been with the worst intentions in mind.'[19] It was his 'Short Tour Policy' in which service in Vietnam would be limited to a one-year tour of duty for soldiers and much less for officers. Battalion commanders were in post for only six months and company commanders for three.

This constant rotation of officers negated the old British Army adage 'Know your men better than their mothers.' The fundamental trust between the leader and the led that is generated by acquaintance and respect for each other's demonstrated competence was eliminated because they were strangers to each other. These American soldiers at every level were conducting S&D missions and being obliged to learn on the job. In the case of officers, the need to have 'command time' logged into their record was a prerequisite for professional advancement, be it at platoon, company, battalion or regimental level. Command was less a privilege and more a box-ticking exercise. The practical effect was that American soldiers lacked combat experience in comparison to their foe, and they paid the penalty:

> Westmoreland's strategy of attrition allied to his short tour policy fostered extraordinarily high ratios of support to 'teeth arm' (UK) or 'combat' (USA) troops which further undermined the potential military productivity of more than half a million men eventually placed under his command. The general was determined to provide American troops with as high a level of creature comforts as possible. The result was a bloated logistic tail and by 1968, no more than 80,000 or 15 per cent of the 536,000 US personnel in the theatre were actually available for sustained front-line employment. Less than 10 per cent of the total served in infantry units.[20]

Overly enthusiastic, incompetent or unpopular officers were at risk of 'fragging', a euphemism for murder/attempted murder at the hands of discontented or disillusioned soldiers. The high number of incidents in the latter years of the Vietnam War was symptomatic of breakdown of discipline in the

US armed forces. Between 1969 and 1972 documented and suspected fragging incidents totalled nearly 900.[21] This topic is revisited in Chapter 2.

The short tours also gave rise to a preoccupation with survival and all were well aware of the date of their repatriation. Westmoreland justified his short-tour policy by claiming that he believed that 'the war would be long and therefore potentially injurious to troop morale and health.'[22] This drew from David Hackworth the observation, 'in and out like clockwork … just long enough to figure out what they didn't know.'

This was the force that Westmoreland pitted against the ruthless, well-trained VC and NVA. At that time, it seemed inconceivable that the Communist forces could maintain their momentum against increasing amounts of American aid and soon the introduction of American bombing and increased combat forces.

Westmoreland got down to 'Search and Destroy'. The methodology was to identify a likely concentration of VC and possible landing zones (LZ) close by. This was the key to the 'search' element. Then helicopter-borne troops were inserted into the LZ to engage the enemy as the 'destroy' part of the exercise. The sole object of the exercise was to kill VC. However, it was not quite as simple as that.

LZs were frequently 'hot' and the air assault troops were ambushed on arrival. Cognizant of the possibility of a 'hot' LZ, the Americans inserted troops beyond the LZ with the intention of snaring the VC as they disengaged from the LZ. The VC countered that by preparing for the arrival of these cut-off troops. The VC had the option, always open to guerrillas, of withdrawing and breaking contact. The US/ARVN force could, usually, only withdraw with a helicopter extraction. US/ARVN wounded *had* to be extracted by air. The aircraft were at their most vulnerable when at very low level, as the photo above illustrates.

The VC accepted battle when it was convenient and melted away into the jungle when it was not. S&D recognized that this was a war without a front line, in which taking and holding territory was unnecessary. Nevertheless, the US often returned and fought over the same ground, sometimes a hill. On occasions the US Army would prepare an LZ by sanitizing it before the landing with an artillery strike. This served to give the VC ample warning of where and when the assault would become susceptible to small-arms fire. The courage of the pilots who flew these missions was extraordinary, and exemplified by Robert Mason who commented:

> When we get farther north, the landing zones are only big enough for one or two ships at a time. The Cong dig a hole in the LZ and cover it with brush. Then they leave one or two men hiding there during our

This photograph shows the vulnerability of a helicopter to small-arms fire during S&D operations. Combat operations at Ia Drang Valley, Vietnam, November 1965. Bruce P. Crandall's UH-1 Huey dispatches infantry while under fire. (*US Army*)

> pre-strikes. They stay concealed in the hole during the strikes and get us as we come with machine-gun fire up through the cockpit.[23]

The logistic effort and the cost of these operations was huge. Approximately 12,000 helicopters were deployed in Vietnam and of these 10,005 were the Bell HU-1 (known as the Huey). The cost of a single HU-1 aircraft in 1964 was $250,000. At 2020 prices this is $2,032,629. The capital investment in 12,000 helicopters was just short of $244 billion, give or take the small change. The training of the pilots, maintenance crews, petrol, oil and lubricants, when added in, drive the expense of this part of Westmoreland's campaign into the financial stratosphere.

No other country could possibly afford operations on this scale, but – and it is a big 'but' – the VC were not quelled. The US and ARVN troops employed on these S&D missions became increasingly sceptical as the large sweeps produced meagre returns. Some Vietnamese were killed, although their membership of the VC or NVA could not always be confirmed. More than 10 per cent of all US/ARVN combat deaths were the result of heliborne operations. Some 2,202 pilots, 2,704 aircrew and 1,269 passengers were killed. Just over 5,000 helicopters were either shot down or crashed.[24]

Captain Chuck Reindenlaugh served as a 'military advisor' at Xuan Loc, east of Saigon. He favoured a policy of 'clear and hold' rather than S&D and when he wrote home in January 1966, he described his life in footballing terms:

> Our weakness is rooted in our inability to garrison every village, hamlet or settlement ... they attack where forces are not stationed ... Imagine a football game in which one of the teams is conventionally uniformed, observes the rules of play. The opposing team, however, wears no uniform and in fact has been deliberately clothed to resemble spectators. This team plays by no rules, refuses to recognize the boundary markers or the Ref's whistle and, when hard pressed by their own goal, the team's quarterback will hide the ball under his shirt and run into the spectator boxes and defy you to find him.[25]

That sums up guerrilla warfare. It is not fair, there are no rules, there are no boundaries and there certainly is no referee. *The only aim of the VC was to win, by any means and at any cost* (author's emphasis). The USA sought to fight the war on its terms, but the VC was not prepared to oblige. Lieutenant General Bernard Trainor USMC was one of many charged with implementing Westmoreland's S&D operations. He said:

> ... there was no subtlety. His idea was to go after people and kill them in great numbers. That's why the body count became such an important standard for evaluating success in the war. It was based on the faith that if you kill more of them than they do of you, in the end you have beaten them.[26]

For the US soldier or Marine deployed in the jungle it was arduous, frustrating and frightening. They were usually soaked to the skin, if not by the rain then with their own sweat. They carried a great deal of ammunition, entrenching tools, medical dressings, morphine and lots of water. The ever-present threat of mines and punji pits was exacerbated by the constant attention of biting insects. At times the patrol would halt and heat their tinned rations. A degree of inventiveness accompanied this process. The soldiers bartered between themselves the contents of their C-Rations and by judicious blending of unlikely components they made the best of unappetizing options. The food did not require to be 'cooked' but heating made it more palatable. They brewed instant coffee or cocoa and accompanied it with dry biscuits spread with melted cheese, a shake of tarragon leaves and dried onion.[27] All soldiers look forward to their next freshly-cooked hot meal; it becomes a focus for fantasy (see the first paragraph of Chapter 1). The meal break was accompanied by a need to prepare a defensive perimeter. Digging even a shallow scrape in the root-laced jungle floor was hard work.

The S&D operations were on a large scale. Multi-battalion or even multi-division, they were often mounted in the deep jungle bordering Laos and Cambodia. Thousands of men, having been inserted, thrashed through high grass, thorn bushes and unyielding vegetation. Invariably, the VC avoided the set-piece battle that all American commanders desired and contented themselves with some sporadic sniping. They had polished their tunnelling skills and had the capacity to disappear underground, especially during bombing or artillery strikes. The willingness of the VC to live underground for extended periods, months or even years is remarkable. Yet this was not a passive tactic; it allowed them to surface in the middle of or behind an American formation, exact a penalty and then just as quickly disappear.

In general, the field craft of the US infantry was vastly different and inferior to that of the Australians and New Zealanders. American patrols did not place any value on silence. They talked and laughed. They carried a comprehensive assortment of kit and their accoutrements were not tied down and so every movement created further sound. The VC, who moved slowly and silently, were well aware of their enemy's position and were thus invariably able to initiate a contact. In any setting the initiator of fire has the advantage. The VC did not carry large supplies of ammunition and accordingly they had to make every round count.

A well-schooled infantry section or platoon is cognizant of the need for fire discipline. Any member of the group who has identified the enemy location can call out a fire order so that *aimed*, *effective* fire can be brought to bear. The American norm was for everyone under fire to expend un-aimed magazines of automatic fire. The logistic implications of poor fire discipline are evident. At the basic level, the VC were better soldiers than the Americans. Tran Thi Gung, a diminutive young woman, explained S&D from a VC perspective when she recorded that

> When I was a young guerrilla, I was smaller than I am today, and the Americans were very big. We knew we could not shoot them from a distance. We had to wait for them to come very close. As soon as I started to fire, I killed an American. After he fell, his friends came rushing to his aid. They held his body and cried a lot. This made them sitting ducks . . . After a few minutes they pulled back, taking the bodies of their friends, but they didn't pick up all their rifles, so I crawled out and grabbed five or six AR-15s . . . In time I could use any weapon including B-40 rockets.
>
> When the Americans pulled back, we knew that they would call in artillery fire, maybe even air strikes. As soon as it was quiet, we returned

to the trenches. The second time they advanced they took more casualties; they were such big targets, so easy to hit. I was no longer scared. They retreated again and once more the shelling began. They did this all day from six in the morning until six at night. Every time they pulled back, I crawled out of my hole to seize more weapons. I shot so many Americans I was awarded the decoration 'Valiant Destroyer of American Infantrymen'.

I think that the Americans lost many people because they were applying conventional tactics against our ambushes and tunnels. Their shells and bombs were extremely powerful and sometimes they killed people in the tunnels, but it didn't happen as often as you might think. The Cu Chi tunnels had such small openings it was very rare for a shell or bomb to land right in the tunnel. As Uncle Ho said, 'a stork can't shit in a bottle, so with our tunnels we shouldn't be afraid of American bombers.'[28]

The American logistic effort in these operations was massive, while that of the VC was minimal. It is easy to understand the frustration felt by young American soldiers who could not get to grips with this elusive enemy. The loss of a comrade to an unseen sniper and the demands of a commanding officer who had to keep up his body count added to the emotional turmoil.

In every company headquarters there was a large sheet of 'talc' upon which the body count could be maintained, platoon by platoon, with the use of a grease pencil. The score sheet was the criteria upon which officers were assessed for future employment and promotion. The numbers were supplied by those engaged with the 'enemy'. The numbers frequently included dead Vietnamese who could not reasonably be described as 'enemy'.

As a management tool, body count was fatally flawed. It was corrupted and was chasing the mythical 'crossover point' that existed only in the minds of Westmoreland and his acolytes. The indifference to losses displayed by the Communist Vietminh in its war with the French should have been noted by the US military in the mid-1950s and before it engaged with the Communist VC and DRV. It was unreasonable to expect the VC/DRV to abandon their successful total war strategy, conducted without quarter, that beat the French, especially when the disarray of their latest opponents was quite evident.

That first Indo-China war was heavily documented, and translated documents were available in the Pentagon Library. David Hackworth, a notable warrior, observed that none of these documents, which detailed French mishaps and Vietminh tactics, were ever checked out.[29] There was a dangerous arrogance abroad in Washington.

It is suggested that it was the body-count policy and free-fire zones that fostered a brutalization of some US soldiers and airmen. For some, human life lost its value and that led inexorably to a series of war crimes in which civilians were butchered; men, women and children. Some 2.5 million Americans served in Vietnam; the vast majority with honour, dignity and courage. However, there were sufficient merciless, homicidal individuals to sully the reputation of their country. These murderers, many of them identified, avoided retribution and that further sullied the reputation of the USA and in particular those officers who swept the crimes under the military carpet. This corporate conduct strengthened the resolve of those opposed to the United States, and so the condoned conduct was doubly damaging.

Robert Kerrey, later the Governor of Nebraska, was a Navy Seal and the raid he led on the hamlet of Thang Phong led to his award of the Medal of Honor. The accuracy of the citation for his medal was challenged and he later agreed that, in the action for which it was awarded, women and children had been murdered. He did not face any legal process and for years has basked in public acclaim as a politician and hero.

There are innumerable other examples of uncontrolled killing by US forces, but it was not until 2006 that the actions of a platoon of the 1st Battalion 327th Infantry Regiment (a constituent of the 101st Airborne Division) were published in *Tiger Force* by Sallah and Weiss.[30] This sickening and damning account is testament to the legacy of the body-count policy. The cover-up that followed compounded the criminality and set to naught America's claim to hold the moral high ground.

The research scientists of the USA and in support of the S&D policy directed their skills at various logistic issues, one of which was the effective interdiction of the Ho Chi Minh Trail and the communist supply line. They sought, by scientific intervention, to increase the rainfall in specific areas and, by so doing, make the ground impassable to NVA motor traffic and to disrupt operations in the south. The concept gave rise to Operations POPEYE and COMMANDO LAVA, both of which were highly-classified weather modification programmes that functioned, principally, between March 1967 and July 1972. The aims of the two programmes were four-fold. They were to soften road surfaces, cause landslides along the trail, deepen river crossings and ensure that soil remained saturated longer than normal.

From late 1966 Operation COMMANDO LAVA was a further innovative exercise designed to make travel along the HCMT difficult. During Operation COMMANDO LAVA, USAF aircraft dropped paper sacks filled with a powdered chemical compound developed by the Dow Chemical Corporation over areas of the trail in Laos. The chemical compound was variously referred to as 'soap' or 'detergent', but was a mixture of trisodium nitrilotriacetic acid and sodium tripolyphosphate. The chemical was developed to destabilize soil to create mud artificially.

The intention was that the chemical would allow US forces to extend the monsoon season indefinitely. The COMMANDO LAVA operations were shrouded in secrecy and classified as 'top secret'. All aircrews for the initial missions of COMMANDO LAVA were required to have at least a secret clearance. Aircraft deployed to Thailand for the missions made use of the Air America/Continental Air Services ramp at Udon Royal Thai Air Base, separating them from regular US Air Force units at the base. The results of the operation were inconclusive, the ground *appeared* to be muddy, but traffic was unaffected. This might have been the result of NVA counter-measures. In December 1967 the operation was abandoned, having cost millions of dollars.[31]

The 54th Weather Reconnaissance Squadron had been formed to implement the two operations and it coined the motto 'make mud, not war'.[32] It operated during every monsoon season, usually March to November, and flew cloud-seeding missions in three C-130 Hercules and two F-4C Phantom aircraft from the Royal Thai Air Force Base at Udon.

To preserve the security of the operation the squadron was deemed to be engaged on 'weather reconnaissance duties' and it did, indeed, provide weather data. In the early stages of Operation POPEYE, the target area was the eastern half of the Laotian panhandle and from July 1967 the target was expanded to the north to include the 20th parallel and the far west of North Vietnam. However, operations over North Vietnam ceased in April 1968 as part of Johnson's restrictions on air operations. The capacity of the 54th Squadron was never fully utilized, and the limits placed upon it reduced its effect. All rain-making operations ceased in July 1972. This little-recognized operation was successful, but hardly war-winning in scope.

Meanwhile, Westmoreland would not be diverted from this attrition policy. There was no doubt that the US armed forces were

> expert in mobilizing huge resources, orchestrating logistic support and developing enormous firepower. In Vietnam these skills led them to fight the war *their* way rather than developing the new skills required to defeat the new kind of enemy they faced. They made the mistake of fighting an unconventional war with conventional tactics.[33]

That was the latter-day judgement of President Richard Nixon with 20/20 hindsight and after the dust had settled. A senior participant was Lieutenant General Bernard Trainor, who said:

> Between my two tours in Vietnam I taught at the Command and Staff College. You could see the disillusionment and unhappiness that officers returning from Vietnam had toward Westmoreland's strategy of 'Search

and Destroy'. We were destroying the North Vietnamese, but we were also destroying innocent civilians and destroying ourselves.

Our hope early on was to win the hearts and minds of the people but that hope was destroyed by the South Vietnamese Government's failure to gain the people's allegiance and by Westmoreland's strategy of attrition.

A lot of people said we should have bombed the North back into the Stone Age and to a certain extent we tried that, but they continued to fight. More bombing wouldn't have worked.[34]

This state of affairs could not continue. Young Americans were being killed in increasing numbers and the arrival of body bags at Dover Air Force Base was raising disquiet. It was against this backcloth that the 'Phoenix Program' was established in 1965 and it was run until 1972 by the CIA but with the active support of US Army Intelligence units of the MACV. On the periphery were Special Forces of the Australian Army training team (AATTV) and the South Vietnamese security service.

The aim of the organization was 'to identify and destroy VC via infiltration, capture, counter-terrorism, interrogation and assassination.'[35] Without any doubt, the VC were a ruthless, cruel enemy waging total war. In that process, they killed 33,052 civilians in South Vietnam.[36] Clearly, the VC had to be confronted and the Phoenix Program was thought to be the answer. However, it was a very blunt, imprecise and murderous weapon and by 1972 Phoenix operatives had 'neutralized' 81,740 suspected VC, their informants or supporters. A staggering number were killed, variously estimated as being about 26,000.[37]

The Phoenix Program, which could only function with the logistic support of the MACV, routinely tortured suspects to the point of death. The techniques were no different to those used by the French and the Vietminh. In addition, there were thousands of targeted killings and Lieutenant Vincent Okamoto who served, very briefly, as an intelligence-liaison officer in 1968, commented by asking rhetorically

How do you find the people on the black list? It's not like you had their address and telephone number. The normal procedure would be to go into a village and just grab someone and say 'Where is Nguyen so-and-so?' Half the time the people were so afraid they would not say anything.

Then a Phoenix team would take an informant, put a sandbag over his head, poke two holes so he could see, put commo wire (telephone cable) around his neck like a long leash, walk him through the village and say, 'When we get to Nguyen's house, scratch your head.' Then that night,

Phoenix would come back, knock on the door and whoever answered the door would get wasted (killed).

As far as they were concerned, whoever answered was a Communist, including family members. Sometimes they'd come back to camp with ears to prove that they had killed people.[38]

The existence of this programme was known to Westmoreland, but he makes only a passing reference to it in his memoir. He saw it as a tool to use in his attempts at 'pacification'. Those who were killed arbitrarily on their doorstep fuelled the body-count statistics. As a pacification device to win hearts and minds, it was more than a little lacking in empathy.

Chapter Thirteen

Hide and Seek

'It is always necessary in battle to do something which
would be impossible for men in cold blood.'[1]
[Colonel Louis Louzeau de Grandmaison]

The campaign in South Vietnam was, in some ways, a vast, open-air military laboratory. The industrial might of the USA was harnessed to provide technological solutions to some of the issues faced by its troops. One of the most pressing of these issues was the inability of Westmoreland's troops to find the VC. They could not kill what they could not find and confront. Three methods to resolve this matter were applied concurrently from 1965. The first was the 'Search and Destroy' forays. The second was the defoliation policy. The rationale for this was very simple: strip the trees of their leaves, kill the jungle foliage and the VC will have nowhere to hide (see Chapter 14). The third element was the air campaign in which heavy bombers would saturate targets, identified in many cases by electronic sensors on the ground, and by so doing satisfy the 'destroy' aspirations of Westmoreland (see Chapter 15). All three of these concurrent programmes had enormous financial and logistic implications, especially the air campaign. There was also a fourth programme; one that did not require killing. That was one of 'pacification' and that is covered in Chapter 16.

On 14 November 1965 Westmoreland launched his biggest air assault to date when he landed three battalions of infantry and one of artillery in the Ia Drang Valley near the Chu Pong Massif in the Central Highlands. The Americans were numerically inferior to the NVA, but counted the battle as a success based on the body count. US losses were 237 KIA and 258 wounded. NVA losses depend on the source consulted but were of the order of 1,070 to 1,753 KIA. The number wounded is unknown. This battle was the blueprint for future American air cavalry operations. Logistically, it had been demanding but for the richest country on earth, cost was not an issue.

On the ground, innovation was alive and well and agile minds were looking for solutions to the 'seek' side of the equation. There was a clear need to develop a means of detecting a human presence deep in the jungle. The first such device was the 'Bed Bug Detector'. This was a gadget carried around, like a mine detector. At the end of the carrying pole there was a little capsule holding a collection of bed bugs. At the front of this capsule was an air sniffer. When the detector was pushed into a bush or hole, the pious hope was that, when the bed bugs smelled a human, they would become agitated. An instrument inside the capsule to measured the degree of agitation of the bugs. A huge amount of money was spent on this interesting device, but it produced more laughs than it did VC.[2]

Along a similar line was the 'XM-2 Personnel Detector' which came in a manpack. It was bulky but did work, although it was more likely to detect the operator than the foe concealed close by. It was not silent and gave away the operator's position.[3] This early and limited technology was pursued and it led to the XM-3, an airborne detector. By 1970, this was in widespread use and was installed on LOH-6, OH-58 and UH-1 helicopters. The development of these devices added to the logistic costs.

Robert McNamara, Secretary of State for Defense, 1961–68. He held his senior military staff in contempt and perceived war to be a matter that required 'management'. (*US Government*)

These XM-3 'sniffers' were not infallible. They could not detect the difference between a civilian and a fully-armed VC; it would be unreasonable to expect them to do so. They could be misled by animals, whose excrement sent similar signals to that of humans.[4] Notwithstanding its limitations, the XM-3 was used to detect smoke and other effluents until the end of the war to the entire satisfaction of some formations.

The Communist forces swiftly moved to establish countermeasures. First, they ensured that their soldiers would recognize a 'sniffer' helicopter. Then they avoided detection by holding their fire, despite the attraction of a low, slow-flying target because the 'sniffer' could identify gun smoke. The VC and NVA placed decoy targets, buckets of urine, and then moved away to watch the US Army firing very expensive artillery rounds into a jungle filled only with trees.[5]

The Communist forces turned the jungle to their advantage: the tree canopy provided cover, shade and some protection from fire, at least until Agent Orange (an herbicide and defoliant) had done its work. The HCMT, where possible, stayed inside the tree line. They were able to construct way stations for truck drivers, porters and soldiers making their way south and for wounded being evacuated to the north. Initially it had all been foot traffic, but by 1961 the first trucks were being used. The HCMT became increasingly sophisticated and along its route, five large Base Areas (BAs) were built and concealed. BA604 was the principal BA and it was from here that the co-ordination and distribution network was managed. BA607, BA609, BA611 and BA612 all had different geographic responsibility. The 559th Transport Group had expanded and, by April 1965, General Phan Trong Tue commanded 24,000 men in six transport battalions, two bicycle transport battalions, a river transport organization, eight engineer battalions and forty-five communication-liaison stations. It was this major force and the traffic moving up and down the HCMT that the communists wanted to conceal from sight and the Americans wanted to find and destroy.

Communist 'research and development' was on an entirely different scale to that of the Americans. They did not have the same degree of industrial muscle and so they concentrated on the basics. The extensive use of tunnels by the VC triggered a need to be able to cook without emitting smoke. Back in 1951 Hoang Cam, a Vietminh soldier, had developed a system in which the smoke was dissipated widely on the surface under cover of thick foliage. It was not a high-tech solution. Although it was practical and at 'no cost', cooking underground still generates heat and some smoke. It was not a popular measure.[6]

The ubiquitous helicopter was a threat that had to be faced and a guerrilla farmer from the Cu Chi village of Nhuan Duc addressed the issue. He produced the 'Cane Pressure Mine'. Previously, potential LZs were crossed by friction fuse wire which would detonate linked hand grenades in the proximity of an American aircraft. This system was hit and miss and depended for success on the helicopter landing on the trap.

The farmer To Van Duc came up with something much more effective. He recognized that the blades of a helicopter produced a significant downdraught and so he suggested that Chinese DH-10 mines be installed *at the top of trees* (author's italics). A sophisticated fuse was connected to the top-most branches of the tree and, when that tree or bush bent under the downdraught, the mine was detonated, very effectively. Initially, the Americans were baffled by this new weapon. Later, they noticed that mines concealed in bushes were often draped in cut foliage. After several days this died and the change in colour gave away the position.[7]

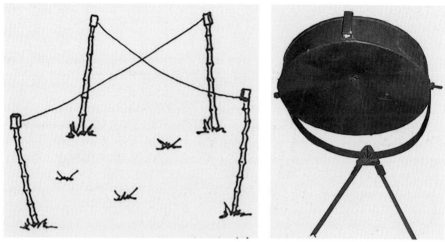

(*Left*) The criss-cross friction fuse wire booby-trap. (*Duc Quyen*)
(*Right*) Chinese DH-10 directional mine, seen here mounted on a stand for deployment on the ground, like the American Claymore. (*jcammo.com*)

In this war the 'seeking' was always done by the Americans because the VC knew where to find Americans if they sought contact. It was the VC who did the 'hiding' and they developed a method in which they dug large, interconnected holes, which developed into very sophisticated tunnel systems. These tunnels were superbly camouflaged and were usually only found by accident. There was no single architect of the communist tunnel systems because they evolved as a response to the military situation that they, a guerrilla force, faced in confronting a technologically and logistically superior enemy in South Vietnam.

The principal tunnel complex originated during the colonial period when the Vietminh were fighting the French. There was an underground haven that, by 1954, had 48 kilometres of tunnels (just short of 30 miles) where the Vietminh lived under the very feet of their enemy. The tunnels connected village communities and this 'facility' grew in sophistication over the following twenty years, when the Vietcong supplanted the Vietminh. By 1965, it was estimated by Major Nguyen Quot that those 48 kilometres of tunnels had expanded to 200 kilometres.

It called for courage and fortitude of the highest order to live underground and conduct a military campaign from that situation. The logistic issues are mundane and legion. For example, how did they carry and store water? How did they cook? How did they dispose of human waste? Why did that waste not identify the tunnel area? How did they wash and dry clothes? How did they ventilate the labyrinthine tunnel complex? How did they dispose of the spoil

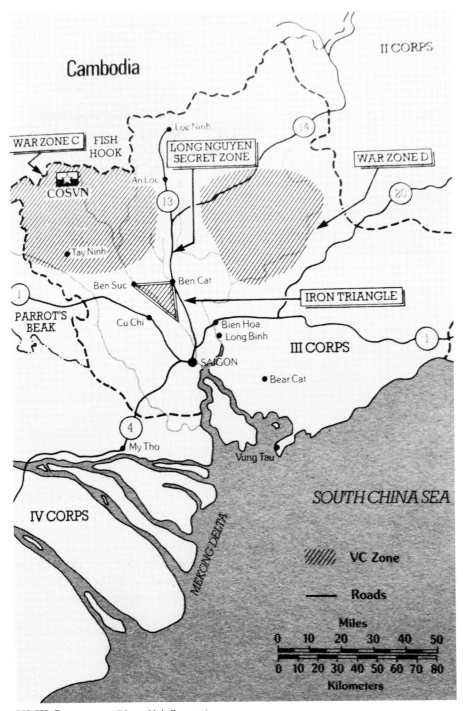

US III Corps area. (*Mangold & Penycate*)

from tunnelling? How did they treat their casualties? What did they do with the dead?

In the West we admire the feats of men who tunnelled their way out of German prison camps in the Second World War, but their exploits pale into insignificance when compared to the VC and its underground warriors.

Westmoreland's campaign really got under way in 1965 as the build-up of US troops continued apace. One of the general's priorities was to protect Saigon and, to this end, he ringed the capital with large base camps provided with every possible domestic convenience. The base areas were inevitably located in places where the Vietcong already dominated the local population. One such place, and where the best of the VC main force units operated, was the 'Iron Triangle'. This was an area of the Central Highlands, approximately 125 square miles of dense rain forest, with some small farming communities, 15 miles north of Saigon and around the small town of Cu Chi.

By chance, the soil of the Iron Triangle provided the VC with a considerable environmental advantage as it was tailor-made for tunnelling. The proximity of the Saigon River had, over millennia, interacted with the laterite clay, a ferric soil with a clay binder which allows some air penetration. The resulting soil was stable, unaffected by water and the roots of adjacent trees served to bind it even further. Captain Linh, a VC commander, commented that 'The earth in Cu Chi is sticky and doesn't crumble. The area is 15–20 metres (50–66ft) above sea level and for some 6 metres (20ft) down we knew there was no water. The water table was much lower; we could not have expected better conditions.'[8]

The dry laterite clay has a reddish colour and when dry the top surface of small roads becomes dusty and gritty, and as abrasive as sand. Dry laterite underground that was not subject to heavy traffic was as hard as masonry. The occupation of these superbly-camouflaged tunnels so close to the national capital by an aggressive guerrilla force ensured night belonged to the VC.

It was not until September 1967 that soldiers of the 9th South Korean Division captured a remarkable document in the course of a sweep north of Saigon. The lengthy document was translated into English and it turned out to be the VC 'Tunnel Manual'. The manual dictated the infrastructure to be used and specified that the passages were not to be straight but 'curved or snake-like'. They were to zigzag at angles of between 60 and 120 degrees because, as it explained, 'if the enemy detects the tunnel entrance, he will set off mines, Bangalores or put in chemicals, all of which are certain to have a disastrous effect on our troops.' Passages were to be no wider than 1.2 metres (just under 4ft) but no narrower than 0.8 metres (2ft 6in), no higher than 1.8 metres (6ft) and no lower than 0.8 metres. The thickness of the roof was to be 1.5 metres (5ft).

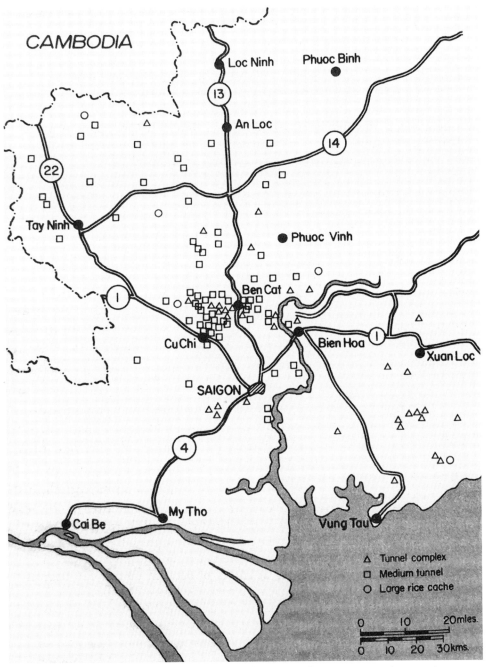

The juxtaposition of the Cu Chi tunnels and American bases. (*Mangold & Penycate*)

The plan for the so-vital trapdoors was specified. They were to be constructed

> with boards 1cm thick (just under 0.5in) and 2 to 3cm wide, make two frames, one with horizontal boards and the other with vertical boards. Insert a nylon sheet between the two frames which later will be glued together. Cover with sponge rubber and fill all openings with wax. A single board should never be used for a trapdoor frame – it is not strong enough.

Trapdoors built to these specifications allowed for the construction of up to four levels in a tunnel complex. The trapdoors were designed to fit tightly into their aperture and so would act as a blast shield and a watertight barrier. The sides of the trapdoor were bevelled downwards at an angle and could sustain considerable pressure. Key to the system was that all trapdoors were to be concealed. The criterion was no less than 'complete invisibility'. Inside a tunnel the trapdoor was covered in soil that concealed small wire handles with which the trapdoor could be lifted. External trapdoors were also covered in soil and foliage was encouraged to grow on top.[9] The success of this concealment was the frequency with which enemy soldiers walked by or sat close to the entrance to a tunnel. When that trapdoor was opened, the tunnel became a weapon pit from which a single sniper could operate.

Underground, every 20 metres or so, the VC dug a water drainage hole to prevent flooding. It was quite small but effective. Much more significant was the special water traps; these were like the U-bend in a toilet. These unsavoury pits were specifically designed to form a block to any smoke, CS gas or other chemical weapons employed by the Americans. It was a very low-tech solution, but it was highly effective. Major Quot believed that one of the most important secrets kept from the Americans was that the tunnels were constructed in a manner that allowed sections to be isolated and evacuated. An assault that appeared to be going well would find no opposition and that was because the fighters in that section had simply decamped.

For the enemy on the surface the entrance to a tunnel could only be found by laborious, hazardous probing with a bayonet. The tunnel entrances were invariably protected by booby-traps. They had to be able to resist fire, flood and chemical warfare. The manual observed that 'such entrances were to be 40 or 50 metres apart (up to 55 yards)' and the dimensions were duly prescribed. The manual said that

> Because the activities of the militia and guerrillas require appearing and disappearing quickly, the entrances to the underground tunnel must be located like the corners of a triangle, so that each can support the other in

combat. Our troops must be able to escape from the underground tunnel through a secret opening so they may continue the fight.[10]

Ventilation was always an issue for those living underground and bamboo ventilation shafts were placed obliquely, to avoid monsoon rain, from the surface down to the first level. Some always pointed east towards the light and others were directed into the prevailing wind. Cooking was an ongoing problem. The fuel was always wood, and smoke was the inevitable product. Every effort was made to disperse the smoke through dispersed shafts to the surface. The smoke was then dissipated over an area where the foliage would also serve to conceal it. However, some smoke swirled through the tunnels. Tom Mangold interviewed several Vietcong fighters after the war about Hoang Cam kitchens and their use.

Major Nguyen Quot (who once lived for five months underground without a break!) said the system worked extremely well. He probably meant that the kitchen was seldom detected by the enemy because he immediately added, 'but it was most unpleasant for the cooks, and there were often leaks in the ducts, leading to some contamination within the tunnels.'

Another Vietcong, Le Van Nong, considered Major Quot's description to be a massive understatement. He averred that

> the tunnels we were in stank and we stank. We met many difficulties. The tunnels were usually very hot, and we were always sweating ... [at night] we tried to come up to cook. It really wasn't possible for us to cook underground, the smoke was always asphyxiating, you just could not breathe, there was no air down there anyway. Sometimes we were driven to attack the Americans and make them go away, just so we could come up and cook at night, cook in the open. You cannot imagine what pleasure it gave us.[11]

Medical Colonel Vo Hoang Le was of the same opinion: 'Usually we ate only dry food. It was possible to cook properly above ground only because the smoke was unbearable if cooking was done underground.'

The Americans were in some ways their own worst enemy. They left behind unconsumed food – tinned meat, dry rice, noodles, cigarettes and chocolate – and the half-empty tins and other detritus were quickly turned to advantage by the VC. All food was consumed, and tins became grenades. Parachute silk was extensively re-used, as were the straps and bindings. Any wooden packing was cannibalized. American ordnance that did not explode was de-fused and then replaced as a mine or booby-trap.

Finding a tunnel was one thing, but dealing with the people inside was something rather different. To counter the tunnel system the Americans

Three VC, the youngest only a child, defusing an American bomb. They are cutting the casing and the kettle is pouring on cold water to cool the saw. This process is hazardous in the extreme.

and Australians asked 'tunnel rats' to enter and fight the VC underground in pitch darkness. This called for soldiers of enormous self-confidence and cold-blooded courage. The encounters were sometimes hand-to-hand, and the initiative was always with the VC fighting on (or under) 'home ground'.

The American Research and Development organization turned its attention to this new-style warfare and sought to manufacture weapons adapted for the purpose. Tunnel rats were unanimous in rejecting the standard issue Colt .45in. It was too unwieldy and too loud. There had to be a better sidearm and the Rats had the option of making their own choice. There was no consensus on the use of silencers; the length of the device when fitted made the weapon cumbersome but with few advantages. Accuracy was not an issue as any fighting underground would be at ranges of 10 yards or less. Shotguns were favoured by some; it was a comfort to know that, when fired, they would not miss. A Major Randy Ellis carried an M2 carbine with an abbreviated stock which folded, reducing the weapon to 22in in length. However, the majority of Rats carried a torch, a knife or bayonet and a handgun of choice.

As early as 1962, the Limited Warfare Laboratory (LWL) at Aberdeen Proving Ground in Maryland developed a counter-insurgency hardware programme and, by 1967, 90 per cent of its projects were geared to the ongoing

The construction of a tunnel. The pace of progress can be judged by the small container of spoil manhandled to the surface. (*RVN*)

An uncovered tunnel entrance of a size that precludes entry to any but the slimmest and the very bravest. (*US Army*)

war in Vietnam. The considerable cost of the 112 staff and their all-embracing and unlimited research was added to the logistic bill. Among its projects there were a host of expensive non-starters, but it did have successes and among those were a helicopter-launched smoke munition, leech repellent, foliage-penetrating radar and a 1,100-calorie meal in a 10oz packet. In the eleven years of its life the laboratory sent 225 items of specialized matériel to troops in the field, 74 of which were accepted for operational use.[12]

On 7 August 1966, the LWL unveiled a 'Tunnel Exploration Kit' for testing. It comprised three components. First, and to replace the hand-held torch, a lamp mounted in a hat was produced. The lamp was activated by a switch held in the mouth. Second was a communication system that came with a 'bone conductor microphone' worn on the bone at the back of the head or around the throat. This device came with wire that trailed behind the operator. Finally, there was an adapted .38 revolver with 4in barrel, silencer and high-intensity aiming light. Earplugs were thoughtfully provided, but could not be used with the communication set-up. Six kits were sent to Vietnam for testing. These kits seemed to be just what was needed and immediately there was a request for a further 450 such kits.

The LWL subsequently developed what they called the 'Tunnel Security and Intelligence Team Protective Equipment Kit', the successor to the original tunnel kit. The recommendations from the evaluation process of the six kits sent to Vietnam had been incorporated in the new development. Among the improvements was the replacement of the modified .38 calibre revolver with a suppressed semi-automatic .22 calibre High Standard pistol. These new kits were turned over to US Army Natick Laboratories, which had been designated as the parent agency for the new request, and sent to Vietnam in May 1968.

The sad fact is that, despite all the work and trials, the kits did not work. The headlight switch often failed, the lamp fell over the Rat's eyes when his hat rubbed against the tunnel roof, this slippage got worse when he started to sweat, the earphones that went with the communication system did not stay snugly inside the ear and the trailing wires snagged on the tunnel floor. The adapted .38 revolver was 'a total disaster'. The aiming light was ineffective because it was diffused and overpowered by the larger hat-mounted lamp. The .38 silencer turned out to be ineffective and even the gun's holster was too bulky for use in a confined tunnel. The use of the kits was discontinued although, sometime later, the communication element reappeared in a different form and with the highly-impressive title of 'Tunnel Explorer, Locator and Communications System' (TELACS). It still did not work.[13]

At the LWL they were not discouraged. Numerous projects were undertaken, such as the counter-ambush weapons with mines mounted on the sides of trucks, a device that alerted a helicopter pilot from which direction he was receiving fire, and the AN-PRC64 radio for jungle use.[14]

The LWL designed a backpack ammunition feeding system for the M60 machine gun. After beginning work in May 1968, it produced an 'Individual Ammunition Feeding Device' capable of being carried like a backpack with a capacity of 400 rounds. The system weighed 36lb and consisted of a backpack frame, a reel-type feed ammunition container and flexible-feed chuting of the kind normally used on aircraft. The system was tested in all the standard firing positions and it was found to not restrict the gunner's field of fire. Seventeen systems were shipped to Vietnam in 1969 for evaluation. Although the system was functional, *it prevented the individual from carrying a standard backpack*.[15]

The LWL admitted that this 'limited its utility when used on long operations away from established base areas'. Machine-gunners invariably operated away from established base areas and this was a prime case of the science being completely divorced from reality. A soldier has to have his personal kit with him at all times, something the LWL had apparently not appreciated.

It will be evident that the 'Tunnel Campaign' involved the USA in considerable logistic effort and inevitable cost. On the other hand, the Vietcong contributed only labour and resolve to their side of the equation.

Initially the VC had the upper hand and it dented the self-assurance of its enemy who was at something of a loss as to how to eliminate the tunnels and the people in them. However, as Voltaire said accurately, 'God is always on the side of the big battalions' and so it would be proved by 1970.[16]

The practicalities of living underground are mundane. Cooking was best done at night on the surface; the daily defecation of perhaps fifty people was conducted over a large ceramic jar sunk into the floor of the tunnel and capped when not in use. The dead were sometimes buried, temporarily, in the tunnel walls. The atmosphere was foul and the tunnels were damp and infested with rats, scorpions, snakes and toxic spiders. Living in these conditions was deeply unpleasant. Some were obliged to conduct their normal affairs, such as the two women pictured above.

The Vietcong turned some of the natural hazards to use. The logistics were very simple. They ate the rats and pronounced them to be more flavoursome than chicken! They boxed up scorpions and attached the box to a trip-wire. Lieutenant Jack Flowers, a tunnel rat, said that 'one of my men got stung: he came out screaming and never went back in another tunnel.'[17] Chi Nguyet, a young female guerrilla, reported that

In our area there is an especially fierce type of bee. They are more than twice the size of an ordinary bee. They don't store honey, but their sting

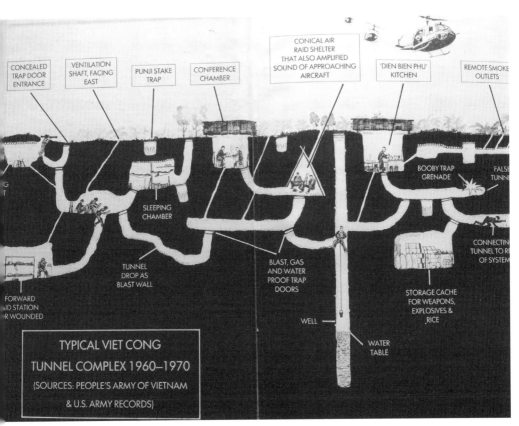

The labels in the diagram (reading from the top):

CONCEALED TRAP DOOR ENTRANCE

VENTILATION SHAFT, FACING EAST

PUNJI STAKE TRAP

CONFERENCE CHAMBER

CONICAL AIR RAID SHELTER THAT ALSO AMPLIFIED SOUND OF APPROACHING AIRCRAFT

'DIEN BIEN PHU' KITCHEN

REMOTE SMOKE OUTLETS

BOOBY TRAP GRENADE

FALSE TUNNEL

SLEEPING CHAMBER

CONNECTING TUNNEL TO REST OF SYSTEM

TUNNEL DROP AS BLAST WALL

BLAST, GAS AND WATER PROOF TRAP DOORS

STORAGE CACHE FOR WEAPONS, EXPLOSIVES & RICE

FORWARD AID STATION FOR WOUNDED

WELL

WATER TABLE

TYPICAL VIET CONG TUNNEL COMPLEX 1960–1970
(SOURCES: PEOPLE'S ARMY OF VIETNAM & U.S. ARMY RECORDS)

A tunnel system. (*PAVN and US Army records*)

is terribly painful. We studied the habits of these bees very carefully and trained them. They always have four sentries on duty and if these are disturbed or offended, they call out the whole hive to attack whatever disturbed them.

We set up some hives in the trees alongside a road leading from an ARVN post to our village. We covered them with sticky paper from which strings led to a bamboo trap we set on the road. The next time an enemy patrol came, they disturbed the trap and the paper was torn from the hive. The bees attacked immediately: the troops ran like mad buffalo and started falling into our spiked punji traps.

From the post they must have radioed for help because the ARVN sent a company by road from another post. By that time, we had set up quite a few hives. When the enemy came, they saw piles of dirt that looked like freshly-dug traps, so the officer ordered the troops to clear away the earth to uncover the 'traps'. But the hives were hidden under the earth and there was a terrible commotion when the bees were disturbed in such a rough way. They attacked and, in no time at all, thirty enemy troops were out of action. We were encouraged by this and started to rear bees especially for our defence.[18]

There were medical facilities in the tunnels and here, two nurses prepare for an operation. Convalescence for patients was underground until they were fit enough to travel. (*NVA*)

Colonel Do Tan Phong underscored the account above and said that in his experience hornets were employed against Americans from 1966. These insects could recognize the scent of their 'trainer' and did not attack him, but nests put in the right place with the use of long poles could be relied upon to sting others. The sting produced a fever in Western troops. Snakes and spiders were used to defend tunnels and they deterred even the most courageous interloper. These natural defences were at the other end of the Research and Development scale employed by the USA. Their cost was minimal, but they worked.

In 1965 the 25th US Infantry Division, commanded by Major General Fred Weyand, was earmarked to move to Vietnam and the staff started to plan the move. Weyand selected a spot about 3 miles outside the town of Cu Chi as his new location because it was well away from the populated centre of Saigon. He expected to 'act as a sort of lightning bolt for the enemy'; moreover, the topography was ideal as it was the one place above the water table. Artillery could reach out from the base and so an area 5,500 yards in diameter could be cleared of any continuous activity.

Just prior to the arrival of the 25th Division in January 1966, 8,000 US and Australian troops swept through the Cu Chi district in a major operation called Operation CRIMP. The ground forces moved into ground that had been extensively bombed by B-52 aircraft. The search that followed found few pickings and in that respect the operation had been unsuccessful.

The plans for Cu Chi Base had been approved and, by mid-1966, the base covered 1,500 acres (around ten golf courses) and here the soldiers of the 25th found a quality of life beyond the wildest dreams of earlier generations of soldiers. They were met by air-conditioned steel offices, modern messing facilities with ice-making machines, walk-in refrigerators, constant electric power, hot-water showers and folding beds. There were separate clubs for officers, NCOs and soldiers. There was a radio station, barbers' shops, retail outlets, sports fields, a miniature golf course, swimming pools and chapels to serve the godly. The claim was that this base replicated everything to be found in the USA. The divisional headquarters was housed in an 'elegant, broad-fronted, single-storey building with three gables in its sloping tin roof'.[19] The base served to emphasize the unbridgeable cultural gap between the Americans and the people they had come 'to save'. All of this in a war zone.

The management of this large, sophisticated military city was a drain on manpower as it employed 4,500 servicemen and thousands of local people, many of whom were VC sympathizers or worse. Every private soldier had a

The base of the US 25th Infantry Division. This sophisticated and very well-served establishment was built on top of the Cu Chi tunnel complex. The enemy was probably below the feet of that parade. (*US Army*)

'hooch maid' who cleaned his living space, his boots and equipment. This was definitely the way to go to war. The construction and running costs of the base were prodigious. Sustaining the occupants of this establishment was a major logistic exercise in its own right. The supply system was known as Operation ROAD RUNNER and it occupied a significant proportion of the residents. It is alleged by Mangold and Penycate that 'four convoys, each of about sixty vehicles' would each day make the short but dangerous journey from Long Binh, the biggest supply depot in the theatre, to Cu Chi Base.[20] Some 240 trucks of supplies each day seems to be excessive, but the source for Mangold and Penycate was *Tropic Lightning News*, the in-house newspaper of the 25th Division. These convoys were subject to regular attack and operations had to be mounted to clear the roads ahead of the convoys. The Americans were experiencing the same problems that faced the French in supplying their border forts by road in the early 1950s. The convoys between Long Binh and Cu Chi, although similar, were commanded from the air, a luxury not available to the French. Whatever the numbers, the fact is that men must have died delivering ice cream.

Weyand quickly discovered that the area he had selected was riddled with tunnels and that the division was likely to be vulnerable in its comfortable new home. Weyand admitted that his choice of the site had caused problems at first, and said that 'We moved into Cu Chi thinking that the area was already secured … the Vietcong could, at that time, with impunity come up in the middle of the night and fire away and cause us that kind of grief.'

Weyand set his tunnel rat team to work and, to the consternation of all concerned, one of them, in the process of making a reconnaissance of a known tunnel, surfaced through a previously unsuspected trapdoor in the middle of the divisional motor pool. The enemy was *literally* under the feet of the 25th US Infantry Division (author's italics).

The Cu Chi base and its egregious comforts was home to a large garrison and, as such, it reinforced the culture gap between those 'in the field' and those who were not. Westmoreland did not restrict the extravagance of Cu Chi Base because it was important, in terms of morale, as it was used as a 'rest and recuperation centre' for soldiers who had been on operations.

Despite the unfortunate location, the upside was that, in Cu Chi, once some of the local tunnels had been cleared, a Tunnel Rat School was established in a preserved length of VC tunnel. The training was a demanding physical and mental test and, in its first five months, only five volunteers completed the course. A dog training school was set up and the dogs could detect anyone who had been exposed to the defoliants being used by the US. The VC responded by buying American toilet soap. The dogs recognized the scent as friendly. Similarly, they were misdirected by pepper spray applied around tunnel entrances.

The locally-employed work force was riddled with spies. Every club, mess hall and sports facility was dependent upon Vietnamese labour and they reported everything that they heard. The intelligence gathered by the VC was timely, accurate and in quantity. One of the agents worked in the base mortuary preparing American dead for repatriation. Thus the VC had a very accurate handle on their enemy's casualties, although the reverse did not apply, where body counts were little more than semi-educated guesses.

The VC made a series of successful attacks inside the 25th Division base until January 1968 and the start of the Tet Offensive that was, in large measure, mounted from Cu Chi. The eradication of the Cu Chi tunnels and their inhabitants followed the failure of Tet (see Chapter 21). The 'Tunnel Campaign' in Cu Chi, if it can be dignified with such a title, tied up thousands of US troops and although causing the US insufficient casualties to be classified as a battle, it spread uncertainty and fear among US soldiers and generated, in the USA, a research programme to counter its effects.

It is interesting to note that a number of distinguished historians, among them Hastings, Davidson and Karnow, make no mention of Cu Chi. Westmoreland in his memoir makes only a slight passing remark. However, Appy quotes at length the experience of Duong Thanh Phong, a combat photographer.

To put the importance of the Cu Chi tunnels into its Vietnamese context, there is a war memorial to the Vietnamese soldiers who died fighting in that part of the world, an area of about 600 square miles:

> There are just over 50,000 names on this single memorial. Had the United States suffered commensurate losses then the wall in Washington would show not 58,193 names but at least 12 million. That simple statistic exemplifies the level of commitment that the Vietnamese applied to the reunification of their country.[21]

Chapter Fourteen

Operation RANCH HAND: Defoliation

'One of the most controversial missions in the short history of the United States Air Force.'[1]

[C.W.T. Jamison]

During the Malayan Emergency (1948–60) Britain used herbicides to destroy bushes and trees to deprive Communist Terrorists (CTs) of concealment. It also targeted their crops as a part of its starvation campaign.[2] A detailed account of these British forays into herbicides was produced by E.K. Wood-ford of the Agricultural Research Council and H.G.H. Kerns of the University of Bristol.[3] After the Malayan conflict ended in 1960, the US considered the British precedent when deciding on its own use of defoliants. It concluded that defoliation was a legal military tactic and Secretary of State Dean Rusk advised President Kennedy accordingly.

It was as early as 6 January 1962 that the Joint Chiefs of Staff (JCS) of the United States authorized the commencement of operations to defoliate selected areas along Route 15 in South Vietnam. This was the start of a major logistic operation that lasted for a decade and cost, in cash terms, billions of dollars. However, in human terms the cost was greater, and the dire results have lasted up to the present day (2020). In 1952, the French had tried de-foliation with manual labour in an attempt to deny cover to the Vietminh ambushing their convoys. It was very hard physical work and in a climate in which vegetation grew quickly, it was also frustratingly unsuccessful.

The Americans would use state-of-the-art herbicides to accomplish what the French had failed to do, and they began the process on 3 October 1964 in south-west Phuoc Long Province, an agricultural area. At the time the US military was focused on its 'advisory' role. In that capacity it was assisting the Government of Vietnam (GVN) in its actions against VC guerrillas.

The herbicide-spraying was remarkably successful, so much so that that the military were quick to recognize its merits and its demand outstripped supply of the requisite chemicals. In its early stage the programme had attracted no attention either in the scientific community or media. Research into defoliant herbicides accelerated and the programme was given the name Operation RANCH HAND. The year 1965 saw a big build-up of US troops in Vietnam and with that came a change in their mission and the advent of 'Search and Destroy'.

In January 1965, and specifically on 'Project 20-32/33', US aircraft made forty sorties in which they sprayed 36,000 gallons of 'Agent Purple'. The effect of these 36,000 gallons on human and animal life was unknown, but they did kill vegetation. The capacity to reduce the concealment provided by the rain forest was an important logistic element in Westmoreland's S&D strategy and he pursued and supported defoliation.

Later in January 1965, in pursuit of 'Project 46', spraying of the Boi Loi forest continued for sixteen days, during which, 78,800 gallons were deposited. The logistic effort and expense were nugatory as the VC had withdrawn before the chemical attack and they were not present when the defoliated area was bombed. By now the botanical facts of life had emerged to show that the defoliant chemicals, although they did enhance vertical visibility, their effect was not permanent. On that basis, some areas were sprayed regularly.

In mid-1965, a less expensive defoliant was obtained to replace the 'purple' and, at the time, the new product was designated 'Orange Herbicide'. The defoliation programme became the victim of its own success and, as demand soared, procurement from the USA became an issue. The reach of RANCH HAND expanded and, for example, in December 1965 the Americans flew (sometimes using helicopters) 897 spraying missions defoliating 253 square miles of forest and 68,000 acres of crops. Spraying is a low-level operation and the airmen claimed to be the most shot-at servicemen in Vietnam. The capacity of the United States to reduce the concealment of the Vietcong was accompanied by carpet-bombing of some of the defoliated areas. An illustration of the effect of the two linked programmes on a stretch of the HCMT is to be seen on page 173. The VC and NVA had no effective counter either to defoliation or bombing. Fifteen bombers were lost to AA or SAM fire over North Vietnam, but that did not hinder their campaign.

In January 1966 new records were established: 188 missions dispersed 177,300 gallons of what was now called 'Agent Orange' over 29 square miles of forest on the slopes of the Chu Pong Mountains near the Ia Drang River valley, south-west of Pleiku. After the spraying there was a pause to let the chemicals do their work and then fighter-bombers dropped napalm. However, it did not have the desired effect because the trees would not burn.

For RANCH HAND it was onwards and upwards. The 148,450 gallons sprayed in March was comfortably exceeded in May 1966 when for the first time 200,000 gallons were used. Usage at this rate was causing a supply problem and so experiments were conducted to establish whether or not a thinner

Agent Orange loaded in 1,500-gallon tanks inside a UC-123K during Operation RANCH HAND. (*US Army*)

spray would suffice. The experiment was conducted in the mangrove forests along the main shipping channel to Saigon. Agent Orange was sprayed at half its usual flow rate; if it was effective it would, at a stroke, double the capacity of the aircraft and halve the cost. Although mangrove was susceptible to Agent Orange, it did not work.

By now the use of Agent Orange in Vietnam was attracting criticism and some experts at the time, including Arthur Galston, opposed herbicidal warfare due to concerns about the side effects to humans and the environment by

A stretch of the HCMT that had been defoliated and heavily bombed. (*US Army*)

indiscriminately spraying the chemical over a wide area.[4] As early as 1966, resolutions were introduced to the United Nations, alleging that the US was violating the 1925 Geneva Protocol which sought to regulate the use of chemical and biological weapons.

The US defence was that Agent Orange was not a chemical or a biological weapon as it could be more accurately described as 'a herbicide and a defoliant and it was used in an effort to destroy plant crops and to deprive the enemy of concealment, and not meant to target human beings.' The American representatives argued that a weapon, by definition, is any device used to injure, defeat or destroy living beings, structures or systems, and Agent Orange did not qualify under that definition. It also suggested, acidly, that if the US were to be charged for using Agent Orange, then Britain and its Commonwealth nations should also be arraigned since they also used it widely during the Malayan Emergency in the 1950s, some sixteen years earlier.[5]

The VC and NVA followed the debates with interest because international outrage was their only defence against Agent Orange. In the meantime, they changed their routes and moved at night.

Westmoreland (who made no mention of defoliation in his memoir) was alert to a section of the DMZ running from the Laotian border to the South China Sea. 'This was a politically sensitive matter because the International Control Commission had been unable to fulfil its obligations under the 1954

Helicopter fitted with spraying equipment. The low altitude of the aircraft makes it very vulnerable to small-arms fire. (*US Army*)

The effect of Agent Orange on mangrove forests. In the top photo the cover available along both sides of the river is evident. In the lower photo the clear space and line of sight works to the considerable advantage of the helicopter-borne US and ARVN troops. (*US Army*)

Geneva Accord to prevent illegal penetration of the neutralized area.' The request was expanded to include defoliation of the northern half of the zone and the adjacent routes into North Vietnam.[6] Washington approved and why not? It was now engaged in outright war with North Vietnam, a country that abided by none of the normal diplomatic or military standards. However, in a decision that exemplified American conduct of the war, Westmoreland was told that he was not to go into the northern section of the DMZ.

Notwithstanding the ongoing supply difficulty, by the end of 1967, the 12th Air Commando Squadron's nineteen aircraft had flown 6,847 sorties and had spread 4,879,000 gallons of Agent Orange and, as a result, 1,226,823 acres in South Vietnam were defoliated.[7] In early 1968 the deluge of Agent Orange increased in volume and in January and February 601,000 gallons were dispensed. One of the aims of defoliation was to dry out the trees and bushes so that they were susceptible to fire. Given the wet climate, this was not usually possible. That is until March 1968, when an unusually dry spell, the first for twenty-five years, worked in favour of the US. Forest fires raged across South-East Asia and one of the biggest was in the U Minh forest on the south-west coast of the Ca Mau peninsula. The fires feasted on defoliated areas and generous helpings of napalm helped them along. The sanctuaries of the VC and NVA were increasingly underground or well into Laos and Cambodia.

The US Department of Defense was under pressure from the environmental lobby and, on 1 March 1968, was obliged to admit that it was directly participating in crop destruction. Four months later it announced that in 1966, that is to say two years earlier, around 59,000 acres of crops had been destroyed. The presumption that these were all 'enemy crops' is patently fallacious. Notwithstanding international disapproval, the consumption of Agent Orange hit dizzying heights. The programme was so successful that the demand outstripped America's industrial capacity. The use of Agent Orange had doubled year on year. The 50,000 gallons in 1962 rose to 400,000 gallons in 1965 and by 1966 it had reached 2,600,000 gallons. The logisticians in Washington forecast a requirement of 6 million gallons in 1967 and 10 million in 1968.[8] Andrew Wells-Dang, writing in August 2002, said:

> In one instance, defoliation in Cambodia resulted in a major international incident. This attack took place on French- and Cambodian-owned rubber plantations in Kampong Cham province between 18 April and 2 May 1969, at a time when the US had no diplomatic relations with the then government of Prince Norodom Sihanouk. The damage caused was substantial. Both the US government and inspection teams confirmed that 173,000 acres were sprayed (7 per cent of Kampong Cham

province) and that 24,700 acres were seriously affected.[9] The rubber plantations totalled approximately one-third of Cambodia's total and represented a loss of 12 per cent of the country's export earnings.[10]

The mystery surrounding the attack has to do with who exactly carried it out. Cambodia was officially neutral in the Vietnam War, though the eastern part of its territory had been subject to infiltration by both US Special Forces (Operation DANIEL BOONE) and guerrillas on southern portions of the Ho Chi Minh Trail (HCMT). No herbicides were admitted being used, however, and large-scale US operations in Cambodia would not begin until the April 1970 covert invasion. The evidence points to Air America, the primary air contractor for the CIA.

The United States never accepted responsibility, but it appeared that the attack had been mounted without the knowledge or consent of either the American Embassy or the USAF. Reparations of $12.2 million were claimed and Kissinger wrote 'Every effort should be made to avoid the necessity for a special budgetary request to provide funds to pay this claim.' Clearly, Kissinger wished to keep the payment secret.

This incident demonstrated that RANCH HAND and the USAF was not the only organization to have herbicide-spraying capability. The use of Agent Orange was uncontrolled. As access to the logistic stocks was insufficiently restricted, the CIA was apparently able to conduct its own private war.

There was vociferous opposition to the principle of herbicide-spraying as a weapon, both in the USA and increasingly in Europe by those with environmental concerns. In Vietnam the weather conditions were limiting operations and then in late 1969 it was announced that the herbicide programme 'would be phased out within a year'. At Westmoreland's headquarters in the MACV there was dismay because Agent Orange was a favoured weapon and commanders were constantly requesting spraying missions. In the last full operational year RANCH HAND flew 5,274 missions and dispensed 4.3 million gallons of herbicides. However, in April 1970 when Melvin Laird, Secretary of Defense (who had replaced McNamara) cut the proposed budget for herbicides in Fiscal Year 1971 from the anticipated $27 million to $3 million, it was the death knell for RANCH HAND. The last spraying operation was on 7 January 1971.

Thereafter there was a logistic problem in disposing of existing stocks of Agent Orange. Laird ordered that all remaining stocks of Agent Orange (and Orange II) in South Vietnam be returned to the United States as quickly as possible after the US Embassy negotiated a formal transfer of title from South Vietnam. On 31 October 1971, all herbicide activities under US control ceased.

Rusting drums of Agent Orange awaiting disposal on Johnson Island. Johnson Atoll is an unincorporated territory of the United States. It is a closed site, having been a secret missile base and a chemical weapon storage and disposal site; the atoll is environmentally contaminated. Remediation and monitoring continue. (*US Army*)

Operation PACER IVY, the removal of all remaining Orange herbicide in South Vietnam, was completed on 28 April 1972. Approximately 5.2 million litres (25,220 drums) were off-loaded on Johnston Island in the Central Pacific Ocean. Operation PACER HO, the destruction of the Agent Orange by at-sea incineration, was conducted between May and September 1977.[11]

The ongoing and tragic history of Agent Orange is beyond the scope of this book, but suffice to say that its legacy is still with the Vietnamese today.

Chapter Fifteen

Prelude

'He, therefore, who aspires to peace should prepare
for war.'[1]

[Flavius Vegetius Renatus]

In 1964, the United States of America was the pre-eminent military power on earth. Its wealth was such that it could fund several carrier groups which provided the capacity to wage war across the globe. In addition, it had a large, well-equipped air force that was able to deliver heavy ordnance from its multitude of installations. Its logistic base was such that, during the war of 1964–1973, the USA built seven jet-capable and seventy-five smaller tactical airfields, six deep-water ports, twenty-six hospitals and twenty-four permanent base facilities, many of them small cities. For example, the base at Long Binh occupied 25 square miles and boasted cinemas, slot machines, steam baths, restaurants, lawns and flower beds. It also employed 20,000 Vietnamese, some of whom were undoubtedly communist agents.[2]

This logistic profligacy did not find universal favour. General Palmer commented that 'Westmoreland's Base Camp idea was an even worse idea than the one-year tour. The manpower it soaked up was appalling, not to mention the waste of material resources and the handicap of having to defend these albatrosses.'[3]

President Johnson recognized that any future bombing of North Vietnam involved a degree of political danger and he was anxious not to do anything to generate a military response from China. It was not his intention to lay waste to North Vietnam, despite

General William Westmoreland, who searched for the elusive 'crossover point', but never found it. (*US Army*)

having ample means to do so. His stated aim was to persuade the North Vietnamese to cease supporting the guerrilla war in the South and negotiate a peace agreement. Military victory by an invasion of the North was never an option. On that basis, no targets were identified close to the Chinese border and the response when it came would be muted.

The history of bombing campaigns is mixed. The Germans failed to quell the British either by bombing their cities during the blitz or, later, with the V-weapons. Curiously, both actually served to strengthen British resolve. Similarly, the Anglo-American bombing campaign of Germany failed to completely destroy the German logistic base and German morale. The bombing of Hiroshima and Nagasaki did have the desired effect, but at a massive cost of lives and moral authority. In May 1964 the American JCS had anticipated the use of bombers as part of a 'thirty-day Vietnam scenario' developed by the State Department. The Joint Chiefs

> proposed air strikes beginning ... against North Vietnam's transportation system. Mining would accompany the effort. Attacks would then occur against targets having maximum psychological effect on the North's willingness to stop the insurgency: POL storage, selected airfields, barracks, training areas, bridges, railroad yards, port facilities, communications and industries. The raids would continue despite expected negotiations, until the United States received evidence that North Vietnam had stopped supporting the insurgency.[4]

That is little more than a statement of the militarily blindingly obvious. Why else would bombers be employed? Their raison d'être is to effect destruction, interdict logistic lines of supply and take lives. Bombing is a strategy not noted for its delicacy or sophistication. It is as the battleaxe is to the rapier.

The posture of the United States and of its strategic bomber force, until 1965, had been entirely focused on the Soviet Union. Those bombers formed part of the Western nuclear deterrent and the Soviet Union had been, correctly, identified as the next likely enemy. The Strategic Air Command (SAC) was designed for a total war scenario but, in American minds, total war did not exist in Vietnam. However, total war did exist most firmly in the minds of the North Vietnamese and its unalterable aim was reunification of North and South, whatever the cost.

Although the transportation system of North Vietnam was vulnerable, the country did not have an economy based on manufacturing. It had no major industrial centres and any factories were decentralized. It was overwhelmingly an agricultural country with a poor transport infrastructure. This was not a target-rich environment. Bundy predicted, on 17 November 1964, that anyway, 'DRV leaders would probably be willing to suffer some damage to the country in the course of a test of wills with the USA.'[5]

The USA was involved in a war with a minor South-East Asian country, described dismissively in Washington as 'piddling'. Despite the cautious resistance of President Johnson and that of his cohort of civilian advisors, it was evident that the increasingly provocative action of North Vietnam had to be either tolerated or confronted.

On 7 February 1965, the VC finally lit the blue touch paper. It provoked an American response with the attack on the US airbase at Pleiku in the Western Highlands, which destroyed ten aircraft and damaged a further fifteen; nine Americans were killed and 125 were wounded. The attack took place against a background of a South Vietnam in political chaos in which the next coup was perceived to be just around the corner. The ARVN had lost control of vast areas of territory and William Bundy wrote that the communists 'see Vietnam falling into their lap in the fairly near future'.[6] He recommended air strikes against the DRV and found powerful support, especially among the military.

Immediately after the attack on Pleiku, President Johnson authorized Operation FLAMING DART and forty-nine retaliatory missions were flown

The remains of a USAF RF-4C Phantom, one of nine that were parked and then destroyed by rockets during a VC attack on an air base. (*USAF*)

on 8–9 February 1965. The targets selected were the People's Army of Vietnam (PAVN, previously referred to as North Vietnam Army, NVA) barracks near Dong Hai and logistic installations just north of the Demilitarized Zone (DMZ). However, tellingly, it was civilian officials who selected the targets. From the very beginning of the air campaign it was 'managed' by civilians in Washington. Their guiding philosophy was that a 'limited war' could be waged and won, to the chagrin of the senior military officers who knew differently.

Predictably, matters did not end there because the VC promptly assaulted a barracks at Qui Nhon and in the process killed twenty-three Americans. FLAMING DART II followed when ninety-nine aircraft from the carriers USS *Hancock*, USS *Coral Sea* and USS *Ranger* struck at Chanh Hoa. Further attacks were mounted by the USAF and South Vietnamese Air Force (SVNAF), the latter operating twenty-eight A-1 propeller-driven Skyraiders. The air war was now joined and bombing targets south of the DMZ started on 19 February when USAF B-57s flew in support of ground operations.

The bombing attacks, mounted from aircraft carriers, had mixed results but they were a watershed and the start of a war that would now escalate in intensity. An operation called ROLLING THUNDER was initiated by Johnson. That programme lasted from 2 March 1965 until 2 November 1968. Its Achilles' heel was that it was in civilian hands.

Chapter Sixteen

Operation ROLLING THUNDER

'I will pay them in their own coin if they wish to carry on the war in that manner.'[1]

[Major General George McClellan]

President Johnson ordered 'a program of measured and limited air action' jointly with the GVN against selected targets in North Vietnam. Operation ROLLING THUNDER brought the heavy bomber to the battlefield. The VC countered massive carpet-bombing air strikes in the south by going underground.

The HCMT was a prime target for bombers. The North Vietnamese called the trail the '*Truong Son*/Strategic Supply Route' and

> the Americans dropped 4 million tons of bombs on the trail alone – over half of the total of 7 million tons. These were sixteen types of 'dumb' bombs and twenty types of guided bombs. As the war progressed, so did the sophistication of these weapons. At its peak 120,000 people worked on the trail and during the war 20,000 were killed, 30,000 were seriously injured and 6,000 are still 'missing', and certainly dead.[2]

The American assumption was that if enough pain and devastation was inflicted, it would motivate the Vietnamese to submit. Major General William DePuy, commanding the 1st Infantry Division, opined that 'the solution in Vietnam is more bombs, more shells, more napalm ... until the other side cracks and gives up.' This simplistic level of strategic thought made a significant contribution to the American defeat because it badly underestimated the tenacity and resolve of the Vietnamese.[3]

The North Vietnamese had established AA artillery around Hanoi and other locations that they deemed to be important, and guns and SAMs were their only defence against high-level bombing; the only alternative was to take shelter, underground if possible, much the same as Londoners did in the 1940s. US intelligence was aware of the location of AA sites but, believing them to be manned by Chinese volunteers, avoided selecting these sites as targets. It may have been politically shrewd, but militarily it was nonsense.

In 1965, at the senior levels of the USAF there was confusion caused by the byzantine chain of command. It started at the very top with the president, Robert McNamara and General Earle Wheeler, the chairman of the JCS. Wheeler proposed targets to McNamara, the decision-maker, but only after a ROLLING THUNDER team of seven officers had reviewed earlier recommendations arriving from Admiral Sharp's Pacific Command (PACOM). Until May 1965 this team included only two officers, and neither was a pilot or a USAF officer.[4]

Despite being appointed as the operational commander of Operation ROLLING THUNDER, Admiral Sharp, who was based in Honolulu, did not take effective control. Instead he delegated responsibility to the commander of the Pacific Fleet (PACFLT) and to the commander of the Pacific Air Forces (PACAF). Each was to direct his own air component. Clodfelter judged that

> the absence of a single air commander produced chaos. The 2nd Air Division in Saigon, the Air Force Headquarters with direct control over fighter wings participating in the campaign, received 'guidance' not only from PACOM and PACAF but also from the 13th Air Force in the Philippines. Meanwhile the US Navy's carrier task force in the Tonkin Gulf received supervision from PACOM and PACFLT. To simplify the multi-layer Air Force command arrangements, PACAF changed the name of the 2nd Air Division to the 7th Air Force in early 1966.

This arrangement actually got worse when the PACAF did not give to the 7th Air Force (previously the 2nd Air Division) command of all its assets. Instead it only delegated to it *operational* direction over the fighter wings. The 13th Air Force retained *administrative* control over the same formations. The product of this cockeyed arrangement was the creation of the 7th/13th Air Force in Thailand, which then assumed *administrative* control of all the fighters. A 7th Air Force officer was quoted as saying that 'the only person in command was the president.'[5] In combination, all of this served to negate the logistic superiority of the USA.

One might enquire what part the ground force commander, Westmoreland, had to play in the target selection process. The reality was that he was some way down the pecking order, in a situation in which these air assets were, ostensibly, on his side and providing his soldiers with support. However, on 1 April 1966 Westmoreland was given authority to schedule strikes but in a strictly limited area, immediately north of the DMZ. He was able to call on air support in South Vietnam.

Inter-service co-operation was in short supply during the early days of ROLLING THUNDER when Navy and Air Force units competed to conduct the most sorties against the North. The conduct of the air war was further affected by President Johnson's artificial numerical limitation on the sorties conducted. The number took no account of the needs of the tactical situation and was as self-defeating as the body-count policy, still firmly in place. Eventually North Vietnam was divided into zones and each service operated only in its allocated zones. Permission was required of the other service if an aircraft was to operate outside its zone. This was not an efficient way to carry out a very expensive military activity.

'Gradualism', which was practised by the Johnson White House, involved the gradual application of pressure through air power on the DRV. The pious hope was that Hanoi would 'get the message' as, initially, 'carefully selected and generally unremunerative targets were attacked'.[6] The subtle plan, manufactured in Washington, was too subtle by half, because the DRV concluded from the very restrained bombing that the USA was not completely committed to fighting the war.

Micro-management of military operations was the name of the game and anathema to the US military leadership. In some cases, the president himself selected bombing targets. Johnson was quoted as saying 'They can't bomb an outhouse without my say-so.' The Joint Chiefs of Staff (JCS) Commander-in-Chief, Pacific (CINCPAC) Military Assistance Command, Vietnam (MACV) all opposed deliberate, incremental slow escalation of the war. They believed that the conduct of the air war against the North was a violation of established principles of warfare.[7]

Making matters worse was the arrogance bordering on contempt for military opinion by McNamara and his 'whizz kids', many of whom were young men trained as economists and having little if any personal military experience or professional appreciation of the military's concerns.[8] Inevitably, McNamara focused on the quantifiable indices of military power and on such countable measures of the war's progress as sorties flown, bomb tonnages dropped, artillery shells fired and enemy killed. Despite the superiority of the USA in logistic terms, by 1966 it had been unable to convert this superiority into the overwhelming military victory that was expected. George Ball is one of very few who understood that 'the quintessential advantage of the North Vietnamese and Vietcong could not be expressed in numbers or percentages. It was the incomparable benefit of superior élan, of an intensity of spirit compounded by the elemental drives of nationalism and anti-colonialism.'[9]

The Defence Intelligence Agency (DIA) inadvertently hampered the bombing campaign because it discounted any announcements by northern agencies or radio broadcasts as propaganda; much of it was, of course, but it still merited evaluation. The DIA applied itself to measuring the destruction inflicted by ROLLING THUNDER and this was much to McNamara's

A GVN F-105D Thunderchief shot down over North Vietnam by a Soviet S-75 Dvina surface-to-air missile. (*PAVN*)

taste. In 1966 the chairman of JCS, General Wheeler, advised President Johnson that the USAF had 'destroyed 4,700 trucks and damaged a similar number, destroyed 4,700 logistic watercraft and damaged an additional 8,700, destroyed over 800 items of railroad rolling stock and damaged a further 1,700. Destroyed sixteen locomotives and damaged fifteen.'[10] It is not suggested that Wheeler would deliberately mislead the president, but he could only reiterate figures he had been given by his staff. From a distance of fifty-four years, these rounded figures are doubtfully positive and about as valid as the body-count statistics. In order to validate the oral reports, post-strike photographs were ordered but the sheer volume of material overwhelmed the photographic interpreters.

The PAVN and VC did not take US aerial superiority lying down and soon realized that if a body of soldiers, armed with rifles, aimed off ahead of a low-flying aircraft, a cone of fire could be produced into which the aircraft would fly. This coordinated use of small arms was remarkably effective. More important was the increased assistance from Russia to the Democratic Republic of Vietnam (DRV, North Vietnam). It provided MiG fighters, AA artillery and SAM missiles. With the equipment came instructors to teach Giap's soldiers and airmen. MiG fighters claimed their first aerial victory in April 1965 and, in July, a SAM downed a second US aircraft.

By August 1967, the DRV had about 200 SAM sites and 7,000 AA guns. To back these up it had a sophisticated ground-controlled radar system and eighty MiG-21s. Hanoi was the most heavily-defended city in the world and this deterred B-52 assaults. In Giap's view, 'the northern skies were turned into a hell of fire and flak' that exacted a considerable toll of American aircraft.[11] Giap was right. American and South Vietnam aircraft losses rose from 171 in 1965 to 280 in 1966 and then on to 320 in 1967.

The DRV infrastructure was damaged, but Hanoi marshalled the population and some 500,000 people were mobilized to repair roads, railways and bridges to ensure the functionality of logistic lines of communication. Frequently the facility was operating again within a single day. River bridges were often replaced with fords. To counter the bombing, steel rails, railway ties and road-building materials were stockpiled near vulnerable sites so that the repair process could start the instant the planes withdrew. The measure of the Vietnamese determination was that, if and when a railway train was halted by damage to the line, bicycle brigades unloaded the cargo and manhandled it to a point where a relief train was waiting beyond the break.[12] While this exercise was going on, another team was repairing the damage, further evidence of the logistic capability of the DRV.

In other measures the DRV restricted travel times, and men and supplies moved only at night or in poor weather. Caches of POL were placed in tanks holding 2,200 and 3,300 gallons along major roads and, in addition, they supplemented these emergency tanks with 55-gallon oil drums concealed close by. The HCMT was re-routed through eastern Laos and Cambodia and neither of those countries was disposed to take preventive action. The weather was a factor and from September to April the thick rain clouds of the monsoon made accurate bombing impossible. In late February, just after the initiation of ROLLING THUNDER, the weather conditions caused bombing missions to be cancelled. In 1966 only 1 per cent of the year's 81,000 sorties flew against proposed fixed targets and again weather was the key reason.

The USAF, US Navy and GVN Air Force carried out the majority of their ROLLING THUNDER operations in North Vietnam with three aircraft types and their variants, none of which had been designed with an Asian campaign in mind. The aircraft were the F-105 Thunderchief, the McDonnell Douglas F-4 Phantom and the same manufacturer's A-4 Skyhawk. This latter plane was specifically designed as a carrier-borne nuclear-attack aircraft for the USN in the early 1950s. The F-105 Thunderchief was the workhorse of the campaign and it was employed on 75 per cent of all ROLLING THUNDER operations.[13]

This single-seater aircraft was huge but not sufficiently agile to excel in dogfights against MiG-21s flown by Chinese volunteers. It was susceptible to

AA fire and posed constant maintenance problems. All in all, it was not ideal. The Phantom was capable of an 8-ton bomb load, but it was also beset with problems. Among these, it was vulnerable to AA fire, had poor rear cockpit visibility and its engines emitted thick black smoke, inconveniently marking its position to AA gunners below. Finally, it had no defensive weapons and was easy meat for enemy fighters. The Skyhawk was a small aeroplane with a bomb load of 4 tons but, like the others, could not deliver those bombs in bad weather.

North of the DMZ a priority was the accurate bombing of strategic targets with minimal civilian casualties. Broadly, the lower the aircraft the more accurate the bombing, but conversely the more accurate the AA fire. US and GVN pilots were not provided with the best of aircraft and 'the combination of political, military and operational controls produced a further operational limitation on ROLLING THUNDER and that was low morale.'[14]

Lieutenant Eliot Tozer III, a Skyhawk pilot, commented, with some bitterness, his feeling and that of his comrades when he wrote:

> The frustration comes on all levels. We fly a limited aircraft, drop ordnance on rare targets in a severely limited amount of time. Worst of all, we do this in a limited and highly unpopular war … All theories aside, what I've got is personal pride pushing against a tangled web of frustration.[15]

Despite Tozer's anger, he and his comrades took the fight to their enemy whenever it was possible. The bravery of these men, many of whom gave their lives in a cause that their commander-in-chief did not seek to win against an enemy with whom he only wanted to negotiate, is remarkable and laudable. The USAF, USN, USMC, GVNAF and RAAF were equipped with myriad aircraft types. All of these had separate maintenance requirements and differently skilled ground staff, working with spares that were not interoperable. These factors added enormously to the logistic burden.

The result of ROLLING THUNDER could be expressed in the numerical terms that were close to the heart of McNamara and his staff. For example, it was reported that in one period when 643,000 tons of bombs were delivered, they destroyed 65 per cent of the DRV's oil storage capacity, 55 per cent of its major bridges, 59 per cent of its power plants, 9,821 vehicles and 1,996 railway cars. These figures are of little value unless they can be related to the declared aim. In this case, however, the aim was not achieved and the DRV still refused to talk.

The loss of aircraft apart, the campaign in 1965 had cost the USA $6.60 to inflict $1 worth of damage. In 1966 that 1 dollar's worth of damage to the DRV cost the US taxpayer $9.60. By most measurements this campaign was failing. 'By war's end, the American bombing campaigns during the Vietnam War amounted to the heaviest aerial bombardment in history, totalling 7,662,000 tons of ordnance.'[16]

In 1967 and south of the DMZ, the estimated 245,000 VC were conducting a guerrilla war. They were usually indistinguishable from the civilian population in whose ranks many were concealed, they did not engage in continuous operations and lived in and on the local economy. Headquarters USAF produced an 'Analysis of Interdiction in South-East Asia: Second Progress Report' in May 1966. It said that

> The present low requirement of 34 tons per day (for VC and PAVN troops in the south) from sources outside the South, though made up largely of ammunition, provides much less than is usually calculated for North Vietnamese forces. 36 percent of the supply support for a soldier in a North Vietnamese Light Division consists of ammunition. When he is deployed to the south this drops to 18 percent. Only 6 percent of supplies furnished to Viet Cong Main Force soldiers is ammunition. Only a 13 percent fire power utilization rate is presently being experienced by the VC/PAVN troops in South Vietnam.[17]

Increasingly, the logistic requirement of the two sides had an ever-widening gap. McNamara acknowledged, in 1967, that Communist forces fought on average only one day in thirty and that their needs from external sources were

An SVNAF pilot jumps into the sea from his fatally damaged aircraft; his fate is unknown.

minimal: 13 tons per day. The needs of the Long Binh base alone exceeded that by multiples of fifty.

Perversely, the bombing campaign actually stimulated the support given to the DRV by Russia and China who answered appeals from Hanoi. The gauge of Vietnamese railway tracks was altered to be compatible with the Chinese gauge and, when that was accomplished, 1,000 tons of supplies arrived daily by way of the North-East Railway.[18]

The influx of logistic support from the two major Communist powers in 1965 alone was around $300 million. The by-product of this was to increase the GNP of the DRV by 6 per cent. The largesse did not stop there, and by 1968 economic aid had reached $600 million and $1 billion in military assistance. In effect, America was now fighting a proxy war and could only take comfort from the fact that China and Russia had very strained relations as both vied for influence over the DRV.

Almost 90 per cent of ROLLING THUNDER's energy was expended on transportation-related targets. The target acquisition gnomes in Washington must have been aware of Churchill's dictum (p. 3). The movement of men and matériel was affected, but not sufficiently to stop the infiltration into South Vietnam or the movement of the relatively small tonnage of supplies. The DRV husbanded its POL and, as an economy, its trains were fuelled by coal or wood. It had a need for 32,000 tons of oil per year, but had amassed a stockpile of 60,000 tons by the end of 1966. The HCMT was no longer a track just for porters, and trucks now plied the north-south routes; they required about 1,000 tons of oil per year.[19] In the 1960s Vietnamese people were accustomed to the use of candles and oil lamps. Electricity was a 'nice to have' for most of the population and so, when power stations were destroyed in 1967, 2,000 portable generators filled the electricity gap.

By the end of 1967 it was starting to dawn on Washington and McNamara in particular that this was an unwinnable war and the prime objective was to find a way to exit the country with as much dignity as possible and at whatever the cost.

Chapter Seventeen

Civil Operations and Revolutionary Development Support (CORDS)

'When we conquer our enemies by kind treatment and by acts of justice, we are more likely to secure their obedience than by victory in the field of battle.'[1]

[Polybius]

In 1966 the USA was committed to Westmoreland's four attrition policies: first, 'Search and Destroy'; second, 'body count'; third and fourth, enthusiastically bombing the large areas of defoliated forest in which the targets lived. There was a clear, complementary and cohesive plan but, by late 1967, it was not producing the desired results. There is one further policy that ran in parallel with the other four. This was the programme, the title of which seems to be contrived to produce the acronym CORDS.

The object of the exercise was the pacification of South Vietnam and, simplistically, to achieve this, the largely rural population of the country was to be housed in areas under the control of either the GVN or the USA. This did not represent original thought. The separation of the civilian population from the Vietcong was vital and the exercise was a very well-trodden path. However, the VC were civilians, they were integrated into their community, they looked and sounded like other South Vietnamese. They were difficult to identify and as such they were the acme of a guerrilla force. The key word in all of this was 'separation'. The Phoenix Programme (see p. 193) sought to address this issue.

Robert Komer, an American civil servant who had the descriptive nickname 'Blowtorch Bob', was selected to lead the 'Hearts and Minds' initiative from its initiation in May 1967. Komer had the responsibility of forming and then leading a mixed organization of civilians and military from both South Vietnam and the USA.[2] He was granted ambassador status and three-star rank (lieutenant general) so that he could command military personnel. The activities of his organization were supported by the MACV, which provided all the considerable logistic requirements.

The background to Komer's appointment is that, in 1965, the US Army Chief of Staff, General H.K Johnson had a meeting with Bernard Fall, the chronicler of Dien Bien Phu. Fall's opinions caused Johnson to reconsider the manner of American operations. He assembled a team of young junior officers with experience as 'military advisors' and told them to develop an alternative to Westmoreland's attrition strategy. In March 1966 the team reported and produced a 'Programme for the Pacification and Long-Term Development of South Vietnam' (PROVN). The report was wide-ranging, innovative, insightful and brutally candid. It rejected body count as a strategy and argued that the highest priority should be pacification. It was critical of the poor and divided management that stemmed from the interface between the MACV and the GVN. Interestingly, it recommended the reduction in the authority of COMUSMACV (Westmoreland) and passing it to an individual, at ambassador level, who would become the pro-consul and, as such, sole manager of United States activity in the country, including the military. Predictably, Westmoreland and his staff bridled at this assault on their well-established status, authority and strategy. They identified PROVN as combatting Phase 1 (Insurgency) and argued that it had been overtaken by events as the war was already into Phase 2 (Insurgency and conventional war). Phase 3 (All-out conventional war) was close to hand.[3] The PROVN report was strong medicine, too much for the MACV, and was quietly allowed to wither but it did not die.

Now, barely a year later Komer had been appointed and his stated aim was to win the support of the civilian population for the GVN and by so doing replace the VC and degrade its malign influence. This was not the first attempt at pacification that the GVN had tried and failed. The Ngo Dinh Diem government of 1955–63 had held sway in the centres of population, but been unable to extend that control into the rural villages. In 1959 Diem activated his version of the 'agroville programme' first tried by the French. The plan was to move peasants from their ancestral land into new settlements with all the advantages of the twentieth century such as schools, medical facilities and transport. The marketing of the programme not only failed to convince the people at who it was aimed, but it was unsympathetically managed and subject to effective, active VC resistance.

The GVN's next move in 1961 had been to copy the successful British pattern that had worked well in Malaya and Sir Robert Thompson assisted in designing the 'Strategic Hamlet Program'. Under this new plan rural peasants were to be moved into fortified villages that they could defend and, furthermore, it would isolate them from VC influence. The programme was rushed into being but, by 1964, 2,600 of the strategic hamlets were under VC control.[4] Clearly, it had failed.

That year, 1964, the MACV and the US Embassy played a part in the organization of the *Chien Thang* (Struggle for Victory) pacification programme. This approach was different, and it envisaged establishing an expanding area of GVN-controlled territory by the provision of armed security, social and material support. It did not succeed as the GVN and its army's (ARVN's) efforts were unable to win over the areas contested by the VC.

It was against a background of successive failure that Komer set out to weld together a diverse group consisting of the MACV, Department of State, CIA and the Agency of International Development. Komer shrewdly did not challenge Westmoreland. He believed that 'Search and Destroy' was an obstacle to his work but appreciated that only the military had the men, matériel and money to make the programme work and he accepted Westmoreland's primacy. He formed the Office of Civil Operations (OCO) to coordinate all the elements of a pacification programme.

Komer decided on a structure that layered his military and civilian staff. Initially he had 4,980 people, a number that rapidly increased to 8,327 after the first six months of operations. By 1968 CORDS personnel were employed in all forty-four provinces and soon after it was functioning in 250 districts of South Vietnam.[5] The CORDS organization was predominantly military: about 85 per cent were uniformed.[6]

Komer made a start by taking responsibility for the training and support of Popular Forces (PF) and Regional Forces (RF), the two para-military organizations concerned with rural security. Komer was a 'doer' and, under his drive and sense of urgency, the strength of both organizations rose, their weapons and equipment were updated and their training improved. At the same time, he set about ruthlessly eliminating identified VC members. Unfortunately, those who operated the Phoenix programme were less than meticulous and an uncounted number of innocent Vietnamese were murdered in the cause of pacification. Brutal as the programme was, it was also ineffective. Komer had his critics, and one judged that

> what Komer erected was a hodgepodge of competing United States and GVN intelligence agencies, manned by incompetent and inexperienced people, tied together in a corporate effort rather than by a unity of command. It never succeeded in identifying and locating the heart of the Viet Cong underground movement.[7]

Another historian commented that CORDS was 'an illusion of progress'.[8] To balance those negative opinions, others saw the programme as 'a successful integration of civilian and military effort' in which, by 1970, allegedly 93 per cent of South Vietnam was thought to be living in 'relatively secure' villages. For unqualified success Komer was dependent upon the totally corrupt GVN and its army. He was betrayed on a constant basis from within and was, in effect, trying to build a castle on sand. Komer himself admitted that CORDS was 'too little, too late'. The programme ceased in February 1973 on the withdrawal of US forces.

Chapter Eighteen

Surprise: Khe Sanh and the Tet Offensive

'Any officer or non-commissioned officer who shall suffer himself to be surprised ... must not expect to be forgiven.'[1]
[Major General Sir James Wolfe]

By late 1967 America's leaders were slowly accepting that this was a war that could not be won even though, by most measurements, it *was* winning. With its allies South Vietnam, Australia, New Zealand and South Korea it mustered 1,173,800 men, of whom a very significant proportion were in the logistic tail.[2] Westmoreland belatedly recognized the merits of the pacification programme; he pronounced that 'the real objective is the people.'[3] The bulk of ARVN assets were to be directed towards pacification and the US and other allies would fight the war. Despite this earnest pronouncement, the financial fact belies it. For the Fiscal Year 1968, $14 billion was spent on bombing and ground offensives, but only $850 million on pacification.

During 1967 Westmoreland had tried, consistently, to bring the enemy to battle and with that aim he mounted two major logistically-demanding operations: CEDAR FALLS and later JUNCTION CITY. These operations were focused near centres of population; however, they had failed to find any significant PAVN headquarters, depots or hospitals. They seized sufficient rice 'to feed a Vietcong division for a year' and small arms and ammunition were taken. The two major sweeps accounted for 3,500 enemy dead at a cost of 354 Americans. Body count apart, the Americans did not consider the operations to be unqualified successes. These operations did, however, have some intangible benefits, not least that Generals Giap and Thanh viewed the incursions as 'disasters' and were convinced that they should not base their main force units anywhere near populated areas. Consequently, they felt obliged to withdraw to their border sanctuaries.

The degree of continuing aggressive hostility of Ho Chi Minh was not fully appreciated in the USA. In April 1967, at the 13th Plenum of the Communist Party's Central Committee, Ho was the leading proponent of a vote to mount

General Giap and General Nguyen Chi Thanh. The men were usually at loggerheads. Thanh commanded the VC in the South. (*PAVN*)

a major offensive against the South to coincide with the Tet holiday at the end of January 1968. Giap was opposed to this because he was not convinced that the people of South Vietnam would rise up in support. Giap favoured a protracted war that the American public would not stomach. Nevertheless, as a good soldier he accepted the decision and planned accordingly. His personal position and standing suddenly improved with the unexpected death of General Nguyen Chi Thanh, who had been his 'deadly rival' for years.[4]

Meanwhile, the Chinese strove to strengthen ties with North Vietnam and when briefed on the strategic plan it promptly 'offered 100,000 logistic troops and truck drivers and 200,000 rail and road maintenance workers. They also promised 107mm and 240mm artillery pieces, the latter having a range of 18 miles.'[5]

At this same time, the US Marines maintained a 'combat base' near the small town of Khe Sanh. It was of no strategic importance, but it had an airstrip and ground access by way of Route 9, although the road was little more than a track. The base dated from 1962 when it was the base for US Army Special Forces. They used it to train 'Civilian Irregular Defense Groups' whose role was to monitor PAVN infiltration and to provide security for the local population.

In March 1967, and while manned by only a single Marine company, the Khe Sanh Combat Base (KSCB) was attacked over a period of twelve days. The Marines were quickly reinforced to four-battalion strength as they confronted two PAVN main force regiments. In the fighting that ensued, 900 PAVN soldiers were killed. The Americans lost 150 dead and 400 wounded.

Later, during the summer of 1967 a build-up of PAVN troops in the area of Khe Sanh was noted and Westmoreland caused the introduction of elements of the 26th Marine Regiment to bolster the garrison. It has been suggested that the initially ill-concealed concentration of PAVN troops was specifically designed to attract American attention and to encourage the reinforcement of Khe Sanh Combat Base (KSCB). If this was the case, then the ploy worked. Intelligence sources noted that, during October 1967, the number of trucks heading south via Laos on the HCMT had increased from a previous average of 480 to 1,116. Significantly, by November there was a veritable flood of 3,823 vehicles and, in December, 6,315.[6] Clearly a major logistic operation was under way and it was sufficient to cause Westmoreland to cable Washington on 20 December, saying that he expected the Viet Cong and North Vietnamese 'to undertake an intensified countrywide effort, perhaps a maximum effort, over a relatively short period of time.'[7]

Military men have striven for centuries to surprise their adversary. The history books are replete with examples and, in the majority of cases, it is surprise that carries the day. Sun Tzu in 500 BC, Thucydides and Xenophon in around 404 BC and Frederick the Great in 1747 all waxed eloquent on the

The USMC combat base at Khe Sanh. (*Captain Moyars S. Shore II*)

merits of surprise. The D-Day landings are a more recent example of successful strategic surprise.

In early November 1967, a Vietcong soldier's notebook fell into American hands and, when translated, the key passage read as follows:

> The central headquarters has ordered the entire army and people of South Vietnam to implement general offensive and general uprising in order to achieve a decisive victory ... Use very strong military attacks in coordination with the uprisings of the local population to take over towns and cities. Troops should flood the lowlands. They should move toward liberating the capital city [Saigon], take power and try to rally enemy brigades and regiments to our side one by one. Propaganda should be broadly disseminated among the population in general, and leaflets should be used to reach enemy officers and enlisted personnel.[8]

The notebook had been captured near the DMZ and in an area where Giap was known to be assembling troops, probably for an attack on Khe Sanh. The US intelligence organization dismissed the notebook as mere disinformation and it was ignored. Later, General Bruce Palmer commented that this was an 'an allied intelligence failure ranking with Pearl Harbor in 1941.'[9]

During January 1968 the PAVN moved thousands of men, and the logistics to support them, into South Vietnam. The Central Office South Vietnam (COSVN) activated all of its Vietcong membership and specially-trained Commando units were infiltrated into cities and towns across the South. Their weapons were transported covertly in loads of farm produce and cached along with ammunition. These extraordinary logistic preparations were made in complete secrecy. Considering the vast numbers of people who were actively involved and, in addition, those who were not involved but nevertheless witnessed the arrangements being put in place, it is amazing that there were no leaks of information. This multitude of men had to be hidden and fed for several weeks, yet the MACV and GVN were entirely unaware of the magnitude of the coming storm. The tunnels of Cu Chi were used as assembly points and logistic bases for the assault on Saigon. The MACV was wary and watchful but anticipated that the Tet holiday would be uneventful.

All the evidence shows that, by late 1967, Giap had selected Khe Sanh for his first Phase III, set-piece 'conventional battle'. He had assembled a major force of two divisions around the KSCB with all the attendant logistic support. The base itself was unimportant; it was the anticipated military victory that was very important. The saga of Khe Sanh is dealt with in Chapter 20.

On the night of 29/30 January 1968 VC forces attacked six cities; these attacks were unsuccessful and were repulsed. It later emerged that these attacks were premature and the result of a communications breakdown between Giap and his subordinates. It had the effect of alerting the MACV and, as a precaution, ARVN soldiers on leave for the holiday were ordered back to duty. Many either did not get the message, ignored it or could not get back in time.

The full fury of the *Tong Cong Kich-Tong Khoi Ngia* (General Offensive, General Uprising, usually referred to as TCK-TKN) was unleashed during the night of 30/31 January 1968. Although some of the initial surprise element had been lost, the range of targeted towns and cities was daunting for both Americans and the GVN. The Communists enjoyed early success, not least in the historic city of Hue.

In Saigon, a unit of nineteen Commandos attacked the US Embassy and got inside the compound and although they did not achieve their aim, all being killed, the impact of that single, well-recorded incident resonated with the American public.

The Tet offensive was 'bold and imaginative'. It had 'an element of surprise', but its deficiencies outweighed its merits. The plan 'violated two of the most hallowed principles of war, those of simplicity and mass.'[10] To succeed, TCK-TKN required sophisticated coordination and communication arrangements, but the PAVN/VC did not have either the equipment or the trained

The US Ambassador, Ellsworth Bunker, views a dead Vietcong who had been sent to kill him.

An American soldier, in the ruins of Hue Fig, engages a target over the bodies of two fallen comrades.

personnel to manage the attacks on multiple targets across the length and breadth of South Vietnam. To compound this weakness Giap spread his forces too thinly on the ground and only in Hue and Saigon did he concentrate sufficient force to have the desired impact. He created a logistic nightmare once battle was joined because efficient re-supply of his soldiers, operating in penny packets, became impossible. The VC had to live off the land, at the expense of the civilian population.

The ARVN soldiers stood firm and acquitted themselves with fortitude and courage. The population did not rise, and the successes of the offensive were limited and impermanent. The VC had no plans for withdrawal and as the offensive faltered, piecemeal retreat was heavily punished by the USAF. Giap should have known much better, but he underestimated the American capacity for mobility.

Westmoreland could deliver reinforcements at will with his aerial superiority, and transport was, as it has ever been, a key component of the American response. Ho Chi Minh's presumptions were that, first, ARVN soldiers would defect; second, that the population would rise in support and third, that the offensive would succeed across the board. This all meant that Giap did not have a 'Plan B'.

Only in Saigon for two weeks and in Hue for almost a month did the fighting extend for any length of time. The majority of the aggressors were members of the Vietcong and it suffered shattering casualties. The Communists lost 'between 45,000 and 84,000' (Davidson). 'Nearly 90,000 replacements' were needed (Currey). '50,000 enemy troops had been killed' (Karnow). '45,267 dead, 61,287 wounded, 5,070 missing' (People's Army of Vietnam Department of Warfare 114th TGi document 1.103. February 1969). Every source consulted gives different figures, but all are huge.

This was probably the closest that Westmoreland got to his derided 'cross-over point'. The Tet Offensive was a resounding defeat for the PAVN and VC. The US and GVN had triumphed and destroyed the VC in South Vietnam. However, unfortunately the offensive was seen live on TV and the images transformed American public opinion.

Tet was a disaster for Giap; COSVN acknowledged that the offensive had failed only two days after the first premature assault. In a captured document, it said

> we failed to seize a number of primary objectives and to destroy mobile and defensive units of the army. We also failed to hold occupied areas. In the political field we failed to motivate the people to stage uprisings ... the troop-proselytizing activities...were not conducted on a broad front. We cannot, therefore, achieve total victory in a short period.[11]

It has to be said that the authenticity of this document is open to question and not least because of the haste of its preparation and distribution. Davidson sums it up by saying 'the document is an enigma, one whose timing is still a mystery. Although the intelligence community, of which he was one (author's

Hue, February 1968; few of the men are armed. Dead VC or civilians lie close by, apparently arranged for the camera.

note), has generally accepted the document as authentic.'[12] The comprehensive defeat of the VC and its virtual eradication worked very much to the advantage of Komer's pacification programme, which was able to continue with markedly less hindrance.

Khe Sanh remained a PAVN/VC objective and Westmoreland was determined to hold it. He saw it as a base for future clandestine forays into Laos and the PAVN heartland and believed that it provided 'flank security'. He also considered that the KSCB was 'even more critical from a psychological viewpoint'.[13] Opinions were divided on the merits of Westmoreland's decision and Dr Arthur Schlesinger, the Harvard University historian, wrote scathingly in the *Washington Post* on 22 March 1968, damning Westmoreland's performance in command. Notwithstanding the victory at Tet, he observed that 'Lincoln had run through a long string of generals before he got to Grant. He would not have suffered Westmoreland for three months.'[14]

The Tet offensive drew to public attention a serious logistic deficiency that, hitherto, had been under wraps. It concerned that most basic of a soldier's equipment: his rifle.

Chapter Nineteen

The M16 Rifle Debacle

'During the Tet Offensive the crisp rattling sounds of AK-47s echoing in Saigon and some other cities seemed to make a mockery of the weaker single-shot Garands and carbines fired by stupefied friendly troops.'[1]

[Lieutenant General Dong Van Khuyen]

The US was in South Vietnam to preserve the GVN and defeat communism. The ARVN was by far its largest and most committed ally and was dependent upon the USA for logistic support. Curiously, when improved weaponry became available to US forces it was not distributed to ARVN soldiers and, in one case, this situation swelled into a public debacle.

It all stemmed from the fact that the ARVN was armed with Second World War cast-off weapons such as the semi-automatic M1 rifle. This rifle weighed in at 11lb and was 43in in length; the Vietnamese soldier who carried it was, in most cases, only about 5 feet (1.5m) tall and weighed about 90lb (41kg). The M1 Garand rifle was obsolete from 1957 and, thereafter, the US National Guard rejected it.

The M1 was a weapon of the 1930s and, when first introduced, it set a new benchmark for military rifles. It was named after its designer John Garand and, in its time, was described by General George Patton as 'the greatest battle implement ever devised'.[2] The general was speaking in about 1944 but, since then, the M1 had been superseded by the M14 in 1957. This was a much-improved selective-fire automatic rifle with a twenty-round magazine which was based upon the M1 and fired the highly-destructive 7.62mm round. The M14 was, in turn, replaced by the M16 and its 5.56mm ammunition. Thus the M1 rifle being used by the ARVN was two full generations out of date.

On the other hand, the PAVN and VC were armed with the automatic AK-47. Most of the fighting in all the Vietnam wars was conducted at short ranges: 200 yards or less and often at ranges of 20 yards or less. In the assault the communist soldiers had a massive fire-power advantage with probably the best weapon of its type in the world. The initials 'AK' represent *Avtomat*

Kalashnikova, Russian for 'automatic Kalashnikov', after its designer, Mikhail Timofeyevich Kalashnikov, who developed the accepted version of the weapon in 1947.

Almost from the moment of its official adoption by the Soviet military in 1949, the AK-47 was recognized as being simple to operate, rugged, reliable under trying conditions and suitable for mass production.

Built around a 7.62mm round with a muzzle velocity of some 700 metres per second, the AK-47 had a cyclic firing rate of some 600 rounds per minute and was capable of both semi-automatic and automatic fire. A long, curved, box magazine held thirty rounds, and a separate gas-return tube above the barrel held a piston that was forced back upon firing to activate the mechanisms that ejected the spent cartridge and cocked the hammer for the next round.[3]

The AK-47 was manufactured in two basic designs, one with a wooden stock and the other, designated the AKS, with a folding metal stock. The AK-47 has made it into *The Guinness Book of World Records* as the most widely-spread weapon in the world, with 100 million Kalashnikov rifles currently in use (as of 2020). It is alleged that AK-47s have caused more deaths than artillery fire, air strikes and rocket attacks combined. An estimated 250,000 people are killed by Kalashnikovs every year.

It was in January 1963, after 'extensive trials' at the Aberdeen Proving Ground and in Vietnam that General Earle Wheeler reported, optimistically, that the new rifle, designated the M16, was 'superior to the Kalashnikov'. The weapon weighed 6.35lb and the stock of black plastic helped to keep the weight down.

In December of that year an order for 104,000 rifles was placed with the Colt's Manufacturing Company. After the first copies of the M16 were issued, initial enthusiasm waned when serious design flaws started to emerge. The army criterion was for an automatic rifle that was effective at 500 yards. This imposed strain on the working parts of a very light automatic weapon and led to malfunction. This was exacerbated by the use of a cartridge powered by 'ball powder'. This extremely powerful propellant dispatched the round the

The 5.56mm M16 Rifle, of which, with its many variants, 8 million were manufactured. It was not superseded until the mid-1980s. (*www.loopjamaica.com*)

required 500 yards, but at a price. The cartridge caused unacceptable barrel fouling. The rifle frequently jammed and usually at highly inconvenient moments. It seems to be extraordinary that after 'extensive trials' these faults had not emerged before.

The army and Colt's had effectively put a prototype into mass production and were fine-tuning it as it failed in the troops' hands.[4]

The M16 rifle with its smaller, lighter 5.56mm round allowed the US soldier to carry more ammunition but that, in turn, led to the profligate, un-aimed and ineffective use of ammunition. The US system was able to cope with this increased use of small-arms' ammunition and its provision was not a significant factor in logistics management. Eugene Stoner, the designer of the original version of the M16, explained the apparent paradox of the smaller bullet's destructive power when he said

> the advantage that a small or light bullet has over a heavy one when it comes to wound ballistics ... What it amounts to is the fact that bullets are stabilized to fly through the air, and not through water, or a body, which is approximately the same density as the water. And they are stable as long as they are in the air. When they hit something, they immediately go unstable [that is to say they tumble, end over end; author's note]. If you are talking about .30-caliber [like that in the M14], this might remain stable through a human body.... While a little bullet, being it has a low mass, it senses an instability situation faster and reacts much faster ... this is what makes a little bullet pay off so much in wound ballistics.[5]

In 1966 the soldiers, now armed with the M16, were not only combatting a capable enemy but doing so with a highly inefficient weapon, notwithstanding the endorsement by its designer. After perhaps only one round was fired, the empty case, which should be ejected, lodged in the working parts, sometimes in the chamber. This eventuality could only be resolved by the pushing of a cleaning rod down the barrel, probably while under fire. This presupposes that the soldier with the jammed rifle had a cleaning rod, but there was a 'chronic shortage of cleaning kits, in which case many men had to rely on phone wire or nylon cord to use as a pull-through. Some men wrote home, asking their families to buy and send out cleaning rods. Of 2,000 M16s tested by armourers, 384 malfunctioned.'[6] Every soldier has to have confidence in his personal weapon upon which his life depends. In this case the propensity to jam was an inhibiting factor on operations and it had a deleterious effect on morale in infantry units. This rifle was a logistic disaster:

> Far from being maintenance-free, the M16 rifle needed maintenance at regular intervals. The M16's gas impingement operating system diverts

hot gunpowder gases that follow the bullet out of the muzzle, through a tube, sending it back into the rifle's upper receiver. This gas pushes the bolt backward, ejecting the empty brass cartridge, picking up a fresh new cartridge, and cycling the weapon action again. In semi-automatic mode this process repeats itself with each pull of the trigger, while in fully automatic mode it will repeat itself as long as the trigger is held down. One issue with the gas impingement system is that in addition to hot gases the tube sends back carbon and other gunpowder residue, which left uncleaned can corrode the chamber, leading to malfunctions. The hot gases and residue issue worsened with the use of the new propellant and subsequently higher rate of fire, increasing the need for regular cleaning. This issue, combined with the tendency of troops to not clean their weapons, led to frequent malfunctions. This worsened with the use of the new propellant and subsequently higher rate of fire, increasing the need for regular cleaning.[7]

The need for frequent cleaning of the rifle was not the only problem. The ammunition was not engineered to cope with the high humidity of South-East Asia and it corroded, a sure-fire cause of jamming. The lips of the magazine bent very easily and the consequence of that was that the rounds were not fed into the breach. The Department of Defense had been offered the option to chrome-plate the chamber but declined, presumably on cost grounds. It was a poor decision because the effect was frequent corrosion of the chamber. The rifle stock was flimsy and had a tendency to crack. Barrel, bolt carrier group and other steel parts rusted. It was found that brass ammunition casings were too soft and that led not only to damage to the rims but also jams during the extraction process. Reports of the failure rate of this allegedly state-of-the-art rifle were disquieting. The malfunctioning rifles were repeatedly blamed for contributing to the deaths of soldiers in firefights, and some soldiers and Marines even elected to carry AK-47s instead.[8] One soldier commented acidly:

> We left with seventy-two men in our platoon and came back with nineteen. Believe it or not, you know what killed most of us? Our own rifle. Practically every one of our dead was found with his (M16) torn down next to him, where he had been trying to fix it.[9]

The US Army sought to conceal what was by now a growing public scandal. Its position was that there were 'teething troubles', but that the prime cause of weapon malfunction was inadequate cleaning. The 'Advanced Research Development Agency', under the direction of Colonel Richard Hallocks, took charge of a policy to conceal the manifest deficiencies of the M16. The object of the exercise was to keep Congress ignorant of the matter, and that borders on malfeasance. Nevertheless, and despite Hallocks' best efforts, news of the dire performance of the M16 was widespread and it was the soldiers who publicized the problem.

Soldiers and Marines wrote home, some to their local newspapers. There was a gathering storm at home to match the anger in Vietnam. Lieutenant Michael Chernevak was one of those who wrote home and he told of how, in one engagement, forty M16s malfunctioned. He sent copies of his letter to his congressman Bobby Kennedy and the *Washington Post*. The USMC did not investigate the cause of Chernevak's letter but the officer himself for corresponding with the press, and he was reprimanded.

Westmoreland laid claim to a fervent wish to equip the ARVN with the M16, but in fact did little to achieve that aim. He conceded that 'upon my departure in the summer of 1968 only a fraction of Vietnamese forces had been equipped'.[10] Apparently, there was a fear that this potent weapon could be captured from the ARVN and used against US forces. No credence was given to it being captured from US soldiers too.

Eventually, and despite the half-hearted political manoeuvring of Westmoreland, the M16 issue reached President Johnson by way of General Bruce Clarke, a retired Second World War commander who had visited South Vietnam at the behest of the president in February 1968. Within three days of Clarke's return to the USA, he recorded that 'a presidential aide called me to say that the president had released 100,000 M16 rifles to the ARVN.'[11]

Two months later, the newly-appointed Secretary of State for Defense, Clark Clifford, announced 'a dramatic increase in the US production of the M16 so as to equip all ARVN units by mid-summer.'[12] This was a significant move away from McNamara's previous policy of ignoring the issue.

In August 1968, on leaving Vietnam, General Fred Weyand emphasized that 'the long delay in furnishing ARVN modern weapons and equipment, at least on a par with that furnished to the enemy by Russia and China, has been a major contributing factor to ARVN ineffectiveness.'[13]

Initially, the rifle's poor performance was the direct result of economies forced on the designers. Some of the problems identified by 1966 were corrected by 1968 and new variants of the M16 were certainly improved and more reliable. It was only after re-design that the M16 and its multiple variants met the aspirations of the men using it. By 1970, the new rifle, now designated the M16A1, had replaced the older rifles. It had taken four years for the rifle to become as reliable as originally advertised but, in those four years, it had caused the death of many of those who carried it. The M16A1 remained in service for a further fifteen years before the US Army and Marines sought new upgrades to the long-serving rifle.[14]

The Tet offensive threw into sharp contrast the disparity between the M1 rifle wielded by the ARVN and the AK-47 in the hands of their enemy. Tet was the catalyst that unlocked a Pandora's Box of logistic mismanagement that was a negative factor in ground operations over a critical period.

Chapter Twenty

The Siege of Khe Sanh

'The objective is not the occupation of a geographical
position but the destruction of the enemy force.'[1]

[General Piotr A. Rumyantsev]

At this point we must backtrack to 1967 and consider one of the more critical battles fought by the Americans in Vietnam. This was the siege of Khe Sanh, named for the adjacent village of the same name. Here a defended perimeter was designated the Khe Sanh Combat Base (KSCB). It was located about 7 miles south of the DMZ and about the same distance from the Laotian border. The military merits of Khe Sanh were few. It straddled Route 9 which went from east to west and continued on into Laos. However, Route 9 was little more than a track, but it did provide a second, fragile line of communication and re-supply. There was, in addition, an airstrip and a water source. The three-month siege of Khe Sanh exemplified the criticality of logistic re-supply and its integral transport system, in this case aerial.

The area is, for the most part, forest with significant hills that rise steeply around the base. It is a wet, dank place, prone to fog and heavy rain. The environment is as hostile as any in South-East Asia. The village had a population of several hundred who worked the coffee plantations which were under French ownership. Some 2 miles north of the village was a plateau 1,447ft above sea level, upon which were the remains of a concrete fort built by the French in de Lattre's time in command. Alongside the fort was the grass airstrip over which, in the early 1960s, a carpet of interlocking metal sheets had been laid to give it an all-weather capability.

The Americans had occupied the village area since July 1962 when Special Forces arrived to befriend the local Bru Montagnards. These people had been persuaded to settle in these parts by the ARVN in order that they could be protected and more importantly not exploited by the VC. These people numbered about 8,000 and were scattered over several square miles. A company of the US Marine Corps (USMC) took up residence in 1966. However, because they and the Special Forces were incompatible, the latter moved out and established a new camp about 5 miles away in the direction of Laos, at the village of Lang Vei.

The United States had a wealth of assets. The Special Forces (Green Berets) reported to the army chain of command and the CIA who, in conjunction with the ARVN, controlled intelligence operations. However, this intelligence was not shared with the Marines, just 5 miles away. The USMC was proud of its self-sufficiency. It had its own air arm, its own artillery and its own culture, procedures and chain of command. The senior USMC officers looked to US Navy headquarters in Honolulu rather than to Westmoreland and the MACV. The tribal attitudes of American forces at Khe Sanh were such that they all but caused a breakdown in effective operations. However, it was the same logistic chain that had to support all American and GVN forces, despite the rifts in personal relations that were a feature of this brief campaign.

There are some who seek to align Khe Sanh with the siege of Dien Bien Phu in 1954, conducted not a million miles away. Ho Chi Minh, Giap and the People's Army of North Vietnam (PAVN) had allowed the victory at DBP to become a national matter of myth and fantasy. It was accorded a value beyond its strictly military worth and it coloured future military decision-making. There are parallels between DBP and Khe Sanh, but they are relatively minor and differ in one key respect.

The principal difference is a matter of logistic support and aerial striking capacity. The French had, at best, 200 assorted and badly maintained aircraft; the Americans 2,000 very well-maintained modern aircraft. It had limitless high-explosive ordnance and the means to deliver it. The two garrisons differed little in scale and both did have a symbolic political importance. By 1967 the war in Vietnam figured large on TV screens in American homes and every day there was a growing anti-war movement. Sight of the constant import of coffins had a profound effect on American public opinion and it nourished the anti-war faction. It follows that the USA could not afford to be defeated at Khe Sanh.

The hierarchy in Hanoi was determined to recreate the DBP scenario and it was encouraged by the US media which was almost unanimously anti-war and anti-South Vietnamese in tone. In French operations at Dien Bien Phu a high proportion of the soldiers killed were colonial troops; in American operations in Vietnam it was very different: the dead were all the 'boys next door'.

In late 1967, the American press reported, or to be more accurate speculated, on American failures and highlighted the corruption of President Thieu's government. This was all grist to Ho Chi Minh's mill. In effect the US armed forces now had two enemies: the Communist forces of North Vietnam and the American media. The only ally was the corrupt and inefficient Government of South Vietnam (GVN). The morale of all soldiers, throughout history, has depended not only on water, food, ammunition and dry boots. It also is dependent upon the wholehearted support of the country

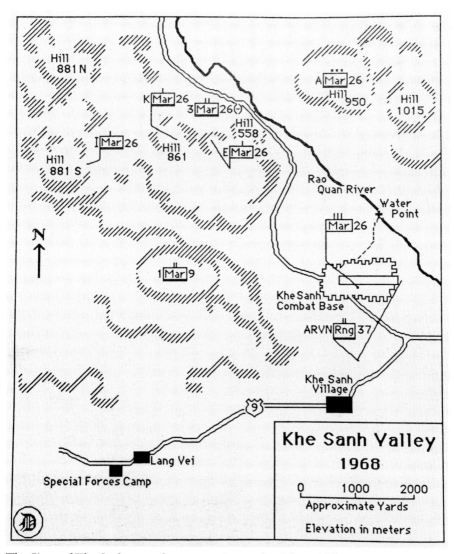

The Siege of Khe Sanh: note the water point on the right, middle. (*Davidson*)

it represents. That wholehearted support of all the American people was now absent, and a vociferous minority was working actively against the war.

Westmoreland's rationale for holding on to Khe Sanh has been a topic of discussion for more than fifty years. In 1964 he had said that

> Khe Sanh could serve as a patrol base blocking enemy infiltration from Laos; a base for . . . operations to harass the enemy in Laos; an airstrip for

reconnaissance to survey the Ho Chi Minh Trail; a western anchor for the defences south of the DMZ; and an eventual jumping-off point for ground operations to cut the Ho Chi Minh Trail.[2]

In March 1967 the defences of KSCB were enhanced by the efforts of a US Navy construction team who built new bunkers and living facilities. This may have provoked the PAVN because, soon after, Marine patrols encountered elements of the 325th Division on Hills 861 and 881 (so named because of their height). These were two of the three high points north and west of the base. Having suffered twelve dead, the Marines helicoptered in a company to occupy Hill 861 and a full battalion into the main base area. There followed a series of savage encounters that came to be known as 'the hill fights' that lasted for a week and cost the PAVN 'about 700 dead'.[3] The PAVN withdrew but refocused on Lang Vei, killing twenty-six of the defenders and wounding thirty-six. The intermittent fighting continued and the body count rose accordingly, and by late July, fifty-two US soldiers had died.

A battery of artillery made its way to the base by way of Route 9 on 9 June, and in August command of KSCB and the 6,000 Marines at Khe Sanh was assumed by Colonel D.E. Lownds, a very experienced officer with thirty-six years of service.

It was at about this time that Westmoreland endorsed his earlier view when he told General Wheeler that Khe Sanh was important as a base for clandestine teams operating cross-border in Laos, that it provided 'flank security' but that it was 'even more critical from a psychological viewpoint because to relinquish this area would be a major propaganda victory for the enemy.'[4] However, Westmoreland did not carry all his officers with him. The decision to hold KSCB was the source of conflict between the senior officers of the USMC and Westmoreland. The questionable strategic value of this area of forest and the logistic support it required was challenged. Lieutenant General Victor Krulak was one outspoken critic who wrote: 'I hated the bad choice to put them there. It was a tactical albatross.'[5] Krulak had a point.

Relationships were not helped when Westmoreland had to seek assurances from General Cushman, the senior Marine Corps officer, because he had had reports that the garrison at KSCB had not yet 'dug in'. The 'digging-in' process is second nature to soldiers the world over whenever they occupy a defensive position. It was not something that should have attracted four-star attention.

The general decided to upgrade KSCB and to ready it for the forays he intended to make into Laos. To do this it was first necessary to further improve the defences. Trees selected for their timber were difficult to cut because in many cases their trunks held shrapnel, relics of artillery fire from

A picture is worth a thousand words!

the earlier fighting. Chainsaw blades were broken on this shrapnel, and any tree, successfully felled, immediately started to rot and provide a haven for termites. The only solution was for prepared hardwood to be imported. This bulky and heavy load added to the logistic burden.

The perimeter of KSCB, initially about 400 yards by 200 yards, started to expand. Stone was quarried from a site about a mile away and building material of all sorts arrived on a succession of aircraft. The metal mats on the airstrip were ripped up and replaced, in itself a significant engineering and labour-intensive task. Logistically, the build-up in Khe Sanh was all-embracing. Ammunition was stockpiled, and artillery tubes, 4.2in mortars and ten tracked vehicles were flown in.

In early January 1968 American technology paid off. Operation MUSCLE SHOALS was testing surveillance equipment in south-east Laos and in that operation a series of electronic sensors had been sown. They revealed increasing activity by the PAVN on the Ho Chi Minh Trail.[6] This was in addition to the earlier and already noted heavy traffic on the trail during October-December 1967 (see p. 197, Chapter 18). The intelligence produced by the CIA road watch teams and the deceptively-named 'Vietnam Studies and Observation Group' combined with aerial reconnaissance photographs was sufficient to alert the MACV that North Vietnam was intent on launching a major operation. These latest hi-tech gadgets identified the sound of trucks or footfall and relayed the intelligence to circling USAF aircraft. Other aircraft carried chemical sniffers that, allegedly, could detect sweat and urine. The full gamut of technologically-advanced weapons and equipment was made available at Khe Sanh.

Giap, meanwhile, had assembled most of the 304th and 308th divisions: 17,200 men. These he deployed over the hills surrounding Khe Sanh and provided his artillery and missile batteries with vantage points that gave them line of sight of KSCB. The PAVN were invisible except to Marine patrols which, from time to time, made chance contact. Aerial reconnaissance showed that the PAVN were, typically, digging encircling trench lines.

Logistically, the American garrison in Khe Sanh wanted for nothing. It had a functioning airstrip and the aerial superiority that secured that airstrip. Giap, on the other hand, had those 17,000 troops and the host of supporting logistic porters, say 20,000, living in most unpleasant conditions in the rain forest. Many more troops were making their way to reinforce Giap. The PAVN was under considerable logistic stress, but Giap was driven by the philosophy of General Piotr Rumyantsev (whose quote heads this chapter). The several square miles of forest and an airstrip were of no value to the PAVN general; he sought a major victory, which he knew would produce rich political rewards, especially in his enemy's heartland. This battle would be Giap's move into Phase III (conventional battle) of Revolutionary Warfare.

Just after midnight on 20 January 1968, Khe Sanh was attacked in strength. Hill 861 was the enemy's first objective; at 0515 it was partially overrun, but by 0530 a counter-attack had regained it. At this moment of success, a salvo of rockets hit the main ammunition compound in the base and 1,500 tons of mixed, stockpiled ammunition exploded. The blast flattened all the buildings

A Marine sniper team in action: Khe Sanh, February 1968. (*David Douglas*)

Re-supply on Hill 861: the reality of logistics. (*Life Magazine*)

that had been so painstakingly constructed in recent weeks. Six parked helicopters were blown over and wrecked; shells, bombs, rockets and grenades rained down; fortunately, most did not explode on contact with terra firma. A significant length of the runway was badly damaged. Piles of stored gasoline exploded and burned. The sky was filled with black smoke. It looked and smelled like Armageddon and got worse as the PAVN poured more artillery shells into the blazing wreckage and onto the runway.

This was a crisis situation, but Giap did not exploit it to the full. A swift, concentrated, all-out ground attack could well have carried the day against a stunned and confused garrison in which 90 per cent of its artillery ammunition had been destroyed.

Amid the ensuing chaos a naval construction detachment flew in and repaired the 1,300-yard runway as its first priority. Only around 600 yards were undamaged. The 834th Air Division was tasked to deliver, by any means, sufficient ammunition to allow the further defence of the base. Every aircraft supporting the KSCB had to run a gauntlet of PAVN .30 and .50 machine guns and, as soon as the aircraft had landed, the enemy directed mortar fire on the stationary target.[7]

This situation was exactly what the 'Low Altitude Parachute Extraction System' (LAPES) had been designed for. LAPES called for a parachute, attached to a pallet of supplies, to be deployed as the aircraft skimmed the airstrip. The deployed parachute dragged the pallet out of the aircraft's hold and onto the ground. There was also an alternative and this was the 'Ground

A C-130 Hercules dropping pallet with 'Low Altitude Parachute Extraction System' on Khe Sanh runway, 1968. (*USAF*)

Parachute Extraction System' (GPES). In this case the aircraft also came in low in order to engage an arresting cable, which in turn yanked the cargo out of the rear. Both procedures were hazardous for the aircraft and also for those on the ground.

Air-drop was the alternative, utilizing the container delivery system for the less bulky items. Despite radar guidance, the weather hampered drop accuracy, just as it had done at DBP.

Urgent appeals for help were quickly answered and very soon 200,000lb of ordnance had been delivered. Medics and reinforcements arrived and the injured were flown out. It had been a disaster, but it could have been much worse. The depth and efficiency of the American logistic system were tested and found to be well up to the task. Despite the vast explosion, the base was well-founded and, thereafter, it beat off the piecemeal attacks, inflicting heavy casualties on the PAVN and VC assailants.

Three days later, Westmoreland felt the need once again to forestall any suggestions that the base be evacuated. He signalled both Admiral Sharp and General Wheeler, saying 'I unreservedly maintain that Khe Sanh is of significant, strategic, tactical and, most importantly, psychological importance.' Operation NIAGRA followed; it was a comprehensive bombing operation.

Westmoreland and General William Momyer, who commanded the 7th US Air Force, initiated Operation NIAGRA 1. This was arguably 'the most concentrated application of aerial firepower in the history of warfare.'[8] From 22 January, B-52 Stratofortresses dropped 60,000 tons of bombs in 2,548 sorties on Giap's troops. The effect was cataclysmic and the body count enormous. Meanwhile, a further 316 acoustic sensors were deployed. The Marines credited 40 per cent of the intelligence available to their 'Fire Support Coordination Centre' to those sensors.[9] The PAVN, as always, made every attempt to 'hold the enemy by his belt'. The point was that the closer they were to the defending US Marines, the more difficult it was to bomb and shell them. Colonel Lownds had stipulated that no bombs were to be dropped nearer than 2 miles to his perimeter, later reduced to 1,300 yards.

KSCB incorporated seven defended localities. Half the garrison was inside the perimeter: 1,000 were at Rock Quarry about a mile to the west; 1,000 were dug in on Hill 558 and a company was holding Hill 881 South on the far west of the base. Hill 861 was held by 200 men and further east fifty men guarded the signallers on Hill 950. Finally, Lang Vei was held by a mixed force of Green Berets and members of the 'Civilian Irregular Defense Group'. Each of these locations came under artillery fire from the 152mm guns of the 68th Regiment concealed on the face of Co Roc across the border and in Laos. PAVN gunners were in constant action and in one day 1,307 rounds impacted on the defenders.

Hill 881 South; re-supply by Chinook. (*www.pinterest.com*)

History repeated itself when active consideration was given to the use of nuclear weapons. It was argued that the PAVN encamped around the perimeter at Khe Sanh provided a valid target, well away from the civilian population which had fled. The political ramifications were evident and a president, who had no intention of invading North Vietnam and who had stated that his sole aim was to start negotiations, was unlikely to acquiesce. He did not, and the matter was quietly dropped.

On 6 February, PAVN infantry, backed by Soviet-built PT-76 tanks, attacked and overran the Special Forces' camp at Lang Vei, about 5 miles west of Khe Sanh Combat Base. This was the first instance of the use of armour by the PAVN during the conflict. Although the North Vietnamese continued to probe the American defences, the attack on Lang Vei was the last major assault by the PAVN. By mid-February 1968, Route 9 was in PAVN hands and so air re-supply, reinforcement and casualty evacuation were all dependent upon Westmoreland's aerial assets. The airstrip was now critical to survival and Giap's artillery never slept, testament to the PAVN logistic system.

Conditions in Khe Sanh were appalling but, despite that, the Marines acquitted themselves with great courage; so too did the Communist enemy.

The Reverend Ray W. Stubbs, a Marine chaplain, commented that 'their fire and camouflage discipline was outstanding, as was their bravery and tenacity.' By the end of the first week of February, 10 per cent of the garrison had been killed or wounded, the majority by artillery fire. It certainly looked and felt like Dien Bien Phu: blood, rain, mud, collapsing bunkers and the constant noise of bombardment. 'There were bandages, bombs, cold food, wet feet, excrement, muck and battlefield litter. There were rats scuttling all over the place, chewing filth, fighting for it, running over men's faces as they slept.'[10] The seasonal fog limited air operations and parachute delivery became more frequent.

Giap did not excel at Khe Sanh as he had at Dien Bien Phu, when he had defeated the French. Then, his astutely-employed artillery and mortar fire-power had cut the French aerial supply line. At Khe Sanh Giap had the artillery but not enough to outgun the Americans. Because of that he was able to interfere with the American logistic operations and inflict casualties, but could not prevent limitless American aerial re-supply. In addition, 'the American combined air power with external artillery gave Westmoreland a tremendous predominance in destructive capacity.'[11]

Giap had assembled a force that outnumbered the garrison by at least 3:1. His force was much larger than was needed to contain the garrison and certainly sufficient to take the position. However, for reasons not fully explained, he subjected his soldiers to blistering air bombardment, incurred

A Soviet-built PT-76 amphibious light tank. (*Sappinen-w*)

vast losses and failed to achieve any discernible aim. If his objective was to start Phase III of the Great Offensive/Great Uprising, then he failed. It is worth noting that this master logistician missed one vital trick, an omission that has intrigued historians ever since.

The fundamental key elements of logistic support are water, food and ammunition. Water is the overriding priority and it is often found in the battlefield but, when it is not, its provision becomes absolutely critical and a major logistic burden. Fresh water for 6,000 men in a tropical theatre, engaged in hard physical work, would entail the daily delivery of about 22,000 gallons of water and then its further distribution. This represents a significant logistic challenge which, if not met, would have a rapid and deleterious effect on the health of the soldiers. The gravity of water deficiency was summarized by Greenleaf and Harrison who made a study of water deprivation. They traced the symptoms of dehydration between a '2 per cent loss of body weight which generates discomfort and thirst to physical collapse at approximately 7 per cent dehydration. A 10 per cent loss of body water, through dehydration, is life-threatening.'[12] This was exemplified during the Six-Day War in the Middle East (5–10 June 1967), in which more than 20,000 Egyptian soldiers died from heatstroke. During the same time, Israeli troops with abundant field water supplies and command-enforced water policies had minimal heat casualties.[13]

At Khe Sanh, the River Rao Quan flowed through a PAVN-controlled area and provided a water point 500 yards north of the garrison perimeter. It would have been an entirely reasonable and legal act of war, on Giap's behalf, if he had either diverted, dammed or contaminated the river. The Geneva Protocol of 1925, which the North Vietnamese had ratified in 1957, makes that position clear. As it was, the PAVN took no action to interdict the water supply. Incredibly, nor did they cut the land-line telephone connection.

The probability is that the PAVN simply did not recognize the vulnerability of the Marines' water supply. It's one of the 'what ifs' of military history. A further enigma is that, given the vulnerability of the water supply, why did the MACV select the spot, elect to stay and reinforce Khe Sanh in the first place? Later Westmoreland told Lieutenant General Phillip Davidson that, by the time he found out about the vulnerability of the water supply, it was too late to evacuate the garrison by air or overland.[14]

On 15 April 1968, seventy-seven days after the siege began, a relieving force got through by way of Route 9. This was at a cost of 130 casualties. The relieving force was faced with a distressing sight, 'completely unpoliced (uncleaned), strewn with rubble, duds and damaged equipment, and with troops living a life more similar to rats than human beings.'[15]

From 17 June the KSCB was bulldozed flat, until it was finally vacated in July. Its bunkers were destroyed and the remains buried. By this means the PAVN was denied the opportunity to take and publicize propaganda photographs. Every vestige of the base disappeared, leaving only a scar of red earth to show where thousands of men had died for a valueless few acres of forest. The last word goes to Giap, who wrote after the event that

> Khe Sanh was not important to us. Or it was only to the extent that it was to the Americans. It was the focus of attention in the United States because their prestige was at stake, but to us it was part of the greater battle that would begin after Tet. It was only a diversion, but one to be exploited if we could cause many casualties and win a big victory.
>
> As long as they stayed in Khe Sanh to defend their prestige they said it was important; when they abandoned it they said it had never been important.[16]

The cost of the battle of Khe Sanh in terms of casualties depends upon the source consulted. It is clear that the body count was vastly in favour of the US. The issue that clouds the arithmetic is the 'where and when' casualties were incurred. However, as a basis for discussion it is suggested that total US and ARVN casualties from 1 November 1967 until the final evacuation on 5 July 1968 were 1,253 killed, 8,015 wounded and seven missing. During Operation CHARLIE for the final evacuation (19 June to 5 July 1968) at least a further eleven Marines were killed; number of wounded unknown. 'Civilian Irregular Defense Group' losses are thought to be of the order of 1,000 to 1,500 killed or missing; at least 250 were captured (in Lang Vei), and the number of injured is unknown.

PAVN casualties estimates cover a very wide range. The US official public estimate is 10,000 to 15,000 killed; the MACV favoured a figure of 5,550. PAVN suggests 2,496.

Whatever the number, the fact is that neither side achieved its aims. This was a siege that achieved nothing, but cost many lives and a great deal of treasure. Giap mishandled the operation and as a result Westmoreland won, less by his brilliance, more by dint of Giap's ineptitude. In Giap's defence he lost to an enemy with an overwhelming logistic advantage. An unwelcome element of the siege that fuelled unrest in the USA was the role of the media, which misrepresented it.

Westmoreland was replaced by General Creighton Adams in April 1968, and it was Adams who ordered the evacuation of Khe Sanh in July.

Chapter Twenty-One

Critical Times, 1968–1969

'Nothing is more dangerous in wartime than to live in the
temperamental atmosphere of the Gallup Poll, always
feeling one's pulse and taking one's temperature.'[1]

[Sir Winston Churchill]

During the war-torn thirty years of armed strife in Vietnam, 1968–69 was
probably the most critical period. At the beginning of the period was fought
the indecisive Battle of Khe Sanh. However, the comprehensive defeat of the
Vietcong during the Tet offensive, early in 1968, brought little reward for the
USA but, perversely, fuelled the anti-war faction at home. One positive outcome was that the pacification programme, which was close to abandonment
in late 1967, was given new life by the destruction of the Vietcong during the
Tet offensive.

Westmoreland's Search and Destroy strategy and its quest to find the
'crossover point' had failed. The policy of attrition with a body-count men-
tality was manifestly bankrupt. It had been a vastly expensive exercise; the
required degree of battlefield mobility had posed a unique logistic challenge
that had been amply satisfied. Notwithstanding the undoubted success of
the air mobility element, there had been less success on the ground. In the
absence of any clear strategy, often the territory was fought for, won and then
abandoned, only to be fought for again soon after. The frustration and anger
of US troops who were subject to these apparently inexplicable tactics as they
fought an elusive enemy is readily understood. Less so the numerous appalling
atrocities committed by US troops in which the perpetrators were never
punished.

President Johnson, who had endorsed the strategies of Westmoreland and
McNamara and had been resistant to altering his policies, could now see the
need for change. He moved the soldier upstairs to be chief of staff of the army
and the latter either resigned or was sacked; history is vague as to the
mechanics of McNamara's demission of office.

The president's carefully-controlled bombing policy, Operation
ROLLING THUNDER, and its absurd intention of only attacking the

enemy gently where it would not hurt too much had failed. Johnson's pious hope that, in gratitude for being spared, Hanoi would hasten to the negotiating table was unfulfilled. ROLLING THUNDER had been a palpable failure and an exhausted Johnson decided not to seek re-election in November 1968.

Hanoi was content to play a long game, aware that, as ever, time was on its side. After its cataclysmic defeat at Tet, it recognized that it would have to revert to guerrilla Phase I tactics because its attempt at Phase III had so seriously misfired. The Americans also had to rethink their position. Davidson summed up the situation when he wrote that hitherto 'the United States was not pursuing *the wrong strategy*: the problem was that it was pursuing *no strategy*.' He continued:

> Military strategy – that is the use of armed forces to achieve a national objective – must spring from a political objective, and the civilian leadership must articulate that political objective. From it, the military leaders are supposed to devise the strategic objectives of the war or campaign. These are transmitted to the theatre commander who, in turn, sets his own strategic and operational objectives.[2]

Just like the PAVN and remnants of the VC, this was really suggesting going back to say 1964. It would now involve new people in new roles, perhaps better able to bring the vast logistic resources of the richest country in the world to bear upon a third-world, non-industrialized, obdurate opponent.

The severe depletion of the VC allowed action to be taken against the tunnels in and around Cu Chi. The finale of Johnson's bombing was on 31 October 1968 when B-52 aircraft bombed extensively in the Cu Chi area. 'The bombs were dropped and left mile-long swathes of total devastation. The strike could be seen, heard and felt for 20 miles: a thunderous symphony of destruction that shook the face of the earth and left it permanently scarred.'[3] The bombs were followed by deep ploughing and levelling of square miles of what had once been jungle. However, the threat posed by the Cu Chi tunnels had been finally eradicated. During 1968 the PAVN and surviving VC carried out little more than nuisance raids, stand-off shelling and small unit actions. On 31 October Johnson cancelled ROLLING THUNDER, which inevitably made access to South Vietnam easier for the PAVN. Negotiations did at least get started, but with the USA starting from a poor bargaining position. It was readily evident to Ho, Giap and Le Duan and the remainder of the Hanoi leadership that not only had the USA no intention of pursuing operations and a military victory, but in addition, and as a very significant plus, the weight of public opinion in the USA was now predominantly anti-war. That public opinion was of great significance, given the upcoming presidential election.

A crater left by a B-52 strike in the Cu Chi area, but it could be almost anywhere in South Vietnam. (*Major Denis Ayoub*)

President Nixon was duly elected in November 1968. McNamara was replaced by Clark Clifford who embraced all of his predecessor's extant policies during the ten months he held office. Henry Kissinger, as Secretary of State, became Nixon's right-hand man. They made for a toxic partnership, as both proved to be devious and dishonest in their management of public affairs.

The maintenance of a major army, 536,000-strong, in a foreign country, in sophisticated, superbly-equipped bases that provided all the facilities normally only available in the Continental United States (CONUS) was, by now, an unavoidable, ongoing and apparently endless expense. The vociferous US media was on the case.

Nixon was an unknown quantity to the North Vietnamese. He was known to be anti-communist, but that was unsurprising. It made all sorts of strategic sense to test Nixon and, to this end, in February 1969 a minor offensive was launched. The object was to attack American installations and cause American casualties. This would set a new base line for further negotiations. In the new offensive, 525 posts and bases across South Vietnam were either shelled

President Richard Nixon and General Creighton Adams. They inherited the Vietnam War in 1968–9. (*Bing*)

or subjected to sapper attacks. The MACV repelled the offensive without undue difficulty, but the loss of 1,140 more soldiers was extensively reported in the US press.

An unexpected product of Giap's initiative was reducing the morale of his troops and increasing the numbers of his adherents defecting to the ARVN. 'By 1 July 1969, 20,000 enemy personnel had changed sides; 2,000 more than during the whole of 1968.'[4]

In June 1969 American public opinion was a factor when Nixon confirmed the convictions of the Hanoi leadership. Ignoring Churchill's dictum at the head of this chapter and swayed by public opinion, Nixon announced that US troops were being withdrawn from South Vietnam. The hitherto tacit but now public acceptance by the USA that it could not win a shooting war served only to strengthen the determination of Giap, Le Duan and others to expel the USA from Vietnam. Nixon's announcement proved to be an illustration of 'the law of unintended consequences'. He and the civilians around him did not take into account the impact his announcement would have on the soldiers fighting and dying in Vietnam. It was culpable naivety and unexpected from a nation that had the technology and sophistication to be engaged in putting a man on the moon on 20 July 1969.

Nixon camouflaged his proposed retreat by asserting, glibly, that the United States would honour its treaty obligations and continue to provide a nuclear shield and military and economic aid, but would look to the nation directly threatened to assume primary responsibility for providing the manpower for its defence. This was all about 'Vietnameseation' of the war. The unambiguous promise was to provide logistic aid in all its forms for South Vietnam when needed. In fact, Nixon had no such intention.

This Vietnameseation of the war was by no means original thought. The French had a similar idea fifteen years earlier, but they called it *jaunissement* (yellowing) and history tells us that it did not work then. In this latest case it was no more than a political device to cover the complete withdrawal of American forces.

Nixon and Kissinger tried manfully to get peace negotiations started, but with few cards to play they were operating from a position of weakness. Hanoi was implacable in its demands; in essence they were 'withdraw all American forces and replace the Government of President Thieu'. This latter demand was totally unacceptable. Although the USA had actively participated in regime change before, the removal of Thieu was, emphatically, not an option.

Henry Kissinger (b. 1923), Secretary of State and National Security Advisor under the presidential administrations of Richard Nixon and Gerald Ford; winner of the Nobel Peace Prize in 1973.

It was while ineffective, nugatory letters were passing between Washington and Hanoi that Ho Chi Minh died, aged 79, on 2 September 1969. During his life he had changed the map of South-East Asia and, in the process, caused the deaths of uncounted hundreds of thousands of those caught up in his political aspirations. Before he died, he had the satisfaction of knowing that, in effect, the war was won, all bar the shouting. Le Duan became the undisputed first among equals in the Government of North Vietnam and consequently Nixon's opponent.

The PAVN held the initiative: it decided where and when to fight and the reversion to guerrilla tactics was as effective as ever. For the US

soldiers on the ground, political machinations in Washington did not stop the shelling, the unutterably miserable conditions in the field or the nagging fear of death or disfigurement. There remained the mental strain of staying alert to the constant threat of booby-traps, always concealed, at the very least disabling but often lethal. The pressure on junior officers and senior NCOs was particularly severe. Just as they had been doing since 1964, US soldiers and Marines spent days forcing a way through flooded paddy fields or thick jungle with no sight of an enemy. Then, in a moment, a shower of grenades, a burst of automatic fire and three, perhaps four or more men were down, probably dead. The elusive enemy melted away as artillery support was called for. When that support came, the probability is that it shelled empty jungle. This pattern was repeated time and time again. Helicopters flew in to remove the dead and dying; the courage and airmanship of the helicopter crews was universally recognized. The logistic requirements were fully met, but the costs swelled.

Nixon's public avowal to reduce US forces in Vietnam was, in effect, a public acknowledgement of defeat, and the effect on his officers and men was catastrophic. Not unnaturally, they asked if we are not here to win, why are we fighting and dying in this benighted place? They were dependent upon Henry Kissinger to bring this now pointless war to a speedy conclusion. Kissinger achieved the conclusion, but it took four years and in that time thousands more soldiers on both sides were killed or maimed.

Chapter Twenty-Two

Disintegration, 1969–1973

'A soldier's trade, if it is to mean anything at all, has to be anchored to an unshakeable code of honour. Otherwise, those of us who follow the drums become nothing more than a bunch of hired assassins ... a disgrace to God and to mankind.'[1]

[Major General Carl von Clausewitz]

The flourishing drive for pacification resulting from the elimination of the Vietcong in South Vietnam in the early months of 1968 caused the re-opening of roads that had been in VC hands for years. The logistic benefits were quickly evident as old, ground-transport links were re-established and in turn they boosted the economy. Unhindered, rice-farming saw production of this staple crop rise to over 5 million tons in 1969. Local markets thrived and trading in vegetables, poultry and livestock exuded normality. One of the aims of Robert Komer's pacification programme was the organization and arming of the People's Self Defence Force (PSDF) (see Chapter 17):

> Post-Tet this initiative moved on quickly and by the end of 1969 over 3 million people had volunteered for duty. They were armed with 399,000 weapons. 90 percent of the villages and hamlets of South Vietnam were rated as 'secure' or 'relatively secure'. 5 million more people lived in GVN-controlled areas than had been the case in 1967.[2]

Defections from the VC rose to dizzy heights and during 1969, 47,000 changed sides, a vast increase over 18,000 in the previous year. On the face of it, it was all going swimmingly well for the USA. General Adams, like his predecessor, was anxious for the big set-piece battle, but Giap was far too wily to oblige. Although the policy was no longer 'marketed' as Search and Destroy, Adams, in army parlance, 'continued the movement'. The difference was that the political wind had changed direction.

Nixon was personally affronted by continuing PAVN aggression and considered how best he could retaliate. One option was to recommence bombing, but the political ramifications need not detain us here. Another option was to mount an offensive in Laos and Cambodia aimed at the PAVN, but that might be judged to be excessive and Nixon was acutely aware of the likely media response. While the unattractive alternatives were considered, the Americans had a windfall.

A VC defector surrendered in January 1969 and claimed to have been serving in the COSVN (Communist, South Vietnam Headquarters); not unreasonably he said that he could pinpoint the location of that headquarters across the Cambodian border. It took time to authenticate the man and his message, but he offered a very juicy and significant target. The merits of a major aerial strike were that it would damage the PAVN, would not cause civilian casualties and it could be delivered in secret without arousing the fury of the anti-war faction at home.

An added bonus was that Prince Sihanouk, who ruled Cambodia, would not object to an attack on his unwelcome oppressors. The North Vietnamese had never admitted to occupying parts of Cambodia and they might accept the assault without comment, perhaps? Any bombing would signal to Hanoi that the USA was quite prepared to continue the war and that the restraint exercised by President Johnson would not apply to this new administration.

As had so often been the case during this war, the clear military need for urgency in eradicating a major enemy installation was superseded by politicians and civil servants. Bombing was authorized on 9 March and rescinded very soon after. It was back on by 15 March but in abeyance. Then the PAVN hit Saigon with five rockets and finally, on 18 March, 'Base Area 353' was struck with overwhelming force. Thereafter other similar bases in Cambodia were attacked, in secret until May 1970.

Meanwhile, the process of Vietnameseation continued. American troops were being withdrawn, despite the covert objections of President Thieu and General Adams. The theory was that to balance US withdrawals, the RVN Armed Forces (RVNAF) would be strengthened and re-equipped. Adams was told that his first priority was Vietnameseation in close support of the pacification programme. Meanwhile the war continued and, every month, it cost \$2.5 billion, 400 American lives and consumed 128,000 tons of munitions. The logistic train continued to function and, inexorably, it fed matériel to an army that was, by now, unsure of its aims.

The machinations of the US government as it tried to extricate itself from Vietnam had a deleterious effect upon the morale and effectiveness of the soldiers and Marines who were still in contact with the enemy. Davidson witnessed the unhappy state of his army and wrote that

> For the United States, 1969 produced one unexpected and pernicious harvest – the *beginning* of the demoralization of the American ground

forces in Vietnam (Davidson's emphasis). Historically, an army becomes demoralized either by a devastating defeat, or by huge and purposeless casualties, or by unbearable living conditions, or by obviously corrupt or incompetent leadership.

Yet there is an 'X' factor, an unknown, which rebuts the above and makes armies rise above disaster, heavy casualties, or debilitating living conditions, or incompetent leadership.

The demoralization of American ground units in Vietnam can be attributed to none of the causes generally accepted as destructive of the spirit of a military force. American troops were never defeated, their casualties (looked at historically) were light, they lived in conditions which previous American armies would have considered sinfully luxurious, and their leaders, at least at the top, were competent professionals.[3]

It is suggested that the deep malaise in the American forces, and specifically the ground forces in Vietnam, started earlier when a platoon from the 101st Airborne Division was designated 'Tiger Force'. The *New York Times* commented later that

> Records showed this unit carried out what's believed to be the longest series of atrocities by a platoon in the war. They hurled grenades into bunkers where women and children were hiding, shot prisoners and then cut off their ears and scalps for souvenirs,

Tiger Force, upper arm, unit title.

murdered villagers for no reason and left many of them behind in mass graves.

Military experts who examined the 'Tiger Force' case said the troops were acting out of rage over the death of comrades, frustration over fighting a canny enemy and fear for their own safety. But some of the soldiers themselves spoke years later of orders that made them treat civilians like adversaries, let them fire weapons with little clear justification and measured success from body counts – the supposed enumeration of enemy dead that was likely to include anyone killed by American troops. As with the My Lai Massacre in 1968, in which American troops killed hundreds of women, children and old men in hamlets near the 'Tiger Force' operations area, commanders had an arm's length role in either encouraging or covering up what happened.

Records show that members of Tiger Force shot or stabbed at least eighty-one civilians in violation of military law. But based on *The Toledo Blade*'s interviews with former soldiers and Vietnamese civilians, the platoon is believed to have killed hundreds of unarmed villagers in the Central Highlands between May and November of 1967.[4] 'We weren't keeping count,' former Private Ken Kerney said in 2003. 'I knew it was wrong, but it was an acceptable practice.'

The Army began a four-year investigation of Tiger Force only in 1971. It lasted four years and led to recommendations that eighteen soldiers be charged with murder, assault and dereliction of duty. But in the end, no one was prosecuted, and the case was concealed in the military archives for the next three decades. 'They just buried it,' said a former platoon medic, Ron Causey.

The platoon's forty-five members were expected to survive for weeks at a time in the bush as they searched for enemy camps and called in air strikes but, in May 1967, Tiger Force was sent to Quang Ngai province to move civilians into relocation centers so the farmers couldn't grow rice, depriving the enemy of a crucial food supply.

Private Ken Kerney, Tiger Force soldier. (*Sallah and Weiss*)

Rather than soldiers fighting soldiers, they were destroying people's lives, uprooting them from their homes. It was hateful work, and a dozen 'Tiger Force' veterans told *The Blade* that it led them to become more brutal and begin taking out their aggression on the people they were supposed to protect. First, they killed prisoners, but soon they were gunning down defenceless civilians.

Two former platoon members told Army investigators that many members from the unit had been drinking beer all afternoon on July 23, 1967 when they came upon the old man with the geese. He was a carpenter named Dao Hue, 68, on his way home to his family. When he began babbling in terror a sergeant clubbed him with an M16 rifle.

Lieutenant James Hawkins was the platoon commander between July and November 1967. In June 1975 he was charged with murder. However, all charges against him were later dropped. (*Sallah and Weiss*)

As a medic treated the man's wounds while he knelt before him, the platoon leader, Lieutenant James Hawkins, lifted Mr Dao and shot him in the face with a CAR-15 rifle. Carpenter (the medic) said he tried to stop Lieutenant Hawkins, but the platoon leader threatened to shoot him for interfering. Mr Hawkins, 76, who retired from the military in 1978 as a major, could not be reached. But in an interview with *The Blade* in 2003, he said he shot the elderly carpenter because he was 'making a lot of noise. I eliminated that right there.'[5]

The adverse changes in the culture of US ground forces were the product of several factors. The first of these was that although Nixon's policy served his political ends, it was a hammer blow to his soldiers' morale. The knowledge that this was a no-win war was debilitating, especially so when operations had to continue and lives were risked in support of Vietnameseation and pacification. No one wanted to be the last man killed in Vietnam.[6]

It was a paradox that, while Vietnameseation and pacification were the stated aims, many members of the ground forces were involved in the wholesale killing of civilians, none more so than those led by Major General Julian Ewell, who assumed command of the 9th Infantry Division in 1968. He was an enthusiastic disciple of the 'body-count' policy and was disinterested in the status of the dead. To Ewell all dead bodies were enemy, and he placed no constraints upon his officers and men who were cajoled into producing higher and higher body counts. Ewell's division mounted Operation SPEEDY EXPRESS in which between 5,000 and 7,000 civilians were killed.[7]

During Ewell's period in command the division claimed to have killed 20,000 enemy but, in that process, only 2,000 weapons were recovered, a figure that utterly belies the military status of those 20,000. Colonel David Hackworth, who served under Ewell in the 9th Division, later wrote *Steel my Soldiers' Hearts*, in which he was highly critical of Ewell's performance.

Nevertheless, Ewell was promoted and decorated. He later wrote a book justifying his actions.[8] The promotion of Ewell to lieutenant general required the recommendation of Creighton Adams and the endorsement of William Westmoreland. By their actions, in supporting Ewell, they became party to his conduct and are thus complicit in the killing of thousands of Vietnamese civilians. Is that a fair judgement? It could be argued that they were nowhere near the scene of the 9th Division and its activities. Westmoreland was even in a different country, thousands of miles away. The counter-argument is that a commander is entirely responsible for any actions taken on his behalf. For example, 'Bomber' Harris did not fly on bombing missions over Germany in 1944–45, but he wholeheartedly accepted responsibility for the actions of his men during that period and answered for them.

After the My Lai massacre by C Company 1/20th Infantry of the 23rd American Division in which 504 old men, women and children were

Major General J.J. Ewell (1915–2009), commander of the 9th Infantry Division 1968–69, responsible for the deaths of thousands of civilians. He was never charged with any offence. (*US Army*)

brutally and criminally killed, a Private Tom Glen wrote to General Adams advising him of the atrocities committed by his formation. A staff officer in HQ 23rd Division wrote the response to Adams but forbore to question Glen. This document asserted that 'relations between American soldiers and the Vietnamese people are excellent'.[9] The officer responsible for this cover-up was Major Colin Powell. He later rose to the top of the army, served as Secretary of State and was considered to be a potential president of the USA. In his memoirs he makes passing mention of My Lai but not of Ewell.

General Colin Powell. (*US Army photo*)

The officers responsible for My Lai were readily identified: Lieutenant William Calley, an officer of limited intellect and ability, was sentenced to imprisonment but served only a few months confined to his quarters. His company commander Captain Ernest Medina was acquitted of murder and the jury took only sixty minutes to reach the verdict. The judge wished Medina a 'Happy Birthday' on his acquittal. The divisional commander Major General Samuel Koster was demoted to brigadier. The My Lai murders were not an isolated incident but were symptomatic of an army that had lost its way. So too had the American public, in which a significant minority viewed Calley and Medina as heroes.

The reader of a book focused on logistics might reasonably ask 'What have these atrocities got to do with a book on logistics?' It is argued that an army is a fully integrated, cohesive organization. It has to be appreciated that, whatever activity US Forces were engaged in, somewhere there was a significant logistic element enabling that activity. In an army the honour and glory (such as it is) is shared; does the converse not apply? Is that view too all-embracing? Does it damn the majority with the sins of a minority? The reader must draw their own conclusions.

The lack of public support for a war in which young men were dying every day bred an anger in those not yet called upon to die in defence of their president's aims. The soldiers and Marines viewed the university war protesters and other well-publicized groups with total contempt. There was a fundamental and deeply-rooted difference in outlook, values and class. That civilians who were safe at home, dry and unthreatened, would presume to question, *to dare to question* (author's emphasis) the value of the sacrifices being made daily in South-East Asia was dangerously morale-sapping.

The constant challenges being made concerning the righteousness of the war had the effect of causing some soldiers to doubt the rectitude of their mission, 'in some cases to conceive that what they were doing in Vietnam was dishonourable, and it furnished a ready-made pretext for those who did not want to fight by giving them an excuse to shirk their combat duties as (being) immoral.'[10]

In addition to the moral issue outlined above, there was by now another factor and that was the racial tension that many of the draftees brought with them. Muhammad Ali was quoted as saying 'No Vietcong ever called me nigger' and, on that basis, he went to prison rather than serve in Vietnam.[11] Racism, in all of its many forms, divided groups of men and struck a severe blow at the cohesiveness and martial spirit of a unit. Along with that division came a breakdown in the respect for authority; it was the junior officers and senior NCOs who had to manage recalcitrant soldiers. Many of these junior leaders were not up to the task.

A black officer commented that

> … a certain ambivalence has always existed among African-Americans about military service. Why should we fight for a country that for so long did not fight for us, that in fact denied us our fundamental rights? How could we serve a country where we could not be served in a restaurant and enjoy the amenities available to white Americans?[12]

Put like that, a disinterested observer can understand the forces that were affecting the performance of the US Army. However, an army, any army, can only function if the chain of command has the unqualified support of all those in that chain of command. In effect, an order reasonably and legally given is expected to be complied with immediately and without question; in a word that is *discipline*. Without discipline an army is just an armed rabble. In 1969 the US Army was in danger of earning that label.

Low morale, racial tension and a breakdown in discipline are, individually, matters that would trouble any commander. When widespread drug abuse is added to the mix, it produces a volatile, toxic and unmanageable army. In 1969, this was the army that General Adams had to lead, and he had more than the PAVN to cope with. The Chinese premier, Chou En-lai, boasted to Colonel Nasser of Egypt that China, with North Vietnamese participation, 'had used drugs on a large scale to undermine the morale and efficiency of United States forces during the Vietnam War.'[13] That policy had been more successful than Chou could possibly have hoped for and it was an example of effective, astute, aggressive logistic management.

Vietnam was an uncomfortable station and the largesse of the logistic system did not compensate for the extreme conditions experienced daily by the teeth-arm troops. In his account of this war Davidson sought an explanation for the disintegration of his army. He cited 'harsh physical conditions, stress, leeches, mud, snakes, booby-traps, mines, fatigue, fear, loss of friends, irregular hours, poor food or no food, torrential rain and humid heat.'[14]

That is a formidable list, and life out in the forest looking for 'Charlie' was, without question, unutterably miserable. However, although 'a soldier's lot is not a happy one', that does not excuse either the murder of officers or the murder of civilians. These two issues have to be considered because, from 1968, they were both the product of frustration and low morale.

First, we shall address the matter of 'fragging', so-called because it often involved the use of the readily-available fragmentation grenades that left no forensic evidence. The first incidents of fragging in South Vietnam occurred in 1966. After the Tet offensive in early 1968 and the assassination of Martin Luther King in April, racial tensions between mostly conscripted white and

African-American soldiers increased.[15] Violence between comrades became more frequent. With soldiers reluctant to risk their lives in what was perceived as a lost war, fragging was seen by some soldiers 'as the most effective way to discourage their superiors from showing enthusiasm for combat.'[16] M18 Claymore mines and other explosives were also occasionally employed, as were firearms. Fragging was confined in the main to the army and Marine Corps and it was a phenomenon very rare in the USN and USAF (see Table 2).

The response of the authorities to these very worrying murders and attempted murders was to limit access to weapons, especially grenades, for soldiers in the logistic chain. After any incident, the entire unit concerned was quarantined until a full investigation had been conducted.

In May 1971, the US Army in Vietnam ceased issuing grenades to nearly all its units in Vietnam. Weapon inventory checks and the searches of soldiers' quarters and personal kit did lead to the confiscation of ammunition, grenades and knives. This was little more than a demonstration because all weapons and grenades were readily available on the black market to any soldier intent on killing someone. Predictably, the MACV went to some pains to 'manage' the adverse publicity fragging incidents could produce. It focused on the security steps being taken to protect officers from their own soldiers!

When a grenade exploded in the middle of the night, it was often difficult to distinguish between a fragging and enemy action. It was on that basis that few men were indicted and, not least, because their comrades refused to assist any prosecution. The issue of fragging was symptomatic of an armed force in which the culture had broken down and its ethics had been abandoned.

Many officers in Vietnam were afraid for their lives simply because they were authority figures and they said so. General Colin Powell (a major at the time he served in Vietnam) remarked: 'I moved my cot every night, partly to thwart Viet Cong informants who might be tracking me, but also because I did not rule out attacks on authority from within the battalion itself.'[17]

Table 2. Known US fragging incidents in Vietnam.

	1969	1970	1971	1972
Army	96	209	222	28
Marine Corps	30+	50+	30+	5
Suspected	30	62	111	31
Total	156+	321+	363+	64
Deaths	46	38	12	3

Source: George Lepre, 2011.
Note: Statistics were not kept before 1969.

It begs the question, what sort of army is it when officers' lives are at risk from their own soldiers? Perhaps surreal is the right word.

The short-tour policy instigated by Westmoreland added to the problem and officers were rarely in any appointment long enough to get to know their soldiers and build the relationships that would usually bind a unit together. Team-building was noticeably absent, and it was a deficiency with serious consequences.

The incidence of a fragging leading to death, when related to the strength of US ground forces, is miniscule. However, there were, in addition to physical attacks, countless threats of extreme violence that had a deleterious effect on the performance of both officers and NCOs. A leader who has to lead while anticipating he is about to be shot from behind will be more than a little inhibited when giving his orders, especially so when those orders put his command in contact with the enemy and by extension his life and that of his men in danger.

This corrosive element that pervaded the US ground forces became all the more corrosive as troop withdrawals accelerated. To put the figures in the table above into context the US strength in 1969 was 475,200. In 1970 it was 334,600 and in 1971, the peak year, it had reduced to 156,850. Although by 1972 only 24,200 Americans, the majority of them logistic troops, remained in South Vietnam, statistically the number of incidents was rising and 1972 was the peak, proportionately.

The overwhelming majority of American soldiers and Marines did their duty, unpleasant though it was. However, the small minority who challenged authority and threatened their commanders had a massively disproportionate effect upon every aspect of the campaign. These men, by their actions, betrayed not only their officers but also their country.

The reader might again, at this stage, ask what has any of this to do with logistics? The answer is 'nothing directly'. There is no evidence that the flow of supplies was disrupted to any significant degree. However, as the logistic system was an integral and large part of every formation, inevitably its personnel were affected, perhaps influenced. Insubordination is contagious and especially so when it is seen to go unpunished. Indiscipline is manifested in many ways: it might be failure to salute an officer's commission (the salute given is never personal to that individual), the carrying of dirty weapons, poor turnout, an insubordinate attitude and countless small but cumulatively important acts or omissions.

Davidson commented painfully that 'the hairline crack in the Army's façade of morale and discipline which appeared in 1969 would become a visible fissure in 1970 and a yawning crevice in 1971.'[18]

The unrest in the army serving in Vietnam was not only a reflection of the breakdown in its morale and discipline, but also of the bitterly divided country it represented. At home, in the United States, the anti-war movement was increasingly powerful, and it spurred President Nixon to end the war at any price.

On 4 May 1970, at Kent State University, an anti-war rally confrontation between students and a unit of the Ohio National Guard led to the shooting of four young people. Five guardsmen were indicted but they claimed to have fired in self-defence, testimony that was generally accepted by the criminal justice system. (*John Filo*, The New York Times)

Chapter Twenty-Three

Cambodia and Laos

'There is no accurate measure of loss of morale: hence in many cases the abandonment of the fight remains the only authentic proof of victory.'[1]

[Major General Carl von Clausewitz]

After Nixon's decision to withdraw from Vietnam, the PAVN added to the irritation and frustration of the MACV by avoiding contact. Nevertheless, air assaults were made on the suspected enemy locations and the usual sweeps were conducted, but with scant success. In some instances, this was a matter of 'search and evade' when the assaulting American troops merely sat tight in the jungle or searched an area known to be free of the PAVN. Even if no enemy were found, casualties still mounted from the ubiquitous booby-traps and mines. The hostile environment also added to the sick list. Vietnamese civilians going about their lawful business were encountered and viewed with increasing suspicion and sometimes hostility.

The marked reduction in fighting did not bring any benefits and this 'decrease in the intensity of combat produced inaction, boredom and lethargy in many American units ... and this increased the problems of drugs, alcohol, civilian relations and discipline.'[2] Vietnameseation and pacification were the name of the game, but as the previous chapter revealed, there were many who did not want to play the army game and were prepared to act unlawfully.

In 1969 the judicial system and the in-house legal system in Vietnam became jammed with unanswered cases. It is said that 'justice delayed is justice denied' and that was the case here. Witnesses returned to the USA at the end of their tour or were otherwise unavailable to give evidence. The lawyers working the case were similarly moved on, tour expired. Witnesses, especially civilians, were often difficult to find and even more difficult to interrogate. The US Army was and is a bureaucratic, paper-choked maze. The result was that 'military justice was neither swift nor certain and transgressors have been comparatively free to repeat their acts with impunity.'[3]

It was evident from the early days of American involvement in Vietnam that there was extensive corruption in the supply chain. It was American money and American ships that delivered the logistic support, but a great deal of South Vietnamese labour was employed in the distribution system. Shops in South Vietnamese cities were stocked with stolen American goods and some-times with items that troops in the field were unable to obtain. In any army there are dishonest quartermasters and the capacity to enrich oneself at public expense is a temptation that some are unable to resist. With the US military judicial system failing, internal corruption flourished. As a result, the effec-tiveness of the vastly expensive American logistic base was reduced.

The nature of South Vietnamese society added impetus to this material corruption. There was, as one American commander put it, comprehensive corruption throughout every structure in the country that

> created a sense of social injustice by creating a small elite which held all the power and wealth, and a majority of middle-class people and peasants who became poorer and poorer and who suffered all the sacrifices … Throughout the twenty-one years of decisive American engagement in South Vietnam, corruption was invariably and routinely identified as a pervasive issue in the country; it had corrosive effects in every aspect of the state and society.[4]

The all-embracing corruption was readily recognized by even the most junior American servicemen. They could see that some were enriching themselves at the expense of their fellows and it was a further factor in the serious decline in American morale and discipline.

Back in 1967, Bob Komer, the leader of the CORDS program, took note of Thieu's reluctance to address corruption and so Komer sought some form of leverage that the Americans could use to encourage a more aggressive approach that would lead to the eradication of corporate corruption. How-ever, in the US Embassy Minister-Counselor for Political Affairs John A. Calhoun had observed that this 'entails an invasion of the sovereignty of the Republic of Viet-Nam so great that it could and would be argued thereafter that the United States is indeed the neo-colonialist power its critics and enemies allege it to be.' The problem was acknowledged, but Calhoun added, *'corruption was not incidental to the political system of South Vietnam; it was an integral and defining characteristic of that system'*[5] (author's italics).

General Adams was faced with a plethora of problems. He did not enjoy the support of the American public and his undisciplined army with low morale was crumbling around him. He was charged with passing all responsibility for fighting the war to his major ally whose operational reliability depended, in some measure, on the dishonest, financial and domestic arrangements of the Vietnamese generals. The Pacification program leaned heavily upon a foundation of Vietnamese goodwill for success, and in addition the strength of his army was being drastically reduced. The massive army of 536,100 in 1968 when Adams assumed command had shrunk to 334,600 by 1970 and it would be more than halved one year later.

Nevertheless, given political support, Adams was ready and willing to tackle the well-entrenched PAVN and VC strongholds in Laos and Cambodia. The Cambodian government of Prince Sihanouk had pragmatically invested in the Hak Ly Trucking Company, which proved to be a shrewd move as that company was an arm of the People's Army of Vietnam and it was moving 14,000 tons of matériel a year from the Cambodian port of Sihanoukville to those well-entrenched bases. Adams wanted to bomb these targets, but was thwarted at every turn by Nixon and Kissinger.

Meanwhile, drug-taking by Americans increased. In 1969 only 2 per cent had experienced heroin but, by 1971, some 60 per cent were using marijuana and 22 per cent heroin. The effect on operational efficiency was dire. A study of twenty-eight fragging incidents revealed that most were carried out by support personnel in the logistic chain and that in 87.2 per cent of these cases the person responsible was either drunk or drugged.

May 1969 saw Operation APACHE SNOW – the now infamous assaults on Ap Bia Mountain or Hill 937, better known as 'Hamburger Hill'.

The succession of eleven attacks cost the 101st Airborne Division 102 dead and 372 wounded, while the ARVN had 31 killed. The hill was of no military significance and, at this stage, nor were the 675 PAVN who were killed. The hill was taken and then abandoned by the MACV just a few weeks later. This pointless, wasteful exercise and the resultant loss of life caused anger in the USA and fuelled the anti-war cause. It even gave rise to a Hollywood film. The operation caused anger in the theatre too and, allegedly, 'bounties, raised by common subscription in amounts running anywhere from $50 to $1,000 have been widely reported put on the heads of leaders who the soldiers want to rub out.'

Shortly after the costly assault on Hamburger Hill, one of the underground newspapers in Vietnam, *GI Says*, publicly offered a $10,000 bounty on the life of Lieutenant Colonel Weldon Honeycutt, the officer who led the attack.[6] Honeycutt won a very well-deserved DSC for his personal bravery and exemplary leadership, clearly conduct that was not appreciated by all those around him.

Nixon's political position weakened in the face of Hanoi's refusal to hold discussions. Hanoi confirmed, in July 1969, its firm move back to guerrilla tactics in which small bodies fired upon ARVN and US installations. The following month the communists attacked more than 100 towns and cities; they did not seek to take ground, only to inflict casualties and unsettle their enemy. Despite the unvarnished aggression of the PAVN, Nixon and

Kissinger toiled to find some form of accommodation with Hanoi, although they were cognizant of the threats posed by the communists' Cambodian and Laotian sanctuaries.

On 18 March 1970 General Lon Nol headed a coup d'état that overthrew the erratic, self-indulgent Prince Sihanouk of Cambodia. Lon Nol's motivation was multi-faceted. He resented the presence of PAVN soldiers in his country, but he also resented the rich pickings that Sihanouk and his family had enjoyed and he wanted a share of the cake.

After Nol's pro-Western takeover, the PAVN and VC found that they were no longer welcome, but they still had between 40,000 and 60,000 soldiers on the ground and Nol found himself under severe pressure. Typically, Nixon prevaricated and procrastinated. However, on 29 April 1970, 19,300 US ground troops invaded Cambodia into an area known as the Fish Hook. At the same time, 29,000 ARVN soldiers attacked Parrot's Beak. This was all in direct response to Nol's appeal for American support. The aim of the invasion was to destroy the COSVN headquarters and logistic bases while, at the same time, making it clear to Hanoi that they faced an obdurate foe in Richard Nixon.

The anticipated set-piece battle at Fish Hook did not happen because the communists had decamped. The tanks met opposition, but occupied the logistic bases with relative ease. The ARVN operations at Parrot's Beak were similar; any opposition met was brushed aside. By 3 May the fighting had finished. The headquarters of COSVN was not found, but a vast logistic city covering an area of 3 square kilometres was discovered and there were rich pickings to be had. An inventory of the spoils had to be made and all installations, barracks, hospitals, classrooms, bunkers and storage barns razed. The list of captured matériel was impressive. It included:

- 23,000 individual weapons, sufficient to equip 74 PAVN battalions;
- 2,500 crew-served weapons, 25 battalions' worth;
- 16,700,000 rounds of small-arms ammunition, a year's worth;
- 14,000,000lb of rice, say 30 tons;
- 143,000 rounds of mortar, rocket and recoilless rifle ammunition; and
- 200,000 rounds of AA ammunition.

There was a price to pay for all this booty: 976 men were killed, of whom 338 were Americans. It was claimed that the communists lost 'about 11,000 dead and 2,500 captured'; although these figures are not verified there is no doubt that the operation had dealt the PAVN and VC a very serious blow and, arguably, from the loss of Sihanoukville, the martial aspirations of Hanoi 'were put back a year or probably eighteen months and possibly two years'.[7]

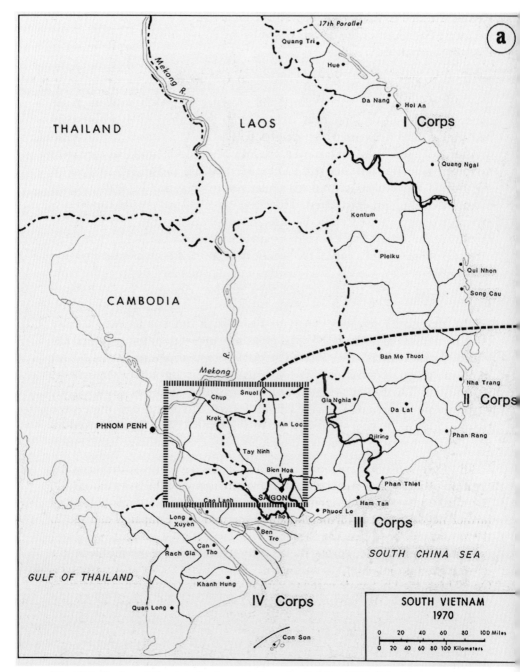

The Fish Hook and Parrot's Beak operations, April–May 1970. (*US Military Academy*)

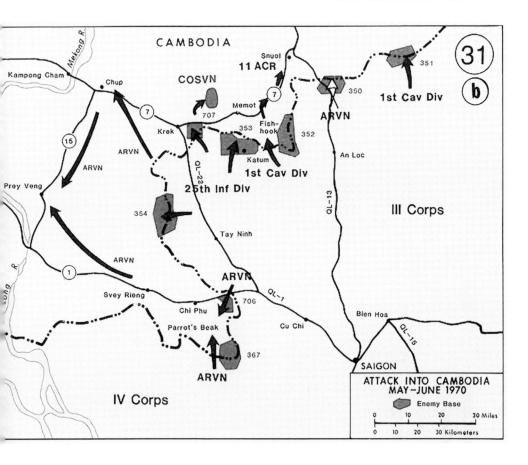

The other effects were mixed. It gave the American withdrawal some breathing space and it augured well for Vietnameseation because the ARVN had apparently performed creditably. However, it did not contribute to any further negotiations; it further inflamed the anti-war campaign and led to the killing of four students at Kent State University on 4 May 1970. Rioting followed in universities across the country and, on 8 May, 100,000 people demonstrated in Washington and almost caused a breakdown in government. On 30 June, the US Senate voted to withhold funds for any further operations in Cambodia but the measure did find favour with the House of Representatives. However, with immediate effect US ground forces were forbidden to enter either Cambodia or Laos.

The further political machinations need not concern us here; suffice to say that stemming from the Cambodian invasion (and swift withdrawal), mounting public dissent became the prime factor in Nixon's policy on fighting the war. Hanoi observed this from a distance and concluded, correctly, that the primary battlefield was thousands of miles away.

An analysis of the ARVN's superficially satisfactory performance at Parrot's Beak revealed that modest success was accomplished despite logistic deficiencies. The armoured component was beset by a range of issues. Patton discovered in 1944 that any armoured thrust must have a rock-solid fuel re-supply system in place. This was missing at Parrot's Beak, as were efficient radio communications. Importantly, the field maintenance of the armour, dependent on the availability of spare parts and skilled mechanics, was sorely inadequate. Many tanks broke down and their recovery, by a tow from a functioning tank, reduced the force by two.

The politicization of the ARVN, the lack of discipline and the convoluted command system all combined to limit Vietnameseation. Meanwhile the US Army continued in its apparently unstoppable decline. Absence without leave (AWOL) became more prevalent and drug use climbed. In 1970 there were 65,000 men using drugs and that resulted in 11,058 arrests which further clogged the judicial system. There were far more instances of insubordination and wilful refusal to obey an order, in some cases amounting to nothing less than outright unvarnished mutiny. Soldiers were unshaven, badly turned out and slothful.[8] The malaise was not confined to Vietnam but also to bases in the USA. The quote at the head of this chapter applied, as defeat was painfully acknowledged. The slump in morale was as von Clausewitz predicted. Senior US officers despaired at a situation created by a political decision and one that they could not now correct.

Kissinger held secret meetings in Paris with Le Duc Tho in Paris on 23 February, 16 March and 4 April 1970; however, he could not reach any agreement with Le Duc Tho who was a seasoned and capable negotiator. Le Duc Tho knew full well that time was on his side as the ferment in the United States grew ever more vociferous.

During 1970 the Pacification and Phoenix programs had put the VC in retreat and South Vietnam was a safer

Le Duc Tho (1911–90), a luminary of the Central Commission of the Communist Party of North Vietnam, winner of the Nobel Peace Prize in 1973. He declined the award. (*DRV*)

place. This was evidenced by the ability to drive south from the DMZ to the southern coast of South Vietnam in safety. VC activity was limited to eleven provinces of the forty-four. Assassinations and kidnapping were much reduced. The People's Self-Defence Force had grown: it had 1,397,000 on its nominal roll and arms were available for 500,000; 91 per cent of hamlets in South Vietnam were said to be 'secure', 7.2 per cent were in the process of being 'contested' and only 1.4 per cent were VC-controlled. By the measurement of 'pacification', alone the war in South Vietnam was being won. The US/GVN was now committing resources to pacification and providing the inhabitants of those hamlets with farming machinery such as tractors, water pumps and generators. This change in logistic priorities meant that non-lethal material was as important as bombs, grenades and small-arms ammunition. The result of this realignment made for an increase in the annual rice harvest from 5.1 million tons to 5.5 million. President Thieu introduced a Land Reform Programme, a further step in the right direction as previously landless peasants were given 8.22 acres to farm.

Despite this largesse, the population did not swing behind its government. It did not miss the oppressive VC, but nor did it feel any affection for either Thieu or his cohorts. This was because, for the most part, the same corrupt officials still managed local affairs. By the end of 1970 the Pacification program had achieved its original aim, which was to counter and defeat VC control of the countryside. This was a success of which the USA could be justly proud.

The incursions at Parrot's Beak and Fish Hook were viewed as successes and in late 1970 it bred an ambition among senior Americans to repeat the exercise, this time in an operation designed to cut the Ho Chi Minh Trail (HCMT). The trail was the sole logistic route from North Vietnam into the South since the loss of the port of Sihanoukville, hitherto the point of entry for 70 per cent of PAVN supplies in the south. The loss of the port had been a serious blow to the PAVN/VC and the HCMT was now critical to the PAVN if it was to operate south of the DMZ.

It was recognized that the ground troops would have to be ARVN, but the US could provide artillery and aerial support. Hanoi was painfully aware of its vulnerability, especially since the earlier invasion and the devastating effect it had had on the COSVN logistic base. Giap reorganized his assets and created 70B Corps with three divisions – the 304th, 308th and 320th – under command. Giap presupposed that any attack would follow the axis of Route 9, that unkempt apology for a road. The 70B Corps was ordered to establish blocking positions along the anticipated line of advance.

The ARVN operation was designated Operation LAM SON 719. It was approved at the very highest military and political levels in both Saigon and

Washington. Approval was given without any recorded dissent. The final decision-maker was Richard Nixon and he signed off on the operation, after typical vacillation, on 18 January 1971. The aim was to destroy the logistic installation in Base Areas 604 and 611, both located in Laos. For the Americans, fully committed to withdrawal from South-East Asia, nevertheless believed it made sense to be party to a tactical offensive operation. There were to be other examples before the final exit in 1973, all of which put the enemy on the back foot and gave the US breathing space.

There was no element of surprise in this operation; there were too many people who were aware of the aims and the timings. Security throughout the ARVN was very lax; an indicator of its inherent corruption.

One of the first major logistic tasks was the repair of the runway at Khe Sanh. It will be remembered that all evidence that Khe Sanh was a military base had been ruthlessly eradicated back in June 1968, only two and a half years earlier. This refurbishment was the first of many LAM SON 719 logistic tasks.

Operations started on 30 January and the logistic function rested on American shoulders. A complication was that although the US would provide artillery support, it could not have its Forward Observation Officers (FOOs) embedded with ARVN armour and infantry. Similarly, air controllers could go no further forward than the Laotian border. This was fighting a war with one arm tied behind the back, and the result of the political storm caused by the earlier invasion. A factor to be considered by the ARVN was the PAVN capacity to reinforce the border area and the 22,000 troops already in place. Giap had between 170 and 200 mixed-calibre AA guns that would challenge the US air sorties in support of the ARVN.

The operation was a succession of blunders. The South Vietnamese had not been tested in major deployments before without accompanying American advisors. The best guess, by American planners, was that four divisions or about 60,000 men would be required to accomplish this mission. Saigon demurred and allocated half that number. It was evident from the very first that Thieu intended to be a player in the operation, having given command of the ARVN Corps to Lieutenant General Hoàng Xuân Lãm. This officer was more noted for his fidelity to Thieu than for his martial ability. Lãm was a bad choice, made for the wrong reasons.

The Laotian town of Tchepone, only about 20 miles inside the border, was the prime objective. This town was already a ruin as it had been a target for earlier US bombing raids. For LAM SON 719 the ruin was bombed again and reduced to rubble. Thieu had ordered General Lãm that he was to halt his incursion as and when he had incurred 3,000 casualties. This was a bizarre, completely non-military instruction that bore no relation to the tactical reality. The weather closed in on 6/7 February and air cover was withdrawn. The following day ARVN formations advanced about 4 miles along Route 9 into Laos and Giap held his fire; he wanted to be sure that this was not just a feint. A Luoi was taken on 10 February and the operation was progressing well, if rather slowly. On 11 February, the 3,000th casualty was incurred. At that point, the ARVN force froze. Lãm issued no orders, nor did his sub-ordinates. Everything just stopped.

Adams, who was playing the role of spectator, was furious. Hard experience had taught him that momentum is critical in armoured warfare. He was unable to restart the advance and he knew that standing still was inviting disaster. Having been invited, disaster duly joined the party.

The ARVN had not even got halfway to its objective, it had not cut or taken control of the HCMT and now it retreated. It was an epic failure with high logistic costs. The retreat rapidly became a rout, trucks ran out of fuel and were abandoned, and men fought to get onto American helicopters. In the USA, the public could see on their TVs ARVN soldiers hanging onto the skids of those helicopters, further damaging the credibility of the war in Vietnam. It was clear that the ARVN was more a leaderless mob than an army. Its deficiencies had been cruelly exposed and Thieu had much to answer for. Although the operation had been agreed at the highest levels, defeat has no father. Nixon, in the face of overwhelming evidence to the contrary and clutching at straws, claimed it as a proof of the success of Vietnameseation and blamed the media for focusing on just a few dreadful scenes.

He convinced very few because, patently, Vietnameseation had just failed miserably. Kissinger, who had been an important player throughout the planning stage, said that the venture had 'fallen far short of our expectations' and went on to blame everyone else, 'characteristically, except himself'.[9]

It is also characteristic that the casualty count varies depending on the source. The ARVN dead are reported as being between 1,529 and 8,483 and the wounded between 5,483 and 12,420; vast disparities. US losses are firmer: between 215 and 253 killed and 1,491 wounded with thirty-eight missing. Thirty-two artillery guns were lost and a further eighty-two captured, it is presumed either to counter-battery fire or when they were overrun in the rout. Some seven fixed-wing aircraft and 107 helicopters were destroyed and around 618 damaged. In addition, fifty-four tanks, eighty-seven armoured vehicles, all engineer plant such as bulldozers and graders and 211 trucks were lost. This was an expensive sortie and the hardware losses incurred during the shambolic, ill-disciplined rout ran into hundreds of millions of dollars.

The PAVN admitted to 2,163 killed and 6,176 wounded. Hastings says that the PAVN's material losses were '670 AA guns, 600 trucks and 88 tanks'.[10] However, he does not provide his source to support these figures. Davidson, on the other hand, asserts the PAVN losses were 2,001 trucks, 106 tanks, 13 guns, 170,346 tons of ammunition and 1,250 tons of rice.[11] The arithmetic is academic from a fifty-year distance. However, the conclusion is that both sides suffered very significant logistic losses. The Chinese and the American taxpayers would pick up the bill.

The failure of LAM SON 719 was a South Vietnamese failure, but illogically the people of that country blamed the USA. There were anti-American demonstrations and American property was attacked. American soldiers were at risk on the streets. The prospect of the USA leaving in the near future bred resentment at the need for the South Vietnamese to fend for themselves. This was an unexpected political consequence of LAM SON 719.

During LAM SON 719 the ARVN M41 light tank had been outgunned by the enemy T-54 medium tank. The MACV promptly re-equipped one ARVN battalion with the M48, and at the same time some self-propelled 175mm guns were introduced to counter Russian 130mm guns fielded by the PAVN. This was a piecemeal, partial arrangement and a half-hearted response.

Chapter Twenty-Four

Operations LINEBACKER
I & II

'He who can modify his tactics in relation to his opponent
and thereby succeed in winning may be called a
heaven-born captain.'[1]

[Sun Tzu]

Following LAM SON 719 there were further military disasters to come and, on 27 March 1971, Fire Support Base Mary Ann was attacked and thirty-one Americans were killed. The defensive arrangements in the isolated hilltop base were inadequate; the troops were indolent, decadent, ill-prepared and ill-disciplined. They were expecting to hand over the base to the ARVN within a few days and, on that basis, had opted out of the war.

Local command was in the hands of poor-quality officers. There were serious repercussions for this avoidable incident and the 23rd Division Commander, Major General Baldwin, was replaced. He received only a letter of admonishment; five other officers suffered administrative penalties sufficient to end their careers. In the great scheme of things FSB Mary Ann was just a minor lost engagement. However, its importance was the slackness and un-soldierly conduct of its garrison and the failure of higher command to identify the situation and correct it. It was symptomatic of the remaining rump of the US Army in Vietnam and demonstrated the lethal folly of attempting, unilaterally, to abandon the war while still within reach of the enemy.[2]

There was political folly too and the part that Nixon played in the war is riddled with intrigue, hypocrisy and dishonesty. His conduct was matched by that of Kissinger and the pair were arch manipulators of people and situations. For example, before flying sorties over Laos and Cambodia navigators were ordered to sign non-disclosure agreements; this applied to the 4,308 sorties made between March 1969 and May 1970. Fake war diaries were compiled to conceal the truth. Nixon was not prepared to regularize his air campaign over Cambodia by seeking changes to the Rules of Engagement (RoE) because that would be subject to public scrutiny.

Later, the White House tapes revealed a telling conversation between the two men in May 1971:

Kissinger: 'So, we get through 72. I'm being perfectly cynical about this, Mr. President.'
Nixon: 'Yes.'
Kissinger: 'If we can, in October '72, go around the country saying we ended the war and the Democrats wanted to turn it over to the Communists . . .'
Nixon: 'That's right.'
Kissinger: 'Then we're in great shape.'
Kissinger: 'If it's got to go to the Communists, it'd be better to have it happen in the first six months of the new term than have it go on and on.'
Nixon: 'Sure.'
Kissinger: 'I'm being very cold-blooded about it.'
Nixon: 'I know exactly what we're up to.'[3]

By the spring of 1971 the political scene was rancid and the military scene little better. Creighton Adams was succumbing to the pressure of the job and he was beset by ill-health and alcohol. His much-reduced army still had a 'ration strength' of 156,800 but the US Army was no longer disposed to take offensive action and so the priorities were the defence of its vast logistic bases and the provision of logistic support to South Vietnamese forces. By year's end the MACV ration strength was down to 24,200 and the American ground military venture was at an end.

On 13 June 1971 a political bomb burst when the *New York Times* published the first extracts of the 'Pentagon Papers', a document leaked by Daniel Ellsberg, a civil servant who had worked on the 'Report of the Office of the Secretary of Defense, Vietnam Task Force'.[4] The document was a history of the political and military involvement of the USA in Vietnam from 1945 until 1967. It revealed that the Johnson White House had 'systemati-cally lied, not only to the public but also to Congress'.[5] The political waters in Washington were muddy and they would get muddier, not least when un-lawful attempts were made to discredit Ellsberg. This was by a group whose function was to plug leaks of sensitive information. They were called the 'White House Plumbers' and, later, their activities inadvertently brought about the downfall of Richard Nixon.

The South Vietnamese re-elected President Thieu on 3 October 1971, to the disbelief of his critics and the chagrin of Nixon and Kissinger who viewed Thieu as an obstacle to peace. Thieu was not everyone's cup of tea, but there could be no doubt as to his total commitment to his country's sovereignty.

The peace negotiations were lengthy and tedious and Thieu's intransigence prolonged the process. For Nixon an agreement was the key to his re-election in 1972. In order to win that re-election, he and Kissinger were prepared to promise Thieu ongoing logistic support after the withdrawal of American forces, a promise that they had no intention of keeping. There was every reason to suppose that the DRV would invade South Vietnam after the withdrawal and they hoped for a decent interval eighteen months to two years before the inevitable happened.

It became clear, in early 1972, that the North was planning an offensive but the where and the when were unknowns because there was an intelligence void. On 30 March, in what was termed 'the Easter Offensive', two PAVN divisions – the 304th and 308th – supported by more than 100 tanks crashed through the DMZ to attack the northernmost provinces of South Vietnam. There was a further invasion from Laos in the west when the 312th Division, with supporting armour, advanced along the line of Route 9 by passing Khe Sanh and into the Quang Tri River Valley. The invasion surprisingly startled the residual Americans and ARVN, giving the PAVN 'the inestimable benefit of shock effect, a crucial psychological edge over defenders who had expected something quite different.'[6] Proof of that surprise is that both General Adams and Ambassador Bunker were out of the country at the time.

On 4 April and in order to forestall a total ARVN collapse, Nixon initiated Operation LINEBACKER I, a bombing attack on the DRV. This operation lasted until 23 October 1972 and its conduct was in military hands, unlike the unsuccessful ROLLING THUNDER. The aim of LINEBACKER I was fourfold and specifically to

> isolate North Vietnam from its external sources of supply by destroying railroad bridges and rolling stock in and around Hanoi and north-eastward toward the Chinese frontier; the targeting of primary storage areas and marshalling yards; to destroy storage and transshipment points; and finally, to eliminate (or at least damage) the North's air defence system.[7]

In effect the bombing was intended to degrade the logistic capability of the DRV. However, to achieve the aim the USA now had less than half their previous air strength. There were three squadrons of F-4s and one of A-37s, in all seventy-six aircraft. However, there were 114 fighter-bombers and eighty-three B-52s stationed in Thailand (now an international airport) and Guam. These considerable USAF assets were supplemented by a USN task force patrolling on the gulf of Tonkin that could provide a further 140 strike aircraft. There was a rapid build-up and by the end of May the number of aircraft had doubled. The naval reinforcement was huge, initially four carriers (later reduced to one), one heavy cruiser, five smaller cruisers and forty-four destroyers. Measurement of the number of sorties flown gives a feel for the scale of LINEBACKER I. During March 1972 there were 4,237 and the South Vietnamese Air Force (VNAF) flew the majority (3,149). Thereafter the pace of the campaign rose and in April there were 17,171 sorties, rising to 18,444 in May. The provision of ordnance and other logistic support for this activity was not all from within Vietnam.

Adams and Ambassador Bunker opposed the bombing of the North on the grounds that the bombing should be directed on the enemy closer to hand in the South. They argued that if the current invasion was not quelled, then the South and the war were both lost. Nixon rejected their advice, increased the intensity of the campaign and deployed 'smart' laser-guided bombs with marked success. Notwithstanding Nixon's resolution, Quang Tri had fallen on 1 May just before the mining of Haiphong harbour and the bombing of Hanoi.

The ARVN was alone on the ground; there were American advisors, but ground operations were Vietnamese. The fighting was ferocious as the PAVN advanced on An Loc, a mere 60 miles north of Saigon. The PAVN was under the command of General Van Tien Dung. This man had spent his life at war and had played a key logistic role at the Battle of Dien Bien Phu. He was

Operations LINEBACKER I & II; B-52 bombers in action. (*USAF*)

---

second only to Giap in the DRV military hierarchy and a formidable adversary.

The air assault on the DRV was huge and amounted to the dropping of 155,548 tons of explosives. The effect was reduced imports into that county from 160,000 tons per month to 30,000 tons and imports by sea from 250,000 tons to nil. Carefully-directed strikes had destroyed most of the DRV's oil storage and 70 per cent of its energy-generating capacity. LINEBACKER won support from the American public and Nixon's political stock rose along with his re-election prospects. There were costs, of course, and the USAF/USN lost forty-four aircraft and crews.

Adams' attitude to LINEBACKER earned the hostility of Kissinger and cost him his job. Adams was 'kicked

General Van Tien Dung (1917–2002), a protégé of Giap and an accomplished commander. (*DRV*)

upstairs' to replace Westmoreland as chief of staff in June 1972. Fred Weyand, erstwhile commander of the 25th Division at Cu Chi, took command of the rump of the MACV until the final withdrawal.

It took time, but the ARVN, now at its peak strength of 1,110,000 with a further 36,000 from South Korea and aided by American air power, slowly and at a cost regained lost ground. However, the enormous size of the ARVN was not, in itself, enough. The quality of its leadership was mixed, ranging from 'very poor' through 'mediocre' to 'competent'. Notwithstanding that, with supporting USAF power, it inflicted such losses on the PAVN that it caused even its most committed communist commanders to take issue with their political leadership, a bold and probably career-inhibiting action.

The impact of air power on guerrilla forces thinly spread and concealed was one thing, but the same air power employed against large bodies of troops, deployed to fight a conventional war, was vastly different and against armour it was utterly devastating. The PAVN had also lost its logistic edge that was the mark of a Giap-led operation. In this case, the great man's role was not operational and his logistic flair was missed by his soldiers, who were short of food, ammunition and medical supplies. This was a protracted operation, the logistic support did not improve, and it led to the eventual retreat.

On 11 July the first operations to retake Quang Tri were initiated by heli-copter assault. As the attrition of the PAVN continued, morale suffered and an ARVN victory became more likely. President Thieu was warned by Kissinger of the importance of taking ground because territorial possession would be an inevitable factor in any forthcoming cease-fire; the communists were unlikely to yield what they already held. Quang Tri was re-taken on 16 September. The USN had played a part in the battles of both Quang Tri and Hue and it fired up to 7,000 rounds a day. In the period April-September 1972, the ships fired 16,000 tons of ordnance into enemy positions, with great accuracy:

> While the B-52s, fighter-bombers AC-119 and 130 gunships were saving Kontum and An Loc, it was the C-130 cargo aircraft and supply heli-copters that kept the defenders supplied, first by landing in and near An Loc and then by air-drops. Army helicopters not only brought in supplies and replacements but evacuated the critically wounded.[8]

As the PAVN suffered from logistic deficiencies, the ARVN was very much better served. The criticality of competent logistic support in any operation has no better exemplar than the battles of the Easter Offensive of 1972. North Vietnam was isolated from Chinese and Russian logistic support as a con-sequence of the mining of Haiphong and the destruction of land routes from the Chinese border.[9] By late 1972, as the PAVN retired to lick its deep wounds, Hanoi recognized that it had probably lost its last chance to inflict military defeat on the USA and that negotiation was the next best option. In an extraordinary repeat of the Tet offensive, although the ARVN/USAF had clearly won the battle, the USA lost the media war, again. The 'Peace Movement' was stirred into renewed activity.

The estimates of casualties suffered in the Easter Offensive were, as ever, imprecise. ARVN losses were of the order of 10,000 killed, 33,000 wounded and 3,500 missing. This was wildly at odds with the claim made by the DRV that they had killed and wounded 213,307. Similarly, US sources spoke of 40,000 to 75,000 enemy killed and 60,000 wounded. PAVN tank losses were thought to be within the vast bracket of between 250 and 700.

The PAVN was highly-skilled and vastly experienced in guerrilla opera-tions, but markedly less so in mobile conventional warfare in which forma-tions with armoured support advances to contact. The logistic requirements of an armoured unit are much more sophisticated than that of a guerrilla force. The provision of ammunition, petrol, oil and lubricants (POL) are as nothing compared to mechanical maintenance, recovery and repair. Without command of the air and without experience to draw upon, the PAVN made a serious error of judgement in March 1972 and it paid the price. Giap had opposed the operation, just as back in 1968 he had opposed the Tet offensive. However, the general's sound advice had been spurned. Notwithstanding the failure of the offensive, General Dung was promoted to full membership of the politburo and given overall command of the PAVN. Giap was demoted and sidelined after twenty-nine years as the country's leading soldier.

All was not sweetness and light with the ARVN and many commanders at all levels were found wanting. Two of the four corps commanders were sacked, as was the commander of a Marine division. A divisional commander was court-martialled. Further down the chain of command there was considerable attrition as the conduct and performance of officers was examined. It did not augur well for military operations after the final American withdrawal.

Meanwhile, LINEBACKER continued, the bombs rained down, and while Kissinger devilled away behind the scenes trying to cobble together a cease-fire, the DRV was reduced to a wasteland and its logistic infrastructure destroyed. The search for an agreement to which all the interested parties would sign up was long and tedious; Thieu was the rock upon which the draft agreements kept foundering.

While the talking went on, the USA mounted Operation ENHANCE PLUS. This was an enormous airlift of military equipment of all sorts. The draft agreement 'specified that equipment would be replaced on a one-for-one basis'. This injection of arms and equipment raised the baseline for further supplies and was designed, theoretically, to improve South Vietnam's capacity to defend itself after the final American withdrawal. However, although the equipment sent to South Vietnam was wide-ranging, it included aircraft for which there were no trained pilots, vehicles of every sort but without spare parts, weapons without ammunition or armourers to maintain them; in fact, all the elements for a rich man's war. ENHANCE PLUS was a hollow gesture from a cynical government without honour to an abandoned government facing a future, cataclysmic defeat.

LINEBACKER attacks above the 20th parallel were paused on 23 October. The DRV demanded that the agreement be signed by 31 October, but Thieu was intransigent and an unfortunate slip of the tongue by Kissinger at a press conference complicated matters. Hanoi was in a hurry because it wanted to stop the re-equipping of the South Vietnamese Air Force which, under ENHANCE PLUS, was proceeding apace. The 31 October deadline came and passed. Relations between Nixon and Kissinger were now 'wary and strained' and between Kissinger and his DRV opposite number they were out-and-out hostile.

Nixon was re-elected on 7 November and this was an invitation to flex America's muscles which, on 29 November, Nixon duly did when he threatened an emissary of Thieu. He warned that, if a peace agreement was not agreed, he would cut off all support to the regime and added, 'without aid you cannot survive, understand?'[10]

It is outside the bounds of this book to cover in detail the labyrinthine machinations of the peace process. They have merited several books and, as there were no discernible logistic issues, suffice to say that in December 1972 talks broke down. On 15 December, Nixon demanded that Hanoi re-open negotiations within seventy-two hours or face renewed bombing. The DRV did not meet the deadline and Nixon initiated LINEBACKER II. This was called the 'Christmas bombing'.

Nixon spoke to the Chairman of the Joint Chief of Staff, Admiral Moorer, and laid his cards on the table. He said to the admiral: 'I don't want any more of this crap about the fact that we couldn't hit this target or that one. This is your chance to use military power effectively to win this war, and if you don't, I'll consider you responsible.'[11]

The gloves were off: the USAF, having already laid waste to most of the DRV, was now to bomb the rubble. It was a brutal demonstration of just how powerful the USA really was. LINEBACKER II was to destroy every military installation in and around Hanoi and Haiphong, specifically AA sites, airfields, railway yards, bridges, roads, powerplants and factories. The vulnerable centuries-old, 2,500-mile labyrinth of earthen dikes around Hanoi were not attacked, despite this exchange between Nixon and Kissinger, which was reported by Ellsberg:

> **Nixon**: 'We've got to quit thinking in terms of a three-day strike in the Hanoi-Haiphong area. We've got to be thinking in terms of an all-out bombing attack, which will continue until they . . . Now by all-out bombing attack, I am thinking about things that go far beyond. I'm thinking of the dikes, I'm thinking of the railroad, I'm thinking, of course, the docks.'
>
> **Kissinger**: 'I agree with you.'
>
> **President Nixon**: 'We've got to use massive force.' (Two hours later at noon, H.R. Haldeman and Ron Ziegler joined Kissinger and Nixon.) 'How many did we kill in Laos?'
>
> **Ziegler**: 'Maybe 10,000–15,000?'
>
> **Nixon**: 'See, the attack in the North that we have in mind, powerplants, whatever's left – POL, the docks. And, I still think we ought to take the dikes out now. Will that drown people?'
>
> **Kissinger**: 'About 200,000 people.'

Nixon: 'No, no, no, I'd rather use the nuclear bomb. Have you got that, Henry?'

Kissinger: 'That, I think, would just be too much.'

Nixon: 'The nuclear bomb, does that bother you? ... I just want you to think big, Henry, for Chrisssakes.'

The bombardment lasted for eleven days (18–29 December 1972) and the unrestrained violence of the campaign made the USA the subject of excoriating comment in the world's media, not least in America. The critics did not seem to understand that, when fighting an enemy committed to total war, extreme violence is required.

In this brief eleven-day time frame there were 724 B-52 sorties and about 640 fighter-bomber sorties. In all, 20,237 tons of ordnance were dropped on a badly-damaged country that quaked under the onslaught. DRV sources claimed that 1,318 of its citizens had been killed, a surprisingly low figure considering the intensity of the attacks. By 28 December the USAF had run out of targets and the DRV had run out of SAMs and was defenceless against further air attack. The USA lost only twenty-six aircraft. It is a measure of the logistic depth of the USA that 20,000 tons of bombs were readily available, that it had the industrial capacity to produce armaments on that scale and the ability to mount air operations from bases thousands of miles away from the targets. LINEBACKER II was a matchless, ruthless and highly effective operation.

By 29 December, the DRV had had enough: its industry, economy and military capacity were all in shreds and it agreed to re-open negotiations. Less than a month later, on 27 January 1973, an agreement was signed, despite Thieu's protestations and, on 27 March, the last American soldier left the country. All the USA's ammunition, weapons, artillery, aircraft, vehicles and domestic facilities were abandoned.

South Vietnam was now on its own, facing a foe that had a devastated homeland but with undiminished aspirations to unify North and South Vietnam, no matter how many Vietnamese lives it would cost.

The scene was set for the Third Vietnamese War.

Chapter Twenty-Five

Reunification: The Finale

'Battles are won by superiority of fire.'[1]

[Frederick the Great]

The victory of North Vietnam (DRV) over the Republic of South Vietnam (RVN) was entirely predictable. It was to be the last of the Vietnamese wars, the third, and was also the shortest: just two years. It was, in effect, a civil war as Vietnamese fought fellow Vietnamese. The DRV, although it was devastated by LINEBACKER II, still aspired to ensure the reunification of both Vietnams and it was only a question of when Hanoi would act.

From April 1973 the economy of the RVN plunged, American support of the economy had ceased, the employment of tens of thousands of people had terminated and the free-spending American soldiers were no more. The economic future looked bleak, but the military situation was, superficially, just a little more promising. The Republic of Vietnam (RVN) controlled 'roughly 75 per cent of South Vietnam's territory and about 85 per cent of its population'.[2] The RVN was sitting on that vast inventory of military equipment which the USA had dumped and to which they now added. However, the RVN Armed Forces (RVNAF) were ineffectively structured, corrupt and badly-led. They were untrained and unable to make use of some of their recently-acquired logistic bounty from Operation ENHANCE PLUS.

In mid-1973 the RVNAF, although about 1 million strong, had only 200,000 infantry. The RVNAF were organized on American lines; they were logistically heavy, and a chronic shortage of capable leaders was unresolved. Nevertheless, the RVNAF outnumbered the communist troops, of whom there were about 219,000 still ensconced in the country. These PAVN/VC troops were quiescent and recovering from the mauling of the Easter offensive a year earlier; they were ill-served logistically and morale was low.

A key player at this time was General Tran Van Tra. He had been in command of PAVN forces during the attack on Saigon during the Tet offensive in 1968 and he reported frankly to Hanoi on the condition of communist forces in South Vietnam. He said that 'our troops are exhausted, and their units are in disarray. We have not been able to make up our losses. We are short of manpower as well as food and ammunition.'[3]

Unabashed by those deficiencies and the recent domestic destruction, Hanoi, despite the agreement so recently signed, started to infiltrate even more men and matériel into the RVN. Incredibly, by mid-April 7,000 PAVN trucks had crossed the DMZ and the much-improved Ho Chi Minh Trail (HCMT) was being put to good use as 73,000 men and up to 500 tanks moved south. Thirteen newly-formed AA battalions were strategically located in South Vietnam and the 263rd Surface-to-Air Missile (SAM) Regiment was in place at Khe Sanh. The fuel line that ran down the HCMT was renewed and expanded. Thirteen airfields were constructed in the sovereign state of South Vietnam by its invasive neighbour. This logistic build-up outdid the logistic effort at Dien Bien Phu some nineteen years earlier. It was the product of a country that had been totally brutalized only months before. The fact that those 7,000 trucks had survived the bombing verges on the miraculous.

The intentions of the DRV (North) were very clear: it had invaded the RVN (South) and now intended to take the state by force of arms. The Third Indochina War was about to commence but, before the shooting started, the DRV worked to destabilize the government of the RVN politically. It embarked on a well-judged and entirely fallacious propaganda campaign that accused the RVN of breaking the peace agreement. This campaign targeted its own soldiers, the people of South Vietnam and the rest of the world. They do say 'if you decide to tell a lie, tell a big one'. The DRV did this and enjoyed a degree of success as a result.

Although Thieu remained firmly in control of his government, he became the architect of his own downfall by taking an uncompromising, intransigent position. He famously had four political and military 'Noes'. These were 'No' territory or outpost was to be surrendered to the enemy. There was to be 'No' coalition government, 'No' negotiation with the enemy and 'No' communist or neutralist activity in the country. The inflexibility that this policy engendered was to prove fatal. Viewing the gathering storm from a distance, Kissinger suggested to a beleaguered Nixon coping with the Watergate affair that the USAF should bomb either the HCMT or the DMZ or both. Nixon was distracted, but authorized some inconsequential strikes on Laos that had no practical effect.

History tells us that when politicians try to play general, it usually ends badly. Hitler, Stalin and Johnson are three examples and now Thieu joined them. His edicts, based on his four 'Noes', committed his troops to a defensive posture, much to the satisfaction of General Dung, leading the PAVN, to whom he had gifted the initiative. Despite being aware of the massive PAVN build-up in South Vietnam, Thieu misread Dung's intentions. Thieu anticipated that Hanoi would seek to overthrow his regime by political means, to include subversion and guerrilla tactics. Having misread Dung's intentions, he also misread the American commitment to his cause and assumed that massive air power was readily available when needed. He had good cause to think that because Nixon had written to Thieu in January 1973, saying 'You have my assurance that we will respond with full force should the settlement be violated by North Vietnam.'[4] Nixon lied: he had no such intention.

There was no American commitment to the RVN, which was on its own. In June 1973, the US Congress reduced the funding of the armed forces and very significantly passed a bill that prohibited direct or indirect combat activities on or near Laos, Cambodia and both Vietnams after 15 August 1973. An RVN naval officer, Commander Nguyen Tri, speaking later said 'the Communists did not win. The Americans simply decided to go home and let South Vietnam lose.'[5]

There was fighting across South Vietnam but a previous kill ratio of 5:1 in favour of the ARVN dropped back to 2:1. By late 1973 the allocation of ammunition was eighty-five rounds and one grenade per month. Soldiers were obliged to fire single shots rather than the favoured short burst of two or three rounds. The economic situation worsened daily. About 2 million people who had previously been employed by the USA were now jobless. TV sets, hi-fi equipment, scooters, imported cigarettes and chocolate vanished from the shops. Car sales dropped to 1 per cent of the previous year. The war in the Middle East in October 1973 added to the financial and economic crisis and inflation rose to 40 per cent.

The RVNAF was created by the Americans in their own likeness, dependent upon state-of-the-art technology and an overly munificent and inflated logistic system. The RVNAF were consuming 56 tons of munitions for every ton expended by the communists. Those communists now determined to attack only in places where they had numerical superiority, the object being to tilt the military balance. To support this policy, the major logistic programme initiated in April 1973 to create a strong platform for the eventual offensive was enhanced and accelerated.

An all-weather highway was constructed from Quang Tri province on the central coast to the Mekong delta. This would expand the road network under PAVN control to 12,000 miles. A network of oil pipelines 3,000 miles long was built with a terminal at Locninh, the site of the PAVN headquarters, about 75 miles north-west of Saigon. A modern radio grid enabled country-wide communications and enhanced the logistic effort. The fact that Hanoi could mount these grandiose programmes is testament to its resilience and amazing recovery from LINEBACKER II. Relations with China and Russia were strained, and in October 1973 approaches to both these previous benefactors for logistic support were rejected.

In late 1973 an offensive was launched and by April 1974, General Tran Van Tra estimated that he had regained all the territory in the Delta lost after the truce. However, Thieu's most determined opponents were not the North Vietnamese, they were his own people. The country was riven with discontent and dissension which Thieu countered with vigorous police action that only served to feed the dissension.

Nixon's malfeasance caused his fall in August 1974 but, before he left office, he signed a bill limiting US aid to the GVN to $1 billion for the next eleven months. This was cut to $700,000 by Congress. President Ford hastened to assure Thieu that 'our support will be adequate'.[6] It was a hollow promise.

General Tran Van Tra was anxious to get on with the conquest of South Vietnam, and by late 1974 he had all the means at his disposal. However, like generals the world over, he met political objections, in this case from Le Duc Tho, the tough negotiator who had dealt with Kissinger but was now back to the centre of the DRV political scene. Le Duc Tho pressed for a continuation of the logistic build-up and General Van Tien Dung supported his view. General Tra was undaunted and now took his case for action to Le Duan, the head of state. A compromise was agreed for a limited offensive; this started in the middle of December 1974 and General Van Tien Dung, despite his earlier opposition, was placed in command.

On 6 January the city of Phuoc Binh, capital of Phuoc Long province, was taken. The garrison was no match for the division-size assault force. The RVN Air Force was deterred by the PAVN anti-aircraft capability and so bombed, ineffectively, from an altitude of 30,000ft. The loss of Phuoc Binh stunned Thieu and his government and the non-response of the US government to the matter heightened the degree of shock. In Hanoi the complete lack of an American reaction was seized upon. It was only the possibility of US bombers that they had to fear because it was clear that ground troops from the USA were most unlikely to be reintroduced. Dung moved four divisions into central South Vietnam and threatened the bailiwick of General Pham Van Phu, the local commander. Phu was no match for Dung and Pleiku and Kontum swiftly fell into communist hands. Thieu ordered that Hue be defended to the last man. The residents of that city decamped en masse and by late March a million refugees jammed roads leading to the south.

The events that followed were viewed on TV screens across the world. The PAVN advance took Hue and by doing so gave rise to massive panic among the civilian population. There were grisly scenes as people fought to save their lives: 'Thousands waded into the sea, among them mothers clutching babies: many drowned or were trampled to death as they fought to reach barges and fishing boats. Sometimes ARVN soldiers shot civilians to make room for themselves.'[7]

It was now only a matter of time. The advancing PAVN was able to rifle abandoned US Army facilities and its logistic needs were met, in part, by captured matériel. The ARVN was being routed and its supply system broke down as individuals looked to their own salvation. The DRV hierarchy in the shape of General Tran Van Tra, Pham Hung, Le Duc An and Le Duc Tho joined Dung at his headquarters in Loc Ninh to plan the encirclement and capture of Saigon. The aim was to take the city in the last week of April 1975. By now Dung's forces numbered 250,000 organized into five corps, fourteen divisions, ten independent brigades and SAM regiments.

The evacuation from Saigon of those likely to face execution by a victorious PAVN is a logistic epic in itself. There were 6,000 Americans and at least 100,000 Vietnamese who had previously been employed by the US in some capacity or another. To this multitude had to be added their kinfolk, pushing the total to almost 1 million. There existed the possibility that disaffected southern troops might turn their weapons on the evacuees to prevent their leaving.

South Vietnamese refugees land on a ship of the US Navy, April 1975. (*US Navy*)

General Duong Van Minh, very briefly the last president of South Vietnam, escorted from his office by PAVN soldiers. (*DRV*)

This is a much-published photograph. It shows only too clearly the atmosphere in Saigon as an officer of the CIA assists refugees on the roof of the US Embassy, Saigon, 30 April 1975.

Ambassador Martin did not excel. He vacillated and appeared to be in thrall to a bureaucratic mindset. He did have the capacity to be flexible and able to make up his own rules to cope with the situation. He was the wrong man in the wrong job at a very critical time.

Thieu was now an isolated, powerless figurehead. On 21 April he resigned and handed over to Tran Van Huong and then he fled to Taiwan. He commented on his desertion by the United States as 'an inhumane act by an inhumane ally'. The USA did, belatedly, seek to save as many of those million as it could. The operation conducted from the US Embassy bordered on the miraculous when the evacuation plan broke down under the weight of emotional and violent mobs. Ambassador Martin left by way of the embassy roof on 30 April and that same day Saigon fell when Colonel Bui Tin accepted the surrender of the city from General Duong Van Minh.

Thirty years of war were at an end, but the killing would go on for years.

Chapter Twenty-Six

Reunification: The Cost

'Money, more money, always more money.'[1]
[Marshal Gian Giacomo de Trivulce]

The first war in Indochina was 'The Logistics War', the second was 'The Helicopter War' and the third was 'The Conventional War'. They all differed, but the Communist Party was common to each. All the wars were fought in the same theatre and in the same climate but, although the logistic requirements were similar, the means of delivery were not.

The costs of war in Indochina in the thirty years from 1945 to 1975 have to be considered under a number of headings. The first and most obvious of these is casualties: dead, wounded and missing. In addition, the injured survivors have incurred ongoing costs. An example is those military and civilians affected by Agent Orange which the Vietnamese Red Cross alleges has caused health problems in 3 million Vietnamese. The chemical dioxin causes cancer, diabetes and birth defects. More than 2.59 million American soldiers were exposed to Agent Orange and 668,000 have suffered ill-health as a result. Those who handled the chemical were a third more likely to have disabled children.[2]

However, there are any number of other headings under which costs might be assessed. These include the intangible and thus immeasurable societal, domestic, psychological, structural and political. Of the others, not least was the financial cost, as the fifteenth-century commander Marshal Gian Giacomo de Trivulce so presciently remarked. The four adversaries would, each in turn, prioritize these costs differently. For example, the financial cost to the USA of Wars One and Two was vast, but they could afford it. Its dead and wounded were far, far more important, even though they were modest in number in comparison with the losses of the other three combatants. Before and after its defeat, the USA had to cope with significant domestic turbulence and political division. The country's prestige and standing, internationally, was degraded. From a military perspective the breakdown in discipline and the resulting abject performance of the US Army was a further serious cost, widely publicized. The cost to the United States could be measured in dollars and deaths alone, but the loss of dignity, respect and governmental authority,

The environmental cost: the effect of Agent Orange in the Mekong delta.

although intangible, were deleterious, long-lasting costs. Despite the lessons to be learned from Vietnam, the second war (1956–73) created a pattern for later unwelcome American incursions across the globe.

The Vietminh/Vietcong/NVA/PAVN, all armed elements of the DRV, spent a miniscule amount of money in comparison with the French and the USA but suffered very heavy casualties. These casualties had a major impact on communities, but were a matter of indifference to the political leaders and their generals. Ultimate victory was overridingly important and, in terms of national pride, it fully justified the human losses. The defeat of the French, Americans and South Vietnamese raised the status of the DRV internationally and its successful struggle for unification attracted a combination of awe and admiration.

For the South Vietnamese there were myriad costs. Initially their culture was heavily influenced by the French, but that lengthy influence, although uncaring, was benign. The Americans who followed came with a presumption of entitlement that adversely affected Vietnamese culture by the imposition of American lifestyles. The injection of generous aid did not generate gratitude but did fuel the inherent corruption that existed in every aspect of public life. By 1975, the cost to South Vietnam was all-embracing. It had lost its sovereignty, democracy, freedom of speech and the rule of law, fragile as that had been under Thieu. It also lost a high proportion of its most capable people either by their emigration or their execution, post-war.

Vietnam was embroiled in conflict for thirty years and during that period death-dealing equipment was in daily use by all sides. The total numbers killed during this period are, at best, an estimate and there is political bias in even arriving at that estimate. Today, on the internet it is possible to obtain speculative statistics that, although they are suspiciously rounded, they are difficult to refute. Paul Shannon worked on the topic in 1996 and arrived at the following:

> 4 million Vietnamese on all sides were killed, wounded or missing during the 1965–1975 period alone. The Pentagon's final estimate of civilian casualties for the South, a nation of about 18 million in 1972, was as high as 1,225,000 for the period between 1965 and 1972.
>
> A US Senate subcommittee report estimated 1,350,000 civilian casualties, including 415,000 killed, for the same period. [What is 125,000 between friends? (Author)] 'Enemy soldiers' killed were at least 850,000, according to both estimates. However, a substantial number of these 'enemy soldiers', were civilians whom the US military defined as 'enemy' because they were within free-fire zones, areas patrolled by US forces.
>
> Estimates of casualties suffered by the PAVN ran from 300,000 to 500,000. During the 'post-war' of 1973–1975, another half a million Vietnamese were killed and wounded – 340,000 of them were civilians – according to the US and South Vietnamese estimates.[3]

The Western casualties are well accounted for: 92,797 French soldiers, many of them colonial troops, were killed during the first Vietnamese War (1945–54) and 76,369 were wounded.[4] What is not recorded is the numbers who suffered life-changing mutilation or mental trauma. Their post-war treatment was an open-ended logistic cost to the French state.

The fall of Dien Bien Phu in 1954 inflicted considerable matériel losses on the French, and Bernard Fall estimated the financial cost of the war to France at $11 billion. Today, after sixty-four years of inflation, that equates to $104.7 billion. Towards the end the USA was meeting 80 per cent of the costs of the war and spent an equivalent $23.8 billion or thereabouts. The USA could well afford to prop up the French, and for the Americans it was a proxy war and a cost-effective way to fight communism.

The first Vietnamese War caused the deaths of about 400,00 North Vietnamese; these people did not all die at French hands because the authoritarian rule of the Vietminh in North Vietnam accounted for the uncounted slaughter of 'dissidents, rich peasants and intellectuals'. The acquisition of power by the Communist Party destroyed the old order and imposed an autocratic, merciless form of government. The social costs are immeasurable but there is no doubt that the DRV was, from its earliest days, utterly single-minded and it provided an unsophisticated peasant society with clear-cut aims that its government pursued ruthlessly.

The DRV had a marked aptitude for logistic management and not just in the jungle. It directed its assets, both human and matériel, with skill and economy. It was unaffected by the human condition and any deaths on government service in any capacity were of little account. The communist system swept away an ancient culture and its values. This cannot be expressed in cash terms.

The first war (1945–54) had any number of unaccounted costs. The first of these was that it gave birth to the second war (1956–73). The USA, with an assumption of entitlement, picked up the reins dropped by the French. Young Americans gave their time, energy and sometimes their lives to hold back what they saw as the scourge of communism. Among all the wars the United States has fought, the Vietnam War is ranked fourth in casualties just below the Civil War and the two world wars:

> Of 2,594,000 personnel who served in Vietnam, 58,220 were killed, 153,303 wounded and 1,643 missing. More than 23,214 soldiers suffered 100 percent disablement. Even afterwards, the war continued to cost many American lives. It is estimated that 70,000 to 300,000 Vietnam veterans committed suicide and around 700,000 veterans suffered psychological trauma.[5]

The Pentagon reported that the United States spent about $168 billion (worth around $1.081 trillion in 2019 dollars) in the entire war. This included $111 billion on military operations (1965–72) and $28.5 billion on economic and military aid to the Saigon regime (1953–75). At that rate, the United States spent approximately $168,000 for every 'enemy' killed. That $168 billion was the thin end of the wedge because it was only the direct costs. In addition, there were the vast and ongoing costs including veterans' benefits.

Warfare is an expensive pastime not to be entered into lightly. It is usually expensive for the winner in some form, but more expensive for the loser. In this case where the communists of North Vietnam overcame the French, the Americans and the South Vietnamese, inevitably logistics were a factor. The final chapter will examine the reasons for the success of the DRV.

Epilogue

'A general who loves luxury can destroy a whole army.'[1]

[The Emperor Maurice]

The three wars in Vietnam had at their core a desire for reunification and the creation of a single state of Vietnam. 'Self-determination' was the cry of all anti-colonialists and no voice was louder than that of the USA which subscribed to the primacy of democracy. It was 'self-determination' that motivated the communists in Vietnam and led to their overwhelming success in which they defeated two Western powers and a well-equipped South Vietnam.

In the first war (1945–54), French colonial aspirations were proved to be out of kilter with its financial and military capacity and with a singular lack of understanding of the price it would have to pay. The French were militarily and financially incapable of wresting back control of Vietnam, and American logistic support was vital. The USA shelved their anti-colonialist views in the belief that supporting the colonial French was preferred to giving the communist Ho Chi Minh unchallenged sway over North Vietnam.

The one single factor that led to French defeat was its failure to overcome its transport deficiencies. It frequently inserted parachute troops with élan and limited success. However, getting the men in was one thing; extracting them without transport, another. The persistent use of wheeled transport on badly-maintained tracks, prone to ambush, was a feature of the war and it played into the hands of a redoubtable foe. The French consistently underestimated the logistic capability of the enemy and, throughout the campaign, were out-generalled and out-fought. The French government was irresolute but, nevertheless, to achieve its ends it appointed a series of mediocre French generals to command in Indochina, none of whom had any experience of Revolutionary War (RW). All, save de Lattre, were out of their depth when confronted by General Vo Nguyen Giap, the master logistician and head of the Vietminh, the embryonic NVA and PAVN. The very fluid and flexible nature of revolutionary war as waged by the Vietminh was in stark contrast to the hidebound, unimaginative Second World War tactics of the French.

The French need to master the thorny transport issue was critical because their road-bound army was facing a foe that moved on his feet. The extraordinarily effective logistic management of the Vietminh allowed it to confront the French at will and, invariably, it held the initiative. Hundreds of thousands of porters supported the Vietminh fighters deep in the forest and Giap was able, consistently, to invest French outposts. The French sought to take and hold ground, and in that process, they killed many thousands of Vietminh, although human losses were an irrelevance to the Vietminh. The French, in seeking to maintain their isolated outposts, relied on aerial re-supply to do so. However, they did not have sufficient air assets or the skills to maintain the aircraft they did have.

The denouement for the French was a direct result of the actions of the logistically illiterate General Navarre. His decision to create a base at Dien Bien Phu and to rely entirely on aerial re-supply would, he hoped, draw the Vietminh into a conventional engagement that he would win. This was military nonsense and Navarre's inability to recognize the logistic capacity of his enemy was made clear when Giap was able to ring the base with AA artillery that negated his only line of supply.

It was not just the courage and superior strategy of the Vietminh that defeated the French, who lacked the political will to win and placed national fortunes in the wrong hands. It was that, combined with the transport/travel/logistic factor, which made the difference for the French. They were deficient and paid a high price. In contrast, the skills of the Vietminh set new benchmarks for military logisticians and, when coupled with the total commitment of the soldiers to their cause, proved to be invincible.

In the event, the French were soundly defeated, despite American aid. They took their colonial ambitions to North Africa, where they were also defeated. The USA had been the closest witness of the capacity of the Vietnamese to wage revolutionary war. Notwithstanding this, the USA was drawn into the Second Indochina War (1956–73) in which it, too, was defeated. After the dust had settled, commentators of every hue examined the performance of the US armed forces in Vietnam in fighting that second war. In 1985, one wrote:

> How could the army of the most powerful nation on Earth materially supported on a scale unprecedented in history, equipped with the most sophisticated technology in an age when technology had assumed the role of a god of war, fail to emerge victorious against a numerically inferior force of lightly-armed irregulars?[2]

This writer, ten years on and with all the evidence to hand, nevertheless expressed a view held by many. Like so very many Americans, he underestimated the DRV and its soldiers. By describing them as 'a numerically inferior force of lightly-armed irregulars', he illustrated his ignorance. Others, less erudite, had called them 'gooks'. Clearly, Krepinevich did not appreciate the extraordinary resolve, tenacity, training and courage of his country's erstwhile enemy. The Americans had never fought a revolutionary war and, faced with the phenomenon of an enemy who would not stay and fight, they were unable to develop a coherent strategy to deal with the increasingly frustrating situation. Lewis Sorley described General William Westmoreland as 'the general who lost Vietnam'. Certainly, Westmoreland's twin policies of search and destroy and short tours achieved very little but cost many lives.

The unequalled wealth of the USA allowed it to resolve the transport problems that had driven the French to defeat. They introduced the helicopter and by so doing changed the face of warfare forever. The gallantry of the men who flew these vulnerable aircraft is to be greatly admired (see Chapter 12). The US Army had no logistic problems. It had more than enough of everything, although the onward transmission from the bases was sometimes problematic and gave rise to antagonism between the teeth-army soldiers who went into the long grass and the rear-echelon soldiers who did not.

Paradoxically, it is suggested that it was not a logistic *deficiency* that affected the performance of the US armed forces but a *surfeit* of goods and services that softened the martial spirit and was divisive among the 'haves' and the 'have nots'. The provision of overly comfortable domestic arrangements when not in the face of the enemy was the root cause of many of the incidents of mounting ill-discipline in army units, many of them in the logistic chain. For bomber crews too, the war had an unreal quality. They would leave luxurious quarters in Thailand or the Philippines, make a lengthy but unchallenged flight and then, having endured a brief, stressful period under fire, return to the air-conditioning and the cinema. The USN never saw action at close quarters and even the soldiers and Marines who provided the sharp edge to the US operations did not spend protracted periods in the field. They rode into battle from and back to a comfortable base where

> they could eat steaks, fries, ice cream and drink ice-cold beer. Army engineers built 2.5 million cubic feet of refrigerated stores. A colonel was awarded a silver star for bravery for delivering frozen turkeys, by helicopter, to Special Forces camp for Thanksgiving … When the Americans left Vietnam, they left behind 71 swimming pools, 160 craft shops, 90 service clubs, 159 basketball courts, 30 tennis courts, 55 softball fields, 85 volleyball fields, 2 bowling alleys and 357 libraries. And there were Post Exchange (PX) shops full of jewelry, perfumes, lingerie and booze.[3]

The USA had limitless resources, but used them in an uncontrolled, profligate and ineffective manner. Under Westmoreland's direction it built vast military cities that had to be staffed and defended. To be fair, the US Army was not entirely self-indulgent and it also built 1,253 schools, 175 hospitals, 155 market places, 1,800 miles of road, 263 churches, 422 dispensaries, 595 bridges and 7,099 dwellings.[4]

During the war the US Army awarded more than 1,250,000 medals for bravery. In comparison, 55,258 were awarded in Korea. The debasing of this particular low-cost but psychologically important symbol speaks volumes about the loss of balance in the US armed forces. Major Powell commented on a change of command ceremony he attended:

> ... the departing CO was awarded three Silver Stars, the nation's third highest medal for valor, plus a clutch of other medals after a tour lasting six months ... his troops had to stand there and listen to an overheated description of a fairly typical performance.
>
> Awards were piled on to a point where writing a justifying citation became a minor art form. The departing battalion commander's 'package', a Silver Star, a Legion of Merit and an Air Medal, just for logging helicopter time became almost standard issue ... these wholesale awards diminished the achievements of real heroes – privates or colonels – who had performed extraordinary acts of valor ... a corrosive careerism had infected the army and I was part of it.[5]

In contrast, their enemy, Pham Van Dong said: 'We fought year after year in extremely hard conditions which went beyond all imagination, but we continued to live, work and fight.' He makes no mention of medals.

During the time frame 1964 to 1968, the USA had the capacity to destroy North Vietnam, had there been the political will to do so. It could be argued that the war could have been won in President Johnson's time had he employed the ruthless tactics of LINEBACKER. However, given 20/20 hindsight, the historian should not ignore the international balance *as Johnson saw it*. The avoidance of a third world war was his aim and a civilian-led, ineffective, limited war was the result. Johnson's military policy was influenced by the need to respond to vociferous domestic opposition to the war. The combination of political timidity and desire to appease public opinion negated the unequalled logistic might of the USA and led directly to its abject defeat.

The North Vietnamese broke new ground in their approach to the logistic support of their forces. The skill to marshal tens of thousands of people, to sustain them, to retain them for protracted periods in one of the most hostile environments on earth invites admiration. The tenacity of the North Vietnamese soldiers and their guerrilla comrades, both with unqualified commitment to their cause, were in stark contrast to the American forces.

The third war was conventional in its conduct. The PAVN, having marshalled its troops, was faced by a large, disorganized, fragile and badly-led ARVN. The outcome was never in doubt, especially so when it became clear that the USA had no intention of intervening. Thieu was no general and he hastened the defeat of his country and his own downfall by interfering in matters military. The PAVN overcame initial logistic deficiencies and, by day's end, it had all the abundance of the American store-houses at its disposal. For example, on the surrender of South Vietnam it captured 800 assorted aircraft; potent weapons of war, but no longer needed.

As a postscript and twenty years later, on 10 November 1995, Robert McNamara met General Giap. He said that he hoped 'to examine misunder-standings and missed opportunities for negotiating an earlier end to the war.' He went on to add that 'we need to draw lessons, which will allow us to avoid such tragedies in the future.' Giap responded by saying 'Lessons are impor-tant. I agree. However, you are wrong to call the war "a tragedy". Maybe it was a tragedy for you, *but for us the war was a noble sacrifice*. We did not want to fight the United States, but you gave us no choice.'[6]

The essence of the first two wars was the unrealistic political aims of the French and the USA, neither of which could understand nor match the '*noble sacrifice*' willingly made by their communist adversary.

The logistics of a 'freshly-cooked meal and a dry pair of socks' (see p. 3), important as they are to Western soldiers, even when provided were not enough to offset the *noble sacrifice* of millions of Vietnamese.

Notes

Chapter 1 – The Way It Is

1. Rommel, Field Marshal E., quoted by Field Marshal Lord Wavell, *Soldiers and Soldiering* (London, Jonathan Cape, 1953).
2. Tepic, J., Tanackov, I. & Gordan, S., 'Ancient Logistics – Historical Timeline and Etymology', *Technical Gazette 18*, 2011.
3. Roy, K., 'From Defeat to Victory: Logistics of the Campaign in Mesopotamia 1914–1918', *First War Studies*, Vol. 1, No. 1 (March, 2010), p. 36.
4. Van Creveld, M., *Supplying War Logistics from Wallenstein to Patton* (Cambridge University Press), p. 231.
5. Clearchus, 401 BC, 'Speech to the Ten Thousand'. Quoted in Xenophon Anabasis 1.3 C 360 BC, *The Persian Expedition*, tr. Rex Warner, 1949.
6. Grassi, D.G., 'Resupplying Patton's Third Army', US Army *Quartermaster Professional Bulletin*, Summer 1993.
7. Field Marshal Viscount Wavell of Cyrenaica. Quoted in *The Greenhill Dictionary of Military Quotations*, p. 276.
8. Churchill, W.S., *The River War: A Historical Account of the Reconquest of the Sudan* (London, Longmans & Green, 1899).
9. Fall, B.B., *Hell in a Very Small Place* (Cambridge, MA, Da Capo Press, 2002 [1966]), Appendix B, pp. 483–4.
10. Thompson, J., *The Lifeblood of War: Logistics in Armed Conflict* (London, Brassey's, 1991), pp. 135-36.

Chapter 2 – The Battleground

1. Lieutenant General William Slim, to the officers of the 10th Indian Infantry Division, June 1941.
2. Davidson, P.B., p. 37.
3. Chapman, S., *The Jungle is Neutral* (London, Chatto and Windus, 1948).
4. Davidson, P.B., *Vietnam at War*, p. 39. Westmoreland, W., *A Soldier Reports* (New York, Dell Publishing, 1976), p. 371.
5. Al Bang interviewed by Hastings on 7 October 2016. Quoted in *Vietnam: An Epic Tragedy*, p. 25.
6. Donovan, D., *Once a Warrior King* (London, Weidenfeld & Nicolson Ltd, 1986), pp. 109–10.
7. HQ, Dept of the Army, Asst. Chief of Staff G-2. *Terrain Estimate of Indo-China* (Washington, 22 December 1950), p. 4.
8. Moberly, F.J., *History of the Great War: The Campaign in Mesopotamia, 1914–1918*, Vol. 2 (London, HMSO, 1924), p. 449.
9. Molkentin, M., *The Centenary History of Australia in the Great War, Vol. 1: Australia and the War in the Air* (Melbourne, Oxford University Press, 2014), p. 94.

Chapter 3 – Why War?

1. Lawrence, T.E., 'The Science of Guerrilla Warfare', *Encyclopedia Britannica*, 1929.
2. Macdonald, P., *The Victor in Vietnam: Giap* (London, Fourth Estate, 1993), p. 22.
3. Davidson, p. 4.
4. Currey, C.B., *Victory at Any Cost* [1997] (Washington, Potomac Books, 2005), pp. 43–4.
5. Ibid., p. 45. In 1982 Brownell was the head of the Vietnam Bibliographical Project at Columbia University.
6. Brownell, W. in a letter to Currey, 13 February 1991. Quoted by Currey, p. 45.
7. Boissarie, D., *Indochina during World War II*: 'An Economy under Japanese Control', *Economies under Occupation*, eds Marcel Boldorf and Tetsuji Okazaki (London, Routledge, 2015), pp. 232–44.
8. Ho Chi Minh (1890–1969) led the Viet Minh independence movement from 1941 onward, establishing the Communist-ruled Democratic Republic of Vietnam in 1945 and defeating the French Union in 1954. Prime Minister (1945–1955) and President (1945–1969).
9. Trang, Truong Nhu, *A Vietcong Memoir* (Vintage, 1986), p. 114.
10. Alphahistory.com.
11. Currey, p. 66.
12. Ibid., p. 68.
13. Giap, Vo Nguyen, 'Stemming from the People', *A Heroic People: Memoirs from the Revolutionary Armed Forces* (Ha No, Foreign Languages Publishing House, 1965), p. 116.
14. Hastings, M., *Vietnam: An Epic Tragedy 1945–1975* (London, William Collins, 2018), p. 9.
15. Major (later Lieutenant Colonel) Archimedes Leonidas Attilio Patti (1913–1998).
16. Hastings, p. 11.
17. 'Vietnam: A Television History; Roots of a War', interview with Archimedes L.A. Patti, 4 January 1981. Part of *The Vietnam Collection*, 1978, p. 12.
18. Ibid.
19. Major General (later General) Sir Douglas David Gracey KCB, KCIE, CBE, MC* (1894–1964).
20. Morgan, T., *Valley of Death: The Tragedy at Dien Bien Phu that Led America into the Vietnam War* (New York, Random House, 2010), p. 67.
21. Macdonald, p. 63.
22. Hastings, pp. 12–13.

Chapter 4 – The 'Dirty War', 1946–1953

1. Lawrence, T.E., 'The Science of Guerrilla Warfare', *Encyclopaedia Britannica*, 1929.
2. Marshal of France Philippe François Marie Leclerc de Hauteclocque (1902–1947).
3. Davidson, p. 9.
4. Ky, Nguyen Cao, *Buddha's Child: My Fight to Save Vietnam* (London, St Martin's Press, 2002), p. 19. Ky was later president of South Vietnam.
5. Windrow, M., *The Last Valley* (London, Cassell, 2005), p. 91.
6. Wall, I.M., *The United States and the Making of Post-War France, 1945–1954* (London, Cambridge University Press, 1991), p. 5.
7. On 29 December 2006 the UK repaid £42.4 million, the last instalment of its debt to the USA. It had taken sixty-one years to meet its obligation.
8. Fohlen, C., 'France, 1920–1970' in C.M. Cipolla (ed.), *The Fontana Economic History of Europe: Contemporary Economics*, Part 1 (1976), pp. 102–3.
9. Macdonald, p. 65.
10. Davidson, pp. 41–2.

11. Macdonald, p. 23.
12. Hastings, p. 18.
13. T'ai soldiers refers to men from a sub-culture in Vietnam. They are the descendants of speakers of a common T'ai language. There are a total of about 93 million Tai people distributed throughout South-East Asia. The T'ai in Vietnam did not have sympathy with the Vietminh.
14. Shrader, C.R., *A War of Logistics* (Lexington, University Press of Kentucky, 2015), p. 33.
15. Tanham, G., *Communist Revolutionary Warfare from the Vietminh to the Vietcong* (New York, Praeger, 1967), p. 110.
16. Shrader, p. 122.
17. Dang Van Viet, *Highway 4: The Border Campaign 1947–1950* (Hanoi, 1990).
18. Currey, p. 116.
19. Lieutenant General Jean Étienne Valluy (1899–1970).
20. Kahn, H. & Ambruster, G., *Can We Win the War in Vietnam?* (New York, Frederick Praeger, 1968), p. 101.
21. Currey, p. 139.
22. Davidson, p. 50.
23. Logevall, F., *Embers of War: The Fall of an Empire and the Making of America's Vietnam* (Random House, 2012), p. 203.
24. Miller, D.M.O., 'Logistic Support in Revolutionary Warfare', *British Army Review*, April 1975, pp. 6–10.
25. Davidson, p. 59. Lieutenant General Phillip Davidson (1915–96) was an intelligence specialist who served in Vietnam between 1967–69 and 1971–72.
26. Ibid., p. 58.
27. Ibid., p. 58.
28. Hoang Van Chi, *From Colonialisation to Communism: A Case History of North Vietnam* (New York, Frederick Praeger, 1964), p. 66.
29. Giap, *Banner of People's War: The Party's Military Line* (New York, Frederick Praeger, 1970), p. 111.
30. Lieutenant General Roger Charles André Henri Blaizot (1891–1981).
31. Giap, 'The Invincible Strength of the Vietnamese People's War in the New Era', Hoc tap *Vietnamese Studies* No. 12, December 1974, p. 13.
32. Giap, *Banner of People's War: The Party's Military Line* (New York, Frederick Praeger, 1970), p. 111.
33. Currey, *Victory*, p. 149.
34. Boettcher, T.D., *Vietnam: The Valour and the Sorrow* (Boston MA, Little, Brown, 1985), pp. 86-7.
35. Davidson, p. 65.
36. Lieutenant General Marcel Maurice Carpentier (1895–1977).
37. Bodard, L., *The Quicksilver War: Prelude to Vietnam, 1955 to the present.* Trans. by Patrick O'Brian (Boston MA, Little, Brown and Co., 1967), p. 204.
38. There are a number of synonyms for 'pacify'. Among them are placate, appease, calm, calm down, conciliate, propitiate, assuage, mollify, soothe, tranquillize, content, still, quieten and silence. The French applied none of these.
39. Giap, 'The Military Art of People's War', ed. Russell Stetler (New York, *Monthly Review Press*, Frederick Praeger, 1970), p. 87–8.
40. Davidson, p. 76.

Chapter 5 – The Debacle of the Border Forts

1. Frederick the Great, *Instructions to His Generals 1747*, tr. Phillips, 1940.
2. Shrader, p. 31.
3. Windrow, p. 98.
4. Lanning, M. & Cragg, D. (1992), *Inside the VC and the PAVN: The Real Story of North Vietnam's Armed Forces* (Williams-Ford Texas, A&M University, Ivy Books, 2008), pp. 120–68.
5. Porch, D., *The French Foreign Legion: A Complete History* (Harper Perennial, 1991), pp. 120–68.
6. Windrow, p. 103.
7. Davidson, p. 77.
8. Karnow, S., *Vietnam: A History* (1983) (London, Penguin Books, 1997), p. 205.
9. Ibid., p. 80.
10. O'Ballance, E., *The Indochina War 1945–1954: A Study in Guerrilla Warfare* (London, Faber & Faber), p. 115.
11. Davidson, p. 85.
12. Ibid., p. 86.
13. Bodard, L., *The Quicksand War: Prelude to Vietnam, 1950 to the Present Time*. Trans. P. O'Brian (Boston MA, Little, Brown & Co., 1967), p. 282.
14. Davidson, p. 87.
15. The British retreat from Kabul, through the Hindu Kush in Afghanistan, cost the lives of 4,500 soldiers and about 11,500 civilians. The final stand was made just outside a village called Gandamack. Of the 16,000 who set out, only one European survived. He was the Assistant Surgeon William Brydon.
16. Currey, p. 169.

Chapter 6 – Escalation, 1951–1953

1. Patton, G.S. Jnr., 'Success in War', *The Infantry Journal Reader*, 1931.
2. Currey, p. 156.
3. General Jean Joseph Marie Gabriel de Lattre de Tassigny, GCB MC (1889–1952).
4. Navarre, H., *Agonie de L'Indochine* (Paris, Plon, 1958), p. 22.
5. Macdonald, p. 101.
6. Davidson, p. 112.
7. Windrow, p. 115.
8. Currey, p. 173.
9. Ibid., p. 174.
10. Truong Chinh (1907–88). Later, and after the death of Le Duan in 1986, he was briefly president of the DRV.
11. Fall, B., *Street Without Joy* (London, Pall Mall Press, 1964), p. 176.
12. Hastings, p. 28.
13. Windrow, p. 117.
14. Hastings, p. 30.
15. UK National Archives FO371/103518, 23 August 1953.
16. *Dinassaut* is an abbreviation of *Division Navale d'Assaut*. These twelve vessels were the creation of General Le Clerc. They were mostly shallow-draft converted landing craft with applied armour. They were well-armed with mounted tank turrets and carried 81mm mortars.

17. Operation MARKET GARDEN was carried out from 17 to 25 September 1944 when the Allies made airborne landings to secure strategically-important bridges in Holland. These troops were to be relieved by ground troops advancing on a single, heavily-defended road. The ground advance was delayed, and the delay resulted in the surrender of the surrounded British troops at Arnhem.
18. General Raoul Albin Louis Salan (1899–1984). Salan later became the head of the OAS that fought for the retention of Algeria as a French colony. He was tried for treason and condemned to death in 1962 but pardoned in 1968.
19. Windrow, p. 118.
20. Davidson asserts French casualties of 5,000, p. 133.
21. Windrow, p. 119.
22. Macdonald, p. 105.
23. Currey, p. 177.
24. A howitzer is characterized by a relatively short barrel and the use of comparatively small propellant charges to propel projectiles over relatively high trajectories, with a steep angle of descent.
25. Buttinger, J., *Vietnam: Dragon Embattled*, Vol. 1 (New York, Frederick Praeger), p. 759.
26. Davidson, p. 138.
27. Ibid., p. 139.
28. Giap, Vo Nguyen, *Dien Bien Phu* (Hanoi, Foreign Languages Publishing House, 1964), p. 63.
29. Windrow, p. 121.
30. Ibid., p. 122.
31. O'Ballance, *Indo-China War*, p. 185.
32. Davidson, p. 155.
33. Recolle, P., *Pourquoi Dien Bien Phu?* (L'Histoire Flammarion, 1968), p. 152.
34. Shrader, p. 24.
35. 'National Intelligence Estimate 91.' 'Probable Developments in Indochina through mid-1954', 4 June 1953. See Shrader, p. 44.
36. Windrow, p. 204.
37. Navarre, H., *Agonie de L'Indochine* (Paris, Plon, 1958), pp. 191–9.
38. Davidson, p. 181.
39. Ibid., p. 188.
40. Navarre, p. 196.
41. Fall, *Street*, p. 317.
42. Navarre, p. 195.
43. Davidson, p. 182.

Chapter 7 – The Siege

1. Sun Tzu, *The Art of War* (c.500 BC), tr. Giles, 1910.
2. Shrader, p. 117.
3. Plating, J.D., 'Failure at the Margins: Aerial re-supply at Dien Bien Phu' (Master's thesis, Ohio State University, 2000), p. 9.
4. O'Daniel, J.W. (Lieutenant General, Chief US Joint Military Mission to Indochina), Progress Report on Military Situation in Indochina (Pearl Harbor, Hawaii, 19 November 1953).
5. Giap, *People's War, People's Army*, p. 174.
6. Fall, B., *Hell in a Small Place* (London, Harper Collins, 1996; Da Capo Press, 1985), p. 37.
7. Ibid.

8. Davidson, p. 195.
9. Cincinnatus (C.B. Currey), *Self-Destruction: The Disintegration and Decay of the United States Army During the Vietnam Era* (New York, W.W. Norton, 1981), p. 10.
10. Fall, *Hell*, pp. 130–3.
11. Rocolle, *Pourquoi*, p. 251.
12. Fall, p. 41.
13. Ibid., p. 44.
14. Ibid., p. 47.
15. Ibid., p. 213.
16. Davidson, p. 204.
17. André, V., 'The Helicopter Ambulance in Indochina', 2–3. Quoted by Shrader, p. 119.
18. Simpson, H.R., *Dien Bien Phu: The Epic Battle America Forgot* (London, Brassey's Inc., 1994), p. 33.
19. Shrader, p. 98.
20. 'La Chaine du Froid', *Caravelle* 256 (12 November 1950). Shrader, p. 60.
21. 4e Bureau EMIFT, 'Note sur le service d'Intendance en Indochine' (Saigon 1953), p. 5. Shrader, p. 62.
22. 'Les Rations Conditionnées', *Caravelle* 256, p. 7.
23. Shrader, p. 128.
24. Windrow, p. 262.
25. Ibid., p. 267.
26. Fall, p. 128.
27. Macdonald, p. 127.
28. Shrader, p. 116.
29. Ibid.
30. Ibid., p. 128.
31. Fall, B.B., *Street Without Joy: Insurgency in Indochina 1946–63*, third revised edition (Harrisburg PA, Stackpole, 1963), pp. 258–9.
32. Davidson, p. 208.
33. Fall, *Hell*, p. 185.
34. Ibid., p. 101.
35. Plating, J.D., *Failure in the Margin*, p. 141.
36. Karnow, S., p. 213.
37. Davidson, p. 241.
38. Davidson, p. 257.
39. Currey, p. 202.
40. Giap, *Dien Bien Phu*, pp. 131–2.
41. Windrow, p. 523.
42. Hastings, p. 67.
43. Dunstone, S., *Vietnam Tracks: Armor in Battle 1945–1975* (London, Osprey Publishing, 1982), p. 18.
44. Windrow, p. 540.
45. Fall, *Hell*, p. 415.

Chapter 8 – The Reckoning

1. Napoleon, 2 December 1805 at Austerlitz, to a captured young Russian officer who was demanding to be shot. Quoted by Claude Manceron, *Austerlitz*, 1966.
2. Karnow, p. 184.

3. Farran, J., 'La Leçon de Dien Bien Phu', *Paris Match*, 12 May 1956.
4. Fall, *Hell*, p. 451.
5. Ibid., p. 452.
6. Giap, *Dien Bien Phu*, pp. 40–1.
7. Karnow, p. 152.
8. Fall, *Hell*, p. 51.
9. Davidson, p. 280.
10. The original source for this widely-cited and conveniently rounded number of 500,000 is Ngo Van Chieu's memoirs, *Journal d'un combatant Vietminh* (Paris, Editions du Seuil, 1955), p. 106. How Ngo Van Chieu, an officer in the DRV's army, compiled this number he has not explained.
11. Lucina, B. & Gleditsch, N.P., 'Monitoring Trends in Global Combat: A New Dataset of Battle Deaths', *European Journal of Population* 21, No. 2 (2005), pp. 145–66.
12. Karnow, p. 53.
13. Ibid., p. 215.

Chapter 9 – Interlude

1. Thucydides, *The Peloponnesian War* (c. 404 BC).
2. Appy, p. xxi.
3. Colonel Edward Lansdale USAF (1908–87). Photographed above when a major general, he was a long-term CIA operative. In 1953, Lansdale was a member of General John Daniel's mission to Indochina and was an advisor to the French. Later, from 1954 until 1957, he was the leader of the Saigon Military Mission (SMM) and he helped to train the Vietnamese National Army (VNA). He was a confidante of both Bao Dai and Ngo Dinh Diem.
4. Karnow, p. 237.
5. Ngo Dinh Diem (1901–63), Prime Minister of South Vietnam June (1954–October 1955). President (October 1955–November 1963).
6. Cavendish, R., 'Failed coup in South Vietnam', *History Today*, Vol. 60, November 2010.
7. Hastings, p. 90.
8. Davidson, p. 284.
9. Nguyen Chi Thanh (1914–67).
10. Davidson, p. 285.
11. O'Neill, *Giap*, p. 168.

Chapter 10 – The Second War: Early Days

1. Winston Churchill (1874–1965), *Greenhill Dictionary of Military Quotations*, p. 34.
2. Giap in an interview with Virginia Morris, *A History of the Ho Chi Minh Trail: The Road to Freedom* (Bangkok, Orchid Press, 2006), p. xvi.
3. Appy, C.G., *Vietnam: The Definitive Oral History told from all Sides* [2003] (London, Ebury Press, 2006), pp. xxvi–xxvii.
4. Ibid., p. xxvi.
5. Davidson, p. 291.
6. Robert Strange McNamara (1916–2009). He had a successful service, academic and business career. He was president of the Ford Motor Company when recruited by J.F. Kennedy, and went on to be president of the World Bank (1968–81).
7. Davidson, p. 293.
8. Gravell, *Pentagon Papers* 11:2, pp. 48, 49, 55.
9. Palmer, D.R., *Summons of the Trumpet: U.S. Vietnam in Perspective* (San Rafael CA, Presidio Press, 1978), p. 20.

10. Hastings, p. 112.
11. Ibid.
12. Jsphfrtz.com US Military Budget Timeline, posted November 2011.
13. Roger Donlan in an interview with Appy, p. 32.
14. Charles Allen interviewed by Hastings, p. 119.
15. Davidson, p. 303.
16. Halberstam, D., *Best and Brightest* (Greenwich, C.T. Fawcett, 1969), p. 364.

Chapter 11: Managing a War

1. Von Clausewitz, C., *On War*, 3.6, 1832. Trans. Howard, M. & Paret, P., 1976.
2. Sorley, L., *Westmoreland: The General who lost Vietnam* (New York, Mariner Books, 2012), p. xviii.
3. Ibid., p. xviii.
4. Sorley, L., p. 67. Telephone interview with Lewis Sorley, 6 November 2009.
5. Record, J., *The Wrong War: Why We Lost in Vietnam* (Annapolis, Naval Institute Press, 1998), p. 51.
6. Karnow, p. 361.
7. Westmoreland interview, 17 April 1981, WGBH Interview Collection Healey Library, University of Massachusetts.
8. Davidson, p. 312.
9. Giap in an interview with Morris, p. xvii.
10. Ibid., pp. 67–8.
11. https://www.militaryfactory.com/vietnam/casualties.asp.
12. Manihot esculenta is commonly called cassava. It is a woody shrub that is a source of carbohydrates. Cassava is the third-largest source of food carbohydrates in the tropics, after rice and maize. It must be prepared correctly and, because it contains cyanide, it can cause partial paralysis or death.
13. Appy, pp. 10–11.
14. Gravel, *Pentagon Papers* III: 531. See also Davidson, p. 313.

Chapter 12 – Search and Destroy

1. Motto of the highest school of the German Army before 1914, quoted in Leon Trotsky, *Military Writings*, 1918.
2. The National Security Action Memorandum 288 was issued on 17 March 1964. Its detail is outside the bounds of this book but, suffice to say, it was subject to endless debate and interpretation.
3. Davidson, p. 316.
4. Gravel, *Pentagon Papers*, III: 186.
5. Palazzo, A., *Australian Military Operations in Vietnam* (Canberra, Army History Unit, Australian War Memorial, 2006).
6. Ham, P., *Vietnam: The Australian War* (Sydney, Harper Collins, 2007), p. 316.
7. Ibid., p. 418.
8. Stone, G., *War Without Honour* (Brisbane, Jacaranda Press, 1966), pp. 53–4.
9. Chanoff, D., *Doan Van Toai, Vietnam: A Portrait of its People at War* (London, Taurus & Co., 1996), p. 108.
10. Palazzo, p. 22.
11. Westmoreland, pp. 335–6.
12. Karnow, p. 362.

13. Record, J., *The Wrong War*, p. 97.
14. Morris, B., 'The Effects of the Draft on US Presidential Approval Ratings during the Vietnam War 1954–1975', Doctoral dissertation (University of Alabama, Tuscaloosa, 2006).
15. Chambers, J. (ed.), (1999), *The Oxford Companion to American Military History*.
16. Clinton, Bush, Trump and Quayle.
17. Abbott, W.F., http://www.americanwarlibrary.com/vietnam/vwc10.htm.
18. US Department of Veterans' Affairs, America's Wars (November 2011).
19. Hackworth, D. & Sherman, J., *About Face: The Odyssey of an American Warrior* (New York, Simon and Schuster, 1989), p. 524.
20. Thayer, T.C., *War without Fronts: The American Experience in Vietnam* (Boulder COL, Westview Press, 1985), p. 94.
21. Lepre, G. (2011), *Fragging: Why US Soldiers Assaulted their Officers in Vietnam* (Lubbock, Texas Tech University Press, 2011).
22. Westmoreland, W., *A Soldier Reports* (New York, Dell Publishing, 1976), p. 358.
23. Mason, R., *Chickenhawk* (London, Corgi Books, 1984), p. 116.
24. Roush, G., Vietnam Helicopter Pilots Association, 2018.
25. West, R., *War and Peace in Vietnam* (London, Sinclair Stevenson, 1995), p. 31.
26. Lieutenant General Bernard Trainor USMC (retd) in an interview with Appy, pp. 3–8.
27. Finlayson, A.R., *Killer Kane* (Jefferson, South Carolina, MacFarland, 2013).
28. Tran Thi Gung in an interview with Appy, pp. 16–17.
29. Hackworth, D. & Sherman, J., *About Face: The Odyssey of an American Warrior* (New York, Simon and Schuster, 1989), p. 598.
30. Sallah, M. & Weiss, M., *Tiger Force: The Shocking True Story of American Soldiers out of Control in Vietnam* (London, Hodder and Stoughton, 2006).
31. https://www.globalsecurity.org/military/ops/commando-lava.htm.
32. Thomas, W., 'Weather Warfare/Global Dominance Over Weather' (willthomas.net, 2007).
33. Nixon, R., *No More Vietnams* (New York, Avon Books, 1985), p. 56.
34. In an interview with Appy, C., p. 3.
35. Summers, H.G. Jr., *Vietnam War Almanac* (New York: Facts on File Publications, 1985), p. 283.
36. McCoy, A.W., *A Question of Torture: CIA Interrogation from the Cold War to the War on Terror* (London, Macmillan, 2006), p. 63.
37. Thayer, T., *War without Fronts: The American Experience in Vietnam* (Boulder COL, Westview Press, 1985), p. 51.
38. Okamoto was interviewed by William Colby at Wayback Machine, a digital archive of the internet on 16 July 1981, WGBH Media Library and Archives, retrieved 9 November 2010.

Chapter 13 – Hide and Seek

1. Colonel Louis Louzeau de Grandmaison in a lecture at the École de Guerre, 1911.
2. Malcolm Brown interviewed by Appy, p. 70.
3. Kirby, R., 'Operation Snoopy: The Chemical Corps People Sniffer' (Wayback Machine, *Army Chemical Review*, June 2007), pp. 20–2.
4. Dunnigan, J.F. & Nofi, A.A., *Dirty Little Secrets of the Vietnam War: Military Information You're Not Supposed to Know* (Macmillan, 2000), p. 236.
5. Davidson, p. 405.
6. Lucus, P., *Ho Chi Minh Noodles and the Trail Through Vietnam* (2011), p. 202.
7. Mangold, T. & Penycate, J., *The Tunnels of Cu Chi* (London, Guild Publishing, 1985), p. 119.

8. Ibid., p. 68.
9. 'Techniques of Constructing and Camouflaging Underground Tunnels' (*Viet Cong Tunnels Manual*) captured 28 September 1967 (Log no. 09-2421-67).
10. Ibid.
11. Mangold & Penycate, p. 81.
12. Progress Report, US Army Land Warfare Laboratory, 30 June 1973.
13. Mangold & Penycate, pp. 108–11.
14. 'Weapons Lab: Small Arms Development at USALWL' (*Small Arms Defense Journal*, http://www.usadefensejournal.com/wp).
15. Ibid.
16. François-Marie Arouet (1694–1778), more usually known by his nom-de-plume 'Voltaire'. He was a French writer, historian and philosopher, famous for his wit.
17. Mangold & Penycate, p. 125.
18. Ibid., pp. 125–6.
19. Ibid., p. 138.
20. Ibid., p. 141.
21. Appy, C.G., *Vietnam: The Definitive Oral History Told from All Sides* (London, Ebury Press, 2006), p. xix.

Chapter 14 – Operation RANCH HAND: Defoliation

1. Jamison, C.W.T., from a PhD dissertation (2001) re-produced in Morris, V. & Hills, C., *The Road to Freedom: A History of the Ho Chi Minh Trail* (Bangkok, Orchid Press, 2006), pp. 170–3.
2. Hack, K., *Defense & Decolonization in South-East Asia* (London, Taylor and Francis, 2001), p. 113.
3. Perera, J.T.A., 'This Horrible Natural Experiment', *New Scientist*, 18 April 1985, pp. 34–6.
4. Arthur W. Galston (1920–2008) was an American botanist and bioethicist.
5. Cambodia: Accession to 1925 Geneva Protocol.
6. Jamieson, p. 171.
7. Ibid.
8. Ibid., p. 172.
9. Telegram from US Embassy Saigon to Secretary of State, Subject: Alleged Defoliation in Cambodia, 12 July 1969; Covering letter to Report on Defoliation in Cambodia from US Ambassador to South Vietnam Bunker, 16 July 1969 (both declassified).
10. G. Deconinck and F. Ninane, 'Report on a Visit to the Krek-Mimot Region After It Was Damaged by Chemical Defoliants', in French with translation (Rubber Research Institute of Cambodia, May 1969); Telegram from Secretary of State to US Embassy Saigon, 24 May 1969 (declassified).
11. Young, A.L., 'The History, Use, Disposition and Environmental Fate of Agent Orange', Environ Health Perspective, 2009.

Chapter 15 – Prelude

1. Flavius Vegetius Renatus, *Military Institutions of the Romans*, AD 378, trans. Clark, 1776.
2. Ebert, J.R., *A Life in a Year: The American Infantryman in Vietnam 1965–1972* (Novato, California, Presidio Press, 1993), p. 89.
3. Palmer, B., *The Twenty-Five-Year War: America's Military Role in Vietnam* (Lexington, University of Kentucky Press, 1984), p. 69.

4. Gravel, M., *Pentagon Papers* III, p. 165; Clodfelter, M., *The Limits of Air Power* (New York, Macmillan, 1989), p. 46.
5. NSC Working Group draft memorandum 17 November 1964; Gravel, M., *Pentagon Papers*, III, p. 215.
6. William Putnam Bundy (1917–2000). Bundy served as a foreign affairs advisor to both presidents Kennedy and Johnson.

Chapter 16 – Operation ROLLING THUNDER

1. Major General George B. McClellan, 9 May 1862. *McClellan's Own Story*, 1887.
2. Morris, V., *The Road to Freedom: A History of the Ho Chi Minh Trail* (Bangkok, Orchid Press, 2006), p. xvii.
3. Appy, p. 200.
4. USAF oral history interview of Colonel Henry Edelen. AFHRC File K239.0512-243 p. 57.
5. Clodfelter, pp. 128–9.
6. Davidson, p. 329.
7. Record, p. 45.
8. Ibid.
9. Ball, G.W., *The Past has Another Pattern: Memoirs* (New York, W.W. Norton, 1982), p. 370. George Wildman Ball (1909–94) was an American diplomat and banker. He served in the US State Department from 1961 to 1966 and was the only major dissenter against the escalation of the Vietnam War in 1965.
10. 'Summary Notes of the 568th NSC Meeting, 8 February 1967.' National Security Files, Vol. 4, Johnson Library, box 2.
11. Currey, p. 252.
12. Van Tien Dung, 'Some Great Experiences of the People's War' (*Visions of Victory*, Stanford, California, Hoover Institution, 1969), p. 158.
13. Clodfelter, M., p. 133.
14. Ibid., p. 134.
15. Mersky, P.B. & Polmar, N., *The Naval Air War in Vietnam* (Annapolis, Nautical and Aviation Publishing, 1981), pp. 180–1.
16. Clodfelter, M., *Vietnam in Military Statistics: A History of the Indochina Wars, 1772–1991* (McFarland & Company, 1995), p. 225.
17. AFHRC File No. K168.187-21, p. 7.
18. Van Dyke, J.M., *North Vietnam's Strategy for Survival* (Palo Alto, California, Pacific Books, 1972), p. 51.
19. Gravel, Edition IV, pp. 110–12.

Chapter 17 – Civil Operations and Revolutionary Development Support

1. Polybius, 'Histories' (c.125 BC) (*Familiar quotations from Greek Authors*, trans. Crawford Ramage 1895).
2. Robert William 'Blowtorch Bob' Komer (1922–2000).
3. Davidson, pp. 409–10.
4. Hunt, R.A., *Pacification: The American Struggle for Vietnam's Hearts and Minds* (Boulder, COL, Westview Press, 1995), pp. 22–3.
5. White, J.P., 'Civil Affairs in Vietnam' Centre for Strategic & International Studies (http://csis.org/files/media/csis/pubs/090130_vietnam_study.pdf).
6. Coffey, R., 'Revisiting CORDS: The Need for Unity of Effort to Secure Victory in Iraq' (*Military Review*, March, 2006), p. 12.

7. Davidson, p. 460. General Davidson was a senior intelligence officer during this period and observed Komer and his activities at first hand.
8. Fisher, C., 'The Illusion of Progress', *Pacific Historic Review*, Vol. 75, No. 1, February 2006, pp. 25–55.

Chapter 18 – Surprise: Khe Sanh and the Tet Offensive

1. Major General Sir James Wolfe, 1789, in his General Orders during the Quebec expedition.
2. Davidson, p. 426.
3. Sharp and Westmoreland, Report, p. 131.
4. Currey, p. 264.
5. Ibid., p. 265.
6. Hayward, S., *The Tet Offensive: Dialogues* (April 2004).
7. Dougan, C., Weiss, S., et al., *Nineteen Sixty-Eight* (Boston, Boston Publishing Company, 1983), p. 11.
8. Wirtz, J.J., *The Tet Offensive: Intelligence Failure in War* (Cornell University Press, 1991), p. 74.
9. Berman, L., *Lyndon Johnson's War* (W.W. Norton & Company, 1991), p. 181.
10. Davidson, p. 446.
11. McGarvey, P.J., *Visions of Victory: Selected Vietnamese Communist Military Writings 1965–1968* (Stanford CA, Hoover Institute on War, Revolution and Peace, 1969), pp. 252–6.
12. Davidson, p. 477.
13. Sorley, L., p. 168.
14. Westmoreland, *A Soldier Reports* (New York, Dell Publishing, 1976), p. 440.

Chapter 19 – The M16 Rifle Debacle

1. Lieutenant General Dong Van Khuyen, the chief logistician of the ARVN. Quoted by Sorley, L., *Westmoreland*, p. 132.
2. Pendergast, S. & Pendergast, T., 'Firearms' (*St James' Encyclopedia of Popular Culture*, St James' Press, 2000), p. 102.
3. *Encyclopaedia Britannica*, 2010.
4. Chivers, C.J., *The Gun* (New York, Simon & Schuster, 2010), p. 316.
5. Fallows, J., 'M-16: A Bureaucratic Horror Story' (*The Atlantic*, June 1981).
6. Hastings, pp. 352–3.
7. Mizokami, K., 'Did the M16 rifle totally fail during the Vietnam war?' (*The National Interest*, 1 October 2018).
8. Ibid.
9. A Marine Corps rifleman quoted in 'Defence: Under Fire' (*Time Magazine*, 9 June 1967).
10. Sorely, p. 132, quoting from Westmoreland's dictated notes, Box 41. WPSCL.
11. Letter, General B.C. Clarke to Brigadier General H.C. Pattison, 29 December 1969. Clarke Papers, Military History Institute.
12. *Time Magazine*, 19 April 1968.
13. Sorely, p. 134, quoting Weyand, Debriefing Report, HQ II Field Force, 4 October 1968.
14. Mizokami, K., 'Did the M16 rifle totally fail during the Vietnam war?'

Chapter 20 – The Siege of Khe Sanh

1. General Piotr A. Rumyantsev (1725–96). Quoted by Parkinson, R., *Fox of the North: The Life of Kutuzov, General of War and Peace* (London, Peter Davies, 1976).
2. Sorley, p. 168.

3. Marino, J.I., 'Strategic Crossroads at Khe Sanh', HistoryNet. Retrieved 4 October 2017.
4. Macdonald, p. 275.
5. Lehrack, O.J. (ed.), *No Shining Armor: The Marines at War in Vietnam* (Kansas, Lawrence University Press, 1992), p. 141.
6. Morocco, J., *The Vietnam Experience: Thunder from Above: Air War, 1941–1968* (Boston Publishing Company, 1984), p. 176.
7. Peeler, M., 'The Aerial Resupply of Khe Sanh' (*33rd Fighter Wing Magazine*, August 2014).
8. Ibid.
9. Nalty, B., 'Airpower and the fight for Khe Sanh' (Office of Air Force History, 1986), p. 95.
10. Macdonald, p. 285.
11. Davidson, p. 554.
12. Greenleaf, J. & Harrison, M.H., 'Water and Electrolytes' (Layman, D.K. (ed.), *Nutrition and Aerobic Exercise*, 1986).
13. Adolph, E.F., 'Heat Exchanges, Sweat Formation and Water Turnover' in Adolph, E.F. (ed.), *Physiology of Man in the Desert* (New York, Inter-Science Publishers, 1947), pp. 33–43.
14. Davidson, p. 570.
15. Ibid.
16. Giap, quoted by Macdonald, p. 289.

Chapter 21 – Critical Times, 1968–1969

1. Sir Winston Churchill, speech in the House of Commons, 30 September 1941.
2. Davidson, p. 529.
3. Mangold & Penycate, p. 263.
4. Davidson, p. 591.

Chapter 22 – Disintegration, 1969–1973

1. Major General Carl von Clausewitz, *On War*, 1832, trans. Howard, M. & Paret, P., 1976.
2. Davidson, p. 611.
3. Davidson, p. 615.
4. The *Toledo Blade* is a daily newspaper in Toledo, Ohio in the United States. It was first published on 19 December 1835 and has a daily circulation of 100,000+.
5. Sallah, M., 'The Tiger Force Atrocities', *New York Times*, 26 September 2017.
6. The last Americans to die in Vietnam were two marines, Charles McMahon and Darwin Judge. They served at the US Embassy in Saigon. Only one day before the fall of Saigon to the North, McMahon, 22, and Judge, 19, who had only been in the country for eleven days, were killed in a rocket attack. Their bodies were eventually repatriated and buried in 1976.
7. 'Look Truth Right in the Eye', US Naval Institute, 2002. Retrieved 4 June 2013.
8. Ewell, J.J. & Ira Hunt, I., *Sharpening the Combat Edge* (Washington, Department of the Army, 1974).
9. Hastings, p. 449.
10. Davidson, p. 616.
11. *New York Times*, 22 June 1967.
12. Powell, C., *A Soldier's Way* (London, Hutchinson, 1995), p. 61.
13. Crozier, B., 'Terror, New Style', *National Review*, 9 August 1985, p. 24.
14. Davidson, p. 617.
15. Lepre, G. (2011), *Fragging: Why US Soldiers Assaulted their Officers in Vietnam* (Lubbock, Texas Tech University Press, 2011), pp. 19–21.
16. Brush, P., 'The Hard Truth about Fragging', Historynet, 2010. Retrieved 25 May 2014.

17. Lock-Pullan, R., *US Intervention Policy and Army Innovation* (London, Routledge, 2006), p. 68.
18. Davidson, p. 619.

Chapter 23 – Cambodia and Laos

1. Major General Carl von Clausewitz, *On War*, 1832, trans. Howard, M. & Paret, P., 1976.
2. Davidson, p. 613.
3. Lewy, G., *America in Vietnam* (New York, Oxford University Press, 1978), p. 160.
4. Randolph, S., 'Foreign Policy and the Complexities of Corruption: The Case of South Vietnam' (Washington, *The Foreign Service Journal*, June 2016).
5. Ibid.
6. 'GI Resistance in the Vietnam war', Libcom.org
7. Thompson, Sir R., *Peace is Not at Hand* (New York, David McKay, 1974), p. 77.
8. Davidson, p. 631.
9. Karnow, p. 646.
10. Hastings, p. 501.
11. Davidson, p. 650.

Chapter 24 – Operations LINEBACKER I & II

1. Sun Tzu, *The Art of War* (c.500 BC).
2. Davidson, p. 511.
3. Apple, R.W., '25 Years Later: Lessons Learned from the Pentagon Papers', *New York Times*, 23 June 1996.
4. Washington Tapes, 29 May 1971. Quoted by Hughes, K., *Fatal Politics: The Nixon Tapes* (University of Virginia Press, 2015), p. 29.
5. In June 2011, the full text of the *Pentagon Papers* was declassified and released to the public.
6. Palmer, D.R., *Summons of the Trumpet: The History of the Vietnam War from a Military Man's Viewpoint* (New York, Ballantine, 1978), p. 317.
7. Head, W.P., *War Above the Clouds* (Maxwell AFB, Air University Press, 2002), p. 65.
8. Davidson, p. 705.
9. Nixon, R.M., *No More Vietnams* (New York, Arbor House Publishing, 1985), p. 150.
10. Hughes, p. 149.
11. Nixon, *Memoirs*, p. 734.

Chapter 25 – Reunification: The Finale

1. Frederick the Great, *Military Testament*, 1768.
2. Karnow, p. 672.
3. Ibid., p. 673.
4. Ibid., p. 672.
5. Hastings, p. 586.
6. Ibid., p. 676.
7. Ibid., p. 680.

Chapter 26 – The Cost

1. Marshal Gian Giacomo de Trivulce (1441–1518) when King François 1 of France asked him what he needed to make war.
2. Shannon, P., 'The ABCs of the Vietnam War' (Indochina Newsletter, Asia Resource Centre Special issue, 1996), pp. 93–7.

3. Ibid.

4. Fall, B., *The Two Vietnams: A Political and Military Analysis* (New York, Praeger, 1967), p. 47.

5. Vietnam war.info/how-much-Vietnam-war-cost.

Epilogue

1. The Emperor Maurice, *The Strategikon*, AD 600.

2. Krepinevich, A., *The Army and Vietnam* (Baltimore, Johns Hopkins University Press, 1985), p. 4.

3. Macdonald, P., p. 302.

4. *Logistic Support*, Library of Congress Catalog no. 72-600389, December 1972.

5. Powell, C., p. 146.

6. Appy, p. 43.

Bibliography

Primary Sources:

'The Military Art of People's War', ed. Russell Stetler, *Monthly Review Press* (New York, Frederick Praeger, 1970).

Banner of People's War: The Party's Military Line (New York, Frederick Praeger, 1970).

Dien Bien Phu (Hanoi, Foreign Languages Publishing House, 1964).

'Stemming from the People', *A Heroic People: Memoirs from the Revolutionary Armed Forces, Ha No* (Foreign Languages Publishing House, 1965).

People's War, People's Army (Foreign Languages Publishing House, Hanoi, 1961).

Banner of People's War: The Party's Military Line (New York, Frederick Praeger, 1970).

Appy, C.G., *Vietnam: The Definitive Oral History, Told from All Sides* (London, Ebury Press, 2006).

Bail, R., *L'Enfer de Dien Bien Phu* (Éditions Heimdal, 1997).

Ball, G.W., *The Past has Another Pattern: Memoirs* (New York, W.W. Norton, 1982).

Bodard, L., *The Quicksilver War: Prelude to Vietnam 1955 to the Present* (Trans. by Patrick O'Brian) (Boston MA., Little, Brown and Co., 1967).

Boettcher, T.D., *Vietnam: The Valour and the Sorrow* (Boston, Little Brown, 1985).

Boissarie, D., 'Indochina during World War II: An Economy under Japanese Control', *Economies under Occupation: The Hegemony of Nazi Germany and Imperial Japan in World War II*, eds Marcel Boldorf and Tetsuji Okazaki (London, Routledge, 2015).

Buttinger, J., *Vietnam: Dragon Embattled*, Vol. 1 (New York, Frederick Praeger, 1967).

Chanoff, D. & Doan Van Toai, *Vietnam: A Portrait of its People at War* (London, Taurus & Co., 1996).

Charlton, M., & Moncrieff, A. (eds), *Many Reasons Why: The American Involvement in Vietnam* (Scolar, 1978).

Churchill, W.S., *The River War* (London, Longmans, Green & Co., 1899).

Cincinnatus (C.B. Currey), *Self-Destruction: The Disintegration and Decay of the United States Army during the Vietnam Era* (New York, W.W. Norton, 1981).

Clodfelter, M., *Vietnam in Military Statistics: A History of the Indochina Wars, 1972–1991* (McFarland & Co., 1995).

Currey, C.B., *Victory at Any Cost* [1997] (Washington, Potomac Books, 2005).

Dang, Van Viet, *Highway 4: The Border Campaign 1947–1950* (Hanoi, Foreign Languages Publishing House, 1990).

Davidson, P.B., *Vietnam at War: The History, 1946–1975* (London, Sidgwick & Jackson,1989).

Donovan, D., *Once a Warrior King* (London, Weidenfeld & Nicolson Ltd, 1986).

Dunnigan, J.F. & Nofi, A.A., *Dirty Little Secrets of the Vietnam War: Military Information You're Not Supposed to Know* (Macmillan, 2000).

Dunstone, S., *Vietnam Tracks: Armor in Battle 1945–1975* (London, Osprey Publishing, 1982).

Ebert, J.R., *A Life in a Year: The American Infantryman in Vietnam 1965–1972* (Novato, Calif., Presidio Press, 1993).

Fall, B.B., *Street Without Shame* (Harrison, USA, Stackpole, 1967).

Fall, B.B., *Street Without Joy: Insurgency in Indochina 1946–63*, 3rd revised edition (Harrisburg PA, Stackpole, 1963).

Fall, B.B., *Hell in a Very Small Place* (Da Capo Press, 2002 [1966]).

Farran, J., 'La Leçon de Dien Bien Phu', *Paris Match*, 12 May 1956.

Finlayson, A.R., *Killer Kane* (Jefferson, South Carolina, McFarland & Co., 2013).

Fisher, C., 'The Illusion of Progress', *Pacific Historic Review*, Vol. 75, No. 1, February 2006.

Fohlen, C., 'France, 1920–1970' in C.M. Cipolla (ed.), *The Fontana Economic History of Europe: Contemporary Economics*, Part One (1976).

Giap, Vo Nguyen, 'The Invincible Strength of the Vietnamese People's War in the New Era', *Hoc Tap Vietnamese Studies*, No. 12, December 1974.

Grassi, D.G., 'Resupplying Patton's Third Army', US Army, *Quartermaster Professional Bulletin* (Summer 1993).

Greenleaf, J. & Harrison, M.H., 'Water and Electrolytes', Layman, D.K. (ed.), *Nutrition and Aerobic Exercise* (1986).

Hack, K., *Defense & Decolonization in South-East Asia* (London, Taylor and Francis Ltd, 2001).

Hackworth, D. & Sherman, J., *About Face: The Odyssey of an American Warrior* (New York, Simon and Schuster, 1989).

Halberstam, D., *Best and Brightest* (Greenwich, C.T. Fawcett, 1969).

Ham, P., *Vietnam: The Australian War* (Sydney, Harper Collins, 2007).

Hastings, M., *Vietnam: An Epic Tragedy, 1945–1975* (London, William Collins, 2018).

Hoang Van Chi, *From Colonialisation to Communism: A Case History of North Vietnam* (New York, Frederick Praeger, 1964).

Hughes, K., *Fatal Politics: The Nixon Tapes* (University of Virginia Press, 2015).

Hunt, R.A., *Pacification: The American Struggle for Vietnam's Hearts and Minds* (Boulder CO, Westview Press, 1995).

Kahn, H. & Ambruster, G., *Can We Win the War in Vietnam?* (New York, Frederick Praeger, 1968).

Karnow, S., *Vietnam: A History* (New York, Viking Press, 1983).

Kaushik, R., 'From Defeat to Victory: Logistics of the Campaign in Mesopotamia 1914–1918', *First War Studies*, Vol. 1, No. 1 (March 2010).

Kirby, R., 'Operation Snoopy: The Chemical Corps People Sniffer', *Army Chemical Review* (Wayback Machine, June 2007).

Krepinevich, A., *The Army and Vietnam* (Baltimore, Johns Hopkins University Press, 1985).

Ky, Nguyen Cao, *Buddha's Child: My Fight to Save Vietnam* (London, St Martin's Press, 2002).

Lanning, M. & Cragg, D., (1992), 'Inside the VC and the NVA: The Real Story of North Vietnam's Armed Forces', *Military History Series* (Williams-Ford, Texas, A&M University, Ivy Books, 2008).

Lawrence, T.E., 'The Science of Guerrilla Warfare', *Encyclopaedia Britannica* (1929).

Lehrack, O.J. (ed.), *No Shining Armor: The Marines at War in Vietnam* (Kansas, Lawrence University Press, 1992).

Lepre, G., *Fragging: Why US Soldiers Assaulted their Officers in Vietnam* (Lubbock, Texas, Tech University Press, 2011).

Lewy, G., *America in Vietnam* (New York, Oxford University Press, 1978).

Lock-Pullan, R., *US Intervention: Policy and Army Innovation* (London, Routledge, 2006).

Logevall, F., *Embers of War: The Fall of an Empire and the Making of America's Vietnam* (London, Random House, 2012).

Lucina, B. & Gleditsch, N.P., 'Monitoring Trends in Global Combat: A New Dataset of Battle Deaths', *European Journal of Population* 21, No. 2 (2005).

Macdonald, P., *The Victor in Vietnam: Giap* (London, Fourth Estate, 1993).

Mangold, T. & Penycate, J., *The Tunnels of Cu Chi* (London, Guild Publishing, 1985).

Mason, R., *Chickenhawk* (London, Corgi Books, 1984).

McCoy, A.W., *A Question of Torture: CIA Interrogation from the Cold War to the War on Terror* (London, Macmillan, 2006).

McGarvey, P.J., *Visions of Victory: Selected Vietnamese Communist Military Writings, 1965–1968* (Stanford CA, Hoover Institute on War, 1969)..

Mersky, P.B. & Polmar, N., *The Naval Air War in Vietnam* (Annapolis, Nautical and Aviation Publishing, 1981).

Moberly, F.J., *History of the Great War: The Campaign in Mesopotamia, 1914–1918*, Vol. 2 (London, HM Stationery Office, 1924).

Molkentin, M., *The Centenary History of Australia in the Great War, Vol. 1: Australia and the War in the Air* (Melbourne, Oxford University Press, 2014).

Morgan, T., *Valley of Death: The Tragedy at Dien Bien Phu that Led America into the Vietnam War* (New York, Random House, 2010).

Morocco, J., *The Vietnam Experience: Thunder from Above: Air War, 1941–1968* (Boston Publishing Company, 1984).

Morris, V. & Hills, C., *The Road to Freedom: A History of the Ho Chi Minh Trail* (Bangkok, Orchid Press, 2006).

Navarre, H., *Agonie de L'Indochine* (Paris, Plon, 1958).

Nixon, R., *No More Vietnams* (New York, Avon Books, 1985).

O'Ballance, E., *The Indochina War 1945–1954: A Study in Guerrilla Warfare* (London, Faber & Faber, 1964).

O'Daniel, J.W., *Progress Report on Military Situation in Indochina* (Pearl Harbor, Hawaii, 19 November 1953).

O'Neill, R.J., *General Giap: Politician and Strategist* (New York, Frederick Praeger, 1969).

Palazzo, A., *Australian Military Operations in Vietnam* (Canberra, Army History Unit, Australian War Memorial, 2006).

Palmer, D.R., *Summons of the Trumpet: US – Vietnam in Perspective* (San Rafael, CA, Presidio Press, 1978).

Peeler, M., 'The Aerial Resupply of Khe Sanh', *33rd Fighter Wing Magazine*, August 2014.

Perera, J.T.A., 'This Horrible Natural Experiment', *New Scientist*, 18 April 1985.

Plating, J.D., *Failure in the Margins: Aerial Resupply at Dien Bien Phu* (Ohio State University, 2000).

Porch, D., *The French Foreign Legion: A Complete History* (London, Macmillan, 1991).

Powell, C.L., *A Soldier's Way* (London, Hutchinson, 1995).

Record, J., *The Wrong War: Why We Lost in Vietnam* (Annapolis, MD Naval Institute Press, 1998).

Rocolle, P., *Pourquoi Dien Bien Phu?* (L'Histoire Flammarion, 1968).

Sallah, M. & Weiss, M., *Tiger Force* (London, Hodder and Stoughton, 2007).

Shrader, C.R., *A War of Logistics* (Lexington, University Press of Kentucky, 2015).

Simpson, H.R., *Dien Bien Phu: The Epic Battle America Forgot* (London, Brassey's Inc., 1994).

Sorley, L., *Westmoreland: The General who Lost Vietnam* (Boston, Mariner Books, 2012).

Stone, G., *War Without Honour* (Brisbane, Jacaranda Press, 1966).

Summers, H.G. Jr., *Vietnam War Almanac* (New York, Facts on File Publications, 1985).

Tanam, G., *Communist Revolutionary Warfare: From the Vietminh to the Vietcong* (New York, Praeger, 1967).

Thayer, T.C., *War Without Fronts: The American Experience in Vietnam* (Boulder, Colorado, Westview Press, 1985).

Thompson, J., *The Lifeblood of War: Logistics in Armed Conflict* (London, Brassey's, 1991).

Thompson, Sir R., *Peace is Not at Hand* (New York, David McKay, 1974).

Trang, Truong Nhu, *A Vietcong Memoir* (Vintage, 1986).

Van Creveld, M., *Supplying War Logistics from Wallenstein to Patton (1971)* (Cambridge University Press, 2004).

Van Dyke, J.M., *North Vietnam's Strategy for Survival* (Palo Alto, California, Pacific Books, 1972).

Van Tien Dung, 'Some Great Experiences of the People's War', *Visions of Victory* (Stanford, California, Hoover Institution, 1969).

Wall, I.M., *The United States and the Making of Post-War France, 1945–1954* (London, Cambridge University Press, 1991).

Westmoreland, W.C., *A Soldier Reports* (New York, Dell Publishing, 1976).

Windrow, M., *The Last Valley* (London, Cassell, 2005).

Wirtz, J.J., *The Tet Offensive: Intelligence Failure in War* (Cornell University Press, 1991).

Young, A.L., 'The History, Use, Disposition and Environmental Fate of Agent Orange', *Environ Health Perspective*, 2009.

Secondary Sources

Abbott, W.F., http://www.americanwarlibrary.com/vietnam/vwc10.htm.

Alphahistory.com.

AFHRC File No. K168.187-21.

Gravell, M.R., *Pentagon Papers*.

HQ, Dept. of the Army, Asst. Chief of Staff G-2, *Terrain Estimate of Indo-China* (Washington, 22 December 1950).

Jsphfrtz.com US Military Budget Timeline, posted November 2011.

Morris, B., 'The Effects of the Draft on US Presidential Approval Ratings during the Vietnam War 1954–1975', Doctoral dissertation (University of Alabama, Tuscaloosa, 2006).

Nalty, B., 'Airpower and the Fight for Khe Sanh' (Office of Air Force History, 1986).

Roush, G., Vietnam Helicopter Pilots Association, 2018.

Thomas, W., 'Weather Warfare/Global Dominance Over Weather' (willthomas.net 2007, Techniques of Constructing and Camouflaging Underground Tunnels. Viet Cong Tunnels Manual captured 28 September 1967).

UK National Archives FO371/103518, 23 August 1953.

US Army Department of Defense Manpower Data Centre.

US Department of Veterans' Affairs, America's Wars (November 2011).

USAF oral history interview of Colonel Henry Edelen. AFHRC File K239.0512-243.

Westmoreland interview, 17 April 1981, WGBH Interview Collection, Healey Library, University of Massachusetts.

Progress Report, US Army Land Warfare Laboratory, 30 June 1973. 'Weapons Lab: Small Arms Development at USALWL', *Small Arms Defense Journal*.

White, J.P., 'Civil Affairs in Vietnam', Centre for Strategic & International Studies.

http://www.usadefensejournal.com/wp.

https://www.militaryfactory.com/vietnam/casualties.asp.

https://www.globalsecurity.org/military/ops/commando-lava.htm.

http://csis.org/files/media/csis/pubs/090130_vietnam_study.pdf.

Index